12/02

Beckett and Philosophy

Also by Richard Lane

JEAN BAUDRILLARD

Beckett and Philosophy

Edited by

Richard Lane

Senior Lecturer in English
South Bank University

Director
The London Network for Modern Fiction Studies

First published 2002 by
PALGRAVE
Houndmills, Basingstoke, Hampshire RG21 6XS and
175 Fifth Avenue, New York, N.Y. 10010
Companies and representatives throughout the world

PALGRAVE is the new global academic imprint of
St. Martin's Press LLC Scholarly and Reference Division and
Palgrave Publishers Ltd (formerly Macmillan Press Ltd).

ISBN 0–333–91879–7

This book is printed on paper suitable for recycling and made from fully managed and sustained forest sources.

A catalogue record for this book is available from the British Library.

Library of Congress Cataloging-in-Publication Data
Beckett and philosophy / edited by Richard Lane.
      p. cm
   Includes bibliographical references and index.
   ISBN 0–333–91879–7
   1. Beckett, Samuel, 1906—Philosophy. 2. Philosophy in literature. I. Lane, Richard J., 1966–
PR6003.E282 Z5695 2001
848'.91409—dc21   2001036889

10   9   8   7   6   5   4   3   2   1
11   10   09   08   07   06   05   04   03   02

Printed and bound in Great Britain by
Antony Rowe Ltd, Chippenham, Wiltshire

For Sarah

Contents

Notes on Contributors

Gary Banham is the Research Fellow in Transcendental Philosophy at Manchester Metropolitan University. He is the author of *Kant and the Ends of Aesthetics* (2000) and co-editor of *Evil Spirits: Nihilism and the Fate of Modernity* (2000). He is also co-editor of a special issue of *Tekhnehma: Journal of Philosophy and Technology* on teleology, and editor of a special issue of *Angelaki: Journal of the Theoretical Humanities* on aesthetics and the ends of art. He is series editor for the new philosophy series *Renewing Philosophy* being published by Palgrave.

Mary Bryden is a Senior Lecturer in the Department of French Studies at the University of Reading, UK, where she is also Joint Director of the Beckett International Foundation. Her books include *Women in Samuel Beckett's Prose And Drama: Her Own Other* (1993), *Samuel Beckett and Music* (1998), *Samuel Beckett and the Idea of God* (1998), and *Deleuze and Religion* (2001). She is now completing a monograph on Deleuze and Literature.

David Cunningham teaches English Literature at the University of Westminster. He has been a guest editor of the *Journal of Architecture* and has previously published work on critical theory and the avant-garde. He is currently working on an edited collection of pieces on postwar avant-garde movements.

Robert Eaglestone works on contemporary and twentieth-century literature, literary theory, and philosophy. His publications include *Ethical Criticism: Reading after Levinas* (1997), *Doing English* (1999), *Postmodernism and Holocaust Denial* (2001), and articles on literature, ethics, contemporary European philosophy, science, the Holocaust, archaeology, and historiography. He is the series editor of Routledge Critical Thinkers.

Andrew Gibson is Professor of Modern Literature and Theory at Royal Holloway, University of London. His many publications include *Towards a Postmodern Theory of Narrative* (1996) and *Postmodernity, Ethics and the Novel: From Leavis to Levinas* (1999). His *Joyce's Revenge:*

History, Politics and Aesthetics in Ulysses will be published in 2002. He is currently working on *Doing Without: Samuel Beckett's Tragic Ethics*, a book which focuses on the relationship between the philosophy of Alain Badiou and Beckett's work. He has essays in print or forthcoming on the Badiou/Beckett relationship in the *Journal of Beckett Studies, Samuel Beckett Aujourd'hui*, and collections in France and Germany.

Richard Lane is Senior Lecturer in English at South Bank University, and an honorary Reader in British and Postcolonial Studies at the University of Debrecen, Hungary. He has published numerous articles on modern and postcolonial fiction and theory, in journals such as *Canadian Literature, Commonwealth, JCL, BC Studies*, and *The Malcolm Lowry Review*. He lectures regularly in Canada and the US, and is involved in an ongoing archival study project at the University of British Columbia, Special Collections Division. Recent publications include a chapter in *Post-Colonial Literatures: Expanding the Canon* (1999), *Jean Baudrillard* (2000), a book-length study of *Mrs Dalloway* (2001). Forthcoming work includes a book on *The Literature of the U.S. Immigrant Experience* (2002) and a co-edited collection on contemporary British fiction (2002); he also writes the Canadian Literature section of *The Year's Work in English Studies*. He is joint founder and Director of the London Network for Modern Fiction Studies.

Ulrika Maude has recently completed her doctoral dissertation on Samuel Beckett's prose and drama at the University of York. She has published articles on Beckett, and is currently co-editing a collection of essays on Beckett and the body with Steven Connor. She teaches at the University of York.

Philip Tew is a Senior Lecturer in English at the University of Central England, and an honorary Reader in English and Aesthetics at the University of Debrecen, Hungary. He has published *B. S. Johnson: a Critical Reading* (2001), and "Reconsidering Literary Interpretation" in *After Postmodernism: an Introduction to Critical Realism* (2001). Other work has appeared variously in *Critical Survey, The Anachronist, and Review of Contemporary Fiction*. A collection on contemporary British fiction co-edited by Dr Tew is scheduled for publication in 2002. He is joint founder and Director of the London Network for Modern Fiction Studies.

Acknowledgements

With thanks to Sarah for her ongoing support, to Joseph Jones at the University of British Columbia for the intellectual stimulation and dialogue that formed the background to the Beckett and Philosophy project, Mary Bryden for additional help and guidance in preparing the collection, James Knowlson and the entire Reading Beckett Seminar, my colleague and co-founder of the London Network for Modern Fiction Studies, Philip Tew, who provided ongoing help and encouragement, and with thanks to Robert Eaglestone, Andrew Gibson, Richard Begam, Gary Banham, Thomas Hunkeler, Ulrika Maude, David Cunningham and Steve Barfield. The two Beckett conferences organized by the London Network for Modern Fiction Studies received valuable input that helped with the preparation of this collection; Lois Oppenheim and Stan Gontarski deserve a special mention. In Hungary, thanks to Tamas Benyei, Nora Sellei and Peter Szaffko at the University of Debrecen; in Canada, thanks to Laurie Ricou, Sherrill Grace, Leonard Angel, Anne Yandle, Alexis, Aleteia and Phyllis Greenwood. At South Bank, thanks to John Thieme, Jeffrey Weeks and Deborah Madsen. Finally, the editorial team at Palgrave have provided unremitting support and encouragement.

Introduction

Richard Lane

One of the key texts for contemporary readings of Beckett and philosophy – or the impossibility of Beckett and philosophy and what this actually signifies theoretically – is Simon Critchley's 'know happiness – on Beckett' in his *Very Little . . . Almost Nothing: Death, Philosophy, Literature.* Critchley suggests that: 'By debating the meaning of meaning, Beckett's work permits us to trace the history of the dissolution of meaning and to delineate some sort of genealogy of nihilism. Such a genealogy would permit neither the restoration of meaning in an ever-falsifiable and faded positivity, some version of the overcoming of nihilism, nor the irrelevant metaphysical comfort of meaninglessness' (1997: 152). A genealogy of nihilism, in the Nietzschean and Foucaultian sense of 'genealogy', would account for the fact that other avenues, for contemporary theorists, remain remarkably problematic when the critical impetus is one of an encounter with, or collision between, philosophy and Beckett's texts. It is a question here of a remainder, with something always escaping the encounter or collision, theorized most famously in his *Acts of Literature* interview by Derrida:

> What Derrida seems to be suggesting is that because one cannot avoid the platitude of metalanguage and the inevitable lagging behind and overshooting of philosophical interpretation, Beckett has to be avoided. One cannot hope to be faithful to the *idiom* of Beckett's language because any interpretation assumes a generality that betrays the idiom, what Derrida will also call a text's *signature* . . . Derrida is suggesting that the work of Beckett's work, its work-character, is that which refuses meaning and remains after one has exhausted thematization. Such a remains (*reste*) would

be the irreducible idiom of Beckett's work, its ineffaceable signature. It is this remainder that is both revealed through reading
and resists reading. (1997: 145)

Critchley gets to this Derridean moment via the work of Theodor
Adorno and the paradox which Zuidevaart sums up: 'Art needs a
philosophy that needs art'. This paradox would simply disappear if
the critic believed that the work of philosophy could completely
account for the artwork, or, if the critic decided that the artwork
was not in need of interpretation: perhaps it is non-conceptual, or,
perhaps it always already communicates what it wants to say, but
in a language entirely other to philosophy.

   If Beckett and philosophy come together now in the project of a
genealogy of nihilism (*not* the reductive reading that Beckett's works
are simply nihilistic), then, for Critchley, this raises the question of
form, or, more precisely, the crisis of form (for example parody):
'where the autonomy of modernist art is a problem because this
autonomy, by definition, can no longer be governed by the constraints and conventions of tradition.' (p. 154). Modernist art does
not emancipate itself from form, but as authentic negation does
need 'formal emancipation' (p. 155). Quoting Zuidervaart quoting
Adorno: 'Beckett's absurdist plays are still plays. They do not lack
all meaning. They put meaning on trial.' (p. 155). Critchley goes on
to examine Beckett's work in some detail, in relation to humour,
narrative, the voice which speaks in the work and, once more, the
problem of meaning. But for this collection, it is Critchley's Adornian
reading which is of most interest; the notion that meaning is on
trial is one examined by a number of contributors. The 'resistance
to philosophy' of Beckett's work is explored by Robert Eaglestone
and touched upon by Steve Barfield as one route to the Heideggerian
moment in Beckett, while Andrew Gibson writes that 'At this moment, the most significant issues in Beckett studies are just beginning
to congeal around the questions raised by Badiou on the one hand,
and Adorno and Critchley on the other.' However, in a sense all of
the contributors are interrogating in different ways this notion of
meaning being 'on trial' if the full Adorno quotation from his *Aesthetic
Theory* is taken into account: 'Beckett's plays are absurd not because
of the absence of any meaning, for then they would be simply
irrelevant, but because they put meaning on trial; *they unfold its
history*' (p. 153; my emphasis). A genealogy of nihilism would account
for the history of 'meaning on trial' as such, but this is not the *only*

critical approach available. In this collection meaning may be on trial, but it is so from a number of competing perspectives and narratives.

Richard Begam, author of the important recent work *Samuel Beckett and the End of Modernity* (1996), argues in the first chapter of this collection that it is essential to examine Beckett's relation to the critical debates concerning foundationalism. Rather than examining philosophical influence (the 'genetic' approach which has largely needed some kind of authorial 'authorization' for critics to proceed, a kind of permission from beyond the grave) or literary-philosophical intertextuality, Begam examines a 'philosophical problem'. This enables Begam to situate Beckett in relation to contemporary debates concerning modernism/postmodernism, existentialism/poststructuralism and humanism/antihumanism. Choosing primary texts that, paradoxically, may seem the most resistant to postfoundationalism – *Company*, radio and stage plays – Begam offers a wide-ranging exploration of the speech/writing opposition, the question of memory, autobiography, and authorial reconstruction, via a Derridean approach. Begam concludes that his close-readings tell 'a remarkably consistent story: again and again, speech yields to writing, foundations give way to contingency.' Robert Eaglestone looks at the notion of 'meaning on trial' from a more literary-theoretical perspective, arguing that Beckett's 'works do clearly test the limits of our ideas about what literature is and the what foundations of "thinking about literature" should be.' However, this is also an interrogation on Eaglestone's part into the entire philosophy/literature division and/ or conflation; thus he examines: Literature as entertainment, Philosophy as the work; Literature as Philosophy; Literature as a parody of Philosophy; Literature as an influence on Philosophy and [literature & philosophy as:] Just texts? His conclusion is that 'the work of Beckett – again, as a test case – reveals a transformative moment, a "real movement" in Heidegger's phrase, in "thinking and writing about literature". This movement has been discussed by Geoffrey Hartman in *Criticism in the Wilderness*, where he writes that literary "commentary may cross the line and become as demanding as literature: it is an unpredictable or unstable genre that cannot be subordinated, a priori to its referential or commentating function."'

The desire to go beyond authorized philosophical/literary connections in the genealogy of meaning on trial has led to some of the most interesting contemporary Beckett criticism, especially in the poststructuralist accounts of critics such as Connor, Critchley,

Derrida and Royle. This collection offers accessible readings of the poststructuralist 'intersections' of Beckett and Derrida (Chapter 3), Foucault (Chapter 4), and Deleuze (Chapter 5) as well as French theorists Badiou (Chapter 6) and Merleau-Ponty (Chapter 7). The Adornian reading is re-addressed within the Part on 'Beckett and German Thought' (Chapter 8), as well as a critical account of Beckett via Habermas (Chapter 9), a survey of Heideggerian moments in Beckett's work (Chapter 10) and the paradoxical 'influence' of Nietzsche (Chapter 11).

In his 'Cinders: Derrida with Beckett', Gary Banham re-examines the Attridge/Derrida interview that is so widely quoted by critics studying a Derridean approach. The 'proximity' to Beckett which is so problematic for Derrida is explored in a highly original way via the 'cinder effect': 'Through associating the works of Beckett and Derrida as bodies of writing which share in the engagement with the "nothing" that brings both to the edge of nihilism this piece will draw out the nature of the difficulty with experiencing the effect of both these bodies of writing.' Banham draws together Beckett's *The Unnamable* and Derrida's *Cinders* (among other texts), to explore how the work of nihilism is also not nihilistic, the aporetics at the heart of Beckett's and Derrida's texts. Thomas Hunkeler examines the proximity of madness in his chapter 'The Role of the Dead Man in the Game of Writing: Samuel Beckett and Michel Foucault', arguing that 'it is the experience of madness that *founds* the works of Beckett and Foucault, but it is precisely this foundation, which in a paradoxical way also *ruins* every construction.' Hunkeler performs a useful critique of the 'misappropriation' of Beckett by Blanchot and Foucault, whereby the experience of madness becomes an avenue to some kind of authentic voice or expression of truth. Hunkeler's reading recovers through a conceptual and historical account the subtle differences between Beckett's and Foucault's positions. Mary Brydon, in 'Deleuze Reading Beckett', writes about the process of recognition in Delueze's experience of Beckett; she examines Delueze's *L'Epuisé*, paying particular attention to the analysis of *Quad*. What is fascinating about Delueze is that in his lack of desire for 'live theatre' his critical abilities were directed towards the earlier prose pieces and the later television plays. Bryden argues, for example that the 'determinacy' which Deleuze 'discerns in Beckett's television plays relates not to a specific cultural or geographical space, but to the disposition of that space. In these plays, the dimensions of the space, and the relation and distance between its inhabiting features, are not incidentals. They *are* the text.' In her chapter, Bryden offers an exceptionally clear and accessible reading of Deleuze's positing of 'three different modes of Beckettian expression, which he calls Langue I, Langue II, and Langue III.' The chapter offers a contextualization and clarification of Deleuze's theoretical reading.

The collection offers an approach to Beckett and French thought beyond the trilogy of Deleuze, Derrida and Foucault; Andrew Gibson, in 'Beckett and Badiou', situates Badiou's reading of Beckett not as some project to 'import' his entire approach into Beckett studies, but more as a way of flagging up a 'different direction' to contemporary critical work which is 'quite different . . . to the postmodern, poststructuralist and deconstructive methodologies that have been most significant for the Beckett criticism of the past decade.' Importantly, 'it does this without any lapse back into the foundationalism, representationalism or existential humanism that so dominated work on Beckett before the arrival of Connor and Trezise.' Gibson elucidates the ethico-political dimension of Badiou's reading in a timely and effective way. Finally, the last chapter in this section is Ulrika Maude's 'The Body of Memory: Beckett and Merleau-Ponty'. Examining the recent 'mutation of the significance of the body into the problem of the body as signification', Maude ties this in critically, and via a wide range of Beckettian texts, with Merleau-Ponty, 'who, with his theory of the incarnate subject, brought the body to the centre of philosophical interrogation.'

In the final Part of the collection, 'Beckett and German Thought', David Cunningham returns to Adorno and the *Aesthetic Theory*. Cunningham argues that 'for Adorno, the challenge Beckett's works make *to philosophy* (and, as such, its dramatic importance), lies, not in the demand for the elucidation of some hidden metaphysical or political thematic present within them, but in the conjunction of these enigmatic modern works' "difficulty" with the critical task of aiding "the non-identical, which in reality is repressed by reality's compulsion to identity".' Through a comparison of Lyotard's not-trying-to-understand Duchamp and Adorno trying-to-understand Beckett, Cunningham examines the genealogy that is often referred to, yet not so often explored via its multiple theoretical ramifications. Philip Tew compares Adorno's approach to Beckett with Habermas's in his chapter 'Philosophical Adjacency: Beckett's Prose Fragments via Jürgen Habermas'. He argues that 'Beckett's world-view would seem opposed to the ultimately positive account of the ontological priority of normative values outlined by Habermas in *The Philosophical Discourse*

of Modernity where those values define human involvement in being and are such that they are seen as providing potentially further
enlightenment.' However, this would not account for 'two oblique
and perhaps surprisingly approving references to Beckett made by
Habermas in *Autonomy and Solidarity*', therefore a critical strategy of
philosophical adjacency is called for to account for such a surprise
move. Tew's chapter provides a powerful critique of the Beckett/
Habermas adjacency via a reading of Beckett's prose fragments. His
concluding questions neatly summarize this approach: 'In a positive
light, is Beckett's curious tension constructive in a performative
manner, or is it the defeat of the communitarian that seeks to refuse
the intersubjective at the heart of the human presence? A web of
dialectical denial sustains the contracted consciousness, which refutes
a series of alternative possibilities: transcendence, acceptance, self-
renewal, altered perception or dialectical reconfiguration of the
lifeworld. If Beckett's central notion remains that of defeat, then its
very thematics haunt Habermas's attempts at renewal of the project
of understanding and socio-philsophical placement that are undercut by his casual literary admiration.' Steve Barfield offers a useful
literature survey of the critical field in his chapter on Beckett and
Heidegger. Barfield examines the restrictions imposed upon scholar-
ship by 'the governing principle of research . . . [that argues for
providing in the first instance] evidence of Beckett's interest in a
particular philosopher (or vice versa).' He then examines the issues
which surround the question of Beckett and Heidegger, with emphasis
upon existentialism, before performing a brief critical reading. Finally,
the collection ends with a chapter by me on Beckett and Nietzsche
which examines the critical and creative possibilities available once
the 'governing principle of research' identified by Barfield is
jettisoned. I argue that an examination of the intertextual relationship
between Beckett and Nietzsche necessitates an aporetic logic whereby
not only does Nietzsche influence Beckett, but paradoxically, Beckett
'influences' Nietzsche.

References

Adorno, Theodor W. (1997) *Aesthetic Theory*, trans. Robert Hullot-Kentor.
   Minneapolis: University of Minnesota Press.
Attridge, Derek (1992) 'This Strange Institution Called Literature: An Interview
   with Jacques Derrida', trans. Geoffrey Bennington and Rachel Bowlby,
   in J. Derrida, *Acts of Literature*, ed. D. Attridge. London and New York:
   Routledge.

Begam, Richard (1996) *Samuel Beckett and the End of Modernity*. Stanford: Stanford University Press.

Critchley, Simon (1997) *Very Little . . . Almost Nothing: Death, Philosophy, Literature*. London and New York: Routledge.

Derrida, Jacques (1991) *Cinders*, trans. N. Lukacher. Lincoln and London: University of Nebraska Press.

Habermas, Jürgen (1990) *The Philosophical Discourse of Modernity*. Cambridge: Polity.

Habermas, Jürgen (1992) *Autonomy and Solidarity*. London: Verso.

Hartman, Geoffrey (1980) *Criticism in the Wilderness*. London: Yale University Press.

Royle, Nicholas (1995) *After Derrida*. Manchester and New York: Manchester University Press.

Part I

Theorizing Beckett and Philosophy

1

Beckett and Postfoundationalism, or, How Fundamental are those Fundamental Sounds?

Richard Begam

> 'What is your aim in philosophy? – To shew the fly the way out of the fly-bottle.'
>
> Wittgenstein

> 'Are all of these eminent thinkers *simply* showing us the way out of a dusty fly-bottle, out of a dilapidated house of Being? I am strongly tempted to say, "Sure. What more did you *think* you were going to get out of contemporary philosophy?"'
>
> Rorty

I

In 1930 Beckett delivered a lecture at Trinity College Dublin about an imaginary French poet named Jean du Chas, founder of an imaginary literary movement called 'le concentrisme.' In many ways, du Chas functioned as Beckett's alter ego, sharing with him a date of birth, childhood memories, a university background, even similarities of attitude and temperament (see Knowlson, 1996: 124–5). Of particular interest is the title of du Chas's putative work, *Discours de la Sortie* or *Discourse on the Exit*, an obvious play on Descartes's *Discours de la Méthode*. Although the lecture was clearly intended as a hoax, a somewhat fatuous piece of graduate school humor, it is instructive to think of Beckett's own writings as an elaborate working out of du Chas's mock treatise. If Descartes's *Discours* lays the groundwork for modern philosophy, establishing the guidelines by which rational discourse might proceed, a kind of road map to analytic inquiry (the word 'method' literally means 'beyond or alongside the road'), then Beckett declines to make the trip, heads for the exit, looks not for the way in but the way out. Du Chas's *Discours* effectively throws open the heated chamber of the Cartesian *poêle*, or better still (note the pun on *du Chas* and *doucher*), douses it with cold water. The result, Beckett observes, is 'un "cogito ergo sum" un peu sensationnel' – a *cogito* that is 'less sensational' both in the sense of being more modest and less grounded in sensation (Beckett, *Disjecta* 42).

That grounding was, of course, crucial for Descartes and the larger enterprise of foundationalism. If philosophy could move beyond skepticism to a form of apodictic knowledge, if it could build its house on the firm ground of a first truth, then it would establish those principles necessary to guarantee the validity of its method.[1] As is well known, Descartes located those principles in the *cogito*: 'And observing that this truth, "*I am thinking, therefore I exist*" was so firm and sure that all the most extravagant suppositions of the skeptics were incapable of shaking it, I decided that I could accept it without scruple as the first principle of the philosophy I was seeking' (Descartes, 1985: 127). Certainly since Descartes – some would argue even before him – philosophy has claimed pre-eminence among the various disciplines on the basis of its status as a master discourse, the system of knowledge that regulates all the other systems of knowledge. The rationalism of Descartes, the empiricism of Locke, Berkeley, and Hume, the logical rigorism of Kant – all of these attempts to systematize thought and construct protocols of logic and reason, represented a desire to establish philosophy as the queen of sciences.

The debate on foundationalism has continued into the twentieth century and in many ways has dominated philosophical discussion since Nietzsche first suggested that truth is a matter of metaphor and therefore as much the province of the poet as the philosopher.[2] Heidegger's break with Husserl and phenomenology, Russell's and the early Wittgenstein's interest in 'simples,' Sartre's 'search for a method,' Rorty's turn away from the analytic tradition, even Lyotard's and Habermas's debate on modernity, have all depended on questions that are directly or indirectly related to foundationalism. One might push the matter further and argue that foundationalism involves the fundamental question of philosophy itself, the question of whether it is possible to establish a discourse that stands outside all other discourses and therefore escapes what Rorty calls contingency (see *Contingency, Irony, and Solidarity*, especially chapter 1).

Now if we are to take Beckett seriously as a philosophical writer – and I think we should – then we will want to know where he stands on one of the defining questions of twentieth-century thought, indeed of philosophy itself. A large and impressive body of commentary exits on the subject of Beckett and philosophy. Generally, this literature has proceeded along one of two lines: either it has been genetic, detailing the kinds of intellectual influence a particular philosopher exercised over the writer – say Descartes, Geulincx, Berkeley, Schopenhauer, Mauthner; or it has been intertextual, mapping areas of theoretical confluence that connect Beckett with thinkers like Hegel, Heidegger, Sartre, Wittgenstein, Derrida.[3] I want to build upon this literature – especially Linda Ben-Zvi's illuminating work on Beckett and Mauthner – but my paper will examine Beckett in relation not to a set of philosophers but to a philosophical problem.[4] In taking such an approach, I propose not only to grapple directly with Beckett's ideas, attempting to give them definitional shape and focus, but also to address a number of allied debates in recent Beckett criticism – i.e., is his work better understood as modern or postmodern, existential or poststructuralist, humanist or antihumanist? In broaching these questions, I am not interested in 'playing the labeling game,' or 'pigeon-holing' one of the most complicated and nuanced writers of the twentieth century. It does, however, seem intellectually disingenuous – even a bit fatuous – to suggest that Beckett embraces both sides of these dichotomies, that he simultaneously believes that the self and reality have deep and essential structures and that they are contingent through and through. Beckett's mind was subtle, not muddled – given to complexity, not to contradiction.

In taking up the matter of Beckett and foundationalism, I would like to begin with a well-known observation he made in a letter to Alan Schneider. 'My work,' he wrote, 'is a matter of fundamental sounds (no joke intended) made as fully as possible . . .' (Beckett, *Disjecta*, 109). The remark is characteristically Beckettian. On the one hand, it seems to strike a universalist note, implying that Beckett's *oeuvre* reduces itself, like a *cri de coeur*, to the bare essentials of the human condition, that it functions as a minimalism in the service of a humanism. On the other hand, the joke, which clearly is intended, argues just the opposite: that the rarefied space of metaphysics – the space where we hear the 'inner voice' of the *cogito* – consists of nothing more than a lot of hot and not very wholesome air. By turning spirit into matter, afflatus into flatulence, Beckett's word play effectively puts the Word or *logos* back into play. At the same time, the passage underscores one of Beckett's dominant concerns: the relation of voice to text, of speech to writing. For like writing, those fundamental sounds serve as a parody of speech, as a second- ary or derivative form of expression, a *parole* which has as it were fallen, becoming in the process its writerly other.

The speech–writing dichotomy provides a useful point of entry into Beckett's corpus – no joke intended – not only because it has frequently appeared as a theme in his own writings, but also be- cause it has emerged as a master trope in Western philosophy, one that bears directly on the issue of foundationalism. As Derrida has argued, thinkers from Plato to Rousseau to Husserl have associated speech with the interiority and self-presence of the *cogito* – Descartes's first principle – and writing with a debased exteriority, an imita- tion of the thing-itself, a second- or even third-order representation.[5] Philosophy has often conceived of its task as essentially recupera- tive, involving the effort to close the gap between representation and reality, between writing and speech.

That effort at recuperation is one of the principal subjects of the trilogy, although recent criticism has tended to agree that no mat- ter how many vice-existers are evoked, the Molloys, Malones, and Mahoods never work their way back to an ur-exister.[6] As the narrator of *The Unnamable* wryly remarks: 'I could employ fifty wretches for this sinister operation and still be short a fifty-first, to close the circuit' (71). One can, however, make a more persuasive case for the proposition that in Beckett's post-trilogy work, especially after the turn to the theater, he discovers the full resources of a living and speaking voice. Two of Beckett's most talented and accomplished interpreters have made precisely that case. In his splendid *Beckett Writing Beckett*, H. Porter Abbott associates a resurgence of character in Beckett – what Abbott calls 'durable individualities' – with the discovery of 'voice' and 'image' as theatrical resources (47). This development is of crucial importance, because in Abbott's view it substantially qualifies and mitigates Beckett's 'postmodernism.'[7] Enoch Brater carries this argument further in his equally impressive *The Drama in the Text*, contending that in Beckett's late fiction voice emerges as the primary and dominant reality: '*Stories were spoken before anyone ever thought of writing them down*. No matter how ill- murmured, ill-recited, or ill-said ... Beckett's story is the old story, the one story, the simple human drama of a voice that calls out to us from the silence and insists on getting itself heard' (13). It is particularly significant, given the issue before us, that Brater takes direct aim at Derrida and the speech–writing dichotomy:

> In Derridean terms Beckett therefore privileges speech over writing, to use that overused nonverb that in some critical circles still resists being a verb. Or, rather, in this instance writing – in-scription – is conceived as a form of heightened speech: a 'script' for that absent voice – *mirabile* and very much *dictu* – that once was in your mouth. (1994: 5)

In what follows, I would like to test the powerful and provoca-tive readings that Abbott and Brater advance by performing two kinds of reading myself. First, I shall examine in some detail one of Beckett's best-known post-trilogy works, *Company*, as a way of in-terrogating the claim that in the 'late fiction' we discover the 'drama in the text,' the speech behind the writing. Second, I shall survey more synoptically a number of radio and stage plays, again with an eye to the role that voice plays in them. Although my approach is necessarily selective (a full-dress analysis of the speech–writing opposition in Beckett would produce a book-length study), the works I have chosen to analyze are representative and, at least on the face of it, resistant to the position I shall take. *Company*, in particular, seems to create problems for a postfoundationalist interpretation. Virtually every commentator agrees that the story dramatizes vocality; indeed an early draft of the work was called 'The Voice VERBATIM,' a title which implies a complete and accurate recovery of a founda-tional speech.[8] At the same time, *Company* is generally schematized as representing two voices – a present-tense voice that cogitates or reflects and a past-tense voice that remembers – thus coordinating two of the defining traditions within the Beckett canon: Cartesian meditation and Proustian recollection. It is also notable that the 'memories' presented are drawn from Beckett's own childhood (diving at the Forty Foot, asking about the distance of the sky, jumping out of the fir tree), rendering the story at least quasi-autobiographical. Hence, the recovery that *Company* enacts appears to be not only of a present *cogito* and a past self, but also of the author himself, opening up the possibility that we are witnessing a post-Barthesian rebirth of the author. As for the radio and stage plays I examine, all of them feature characters who listen to voices – inner voices, repressed voices, past voices – or who themselves become voices. If ever a writer gave pride of place to voice, so it would seem, it is Beckett in the texts I consider. It is my hope that if I can demonstrate that in these works – so apparently at odds with my argument – 'writing' undermines and supplants 'speech,' then I will have gone a long way toward making the case for Beckett as a postfoundational writer.

II

Understanding how the speech–writing dichotomy functions in Beckett depends on understanding the somewhat specialized meanings that have attached to its terms, especially within a philosophical context. Because Derrida shares with Nietzsche the view that philosophy is based not on a set of founding principles but on a series of metaphors and metonyms, one of his larger projects has consisted in revealing the way Western thought has used – or more precisely abused – the figures of speech and writing.[9] The former, Derrida argues, has consistently been identified with positive attributes (spirit, nature, consciousness, authenticity, the living word), the latter with negative attributes (matter, technology, representation, supplementarity, the dead letter). Thus, in Plato, speech or *logos* gives us access to Truth; in Rousseau, speech or *parole* gives us access to Nature (human and physical); and in Husserl speech or *phōnē* gives us access to the Self. There is, of course, a good deal of overlap among the different accounts of the speech–writing dichotomy, so that in Plato and Rousseau speech involves the interiority of consciousness (in Plato through *mnēmē* or 'good memory' and in Rousseau through the compassion of human nature), while for Husserl truth or nature are available through the 'intentionality' of consciousness. Yet, however we schematically represent these three thinkers (and one could add Saussure, Hegel, Lévi-Strauss to their ranks), what must be stressed is that for them speech gestures toward what is foundational, a first principle relating to Truth (Plato), Nature (Rousseau), or Consciousness (Husserl).

Much confusion will be avoided if we understand that in Derrida the opposition between speech and writing effectively functions as the opposition between foundationalism and postfoundationalism. Thus, the apparently paradoxical claim that writing takes precedence over speech makes sense precisely insofar as there is no 'speech,' no 'originary voice' in which Truth, Nature, or Consciousness 'speak to us' before they have been contaminated with the contingency of language. Because we can know neither the self nor the world in a prelinguistic state, these forms of knowledge are always culturally mediated, which is to say available to us as forms of 'writing' rather than forms of 'speech.'[10]

As I indicated earlier, the debate on foundationalism has engaged a wide range of philosophers in the twentieth century, but the view that I will be developing was perhaps most clearly articulated by Wilfred Sellars in his famous critique of the 'myth of the given' (*Science, Perception and Reality*; see especially chapter 5). Linda Ben-Zvi has persuasively argued that the philosopher who most directly shaped Beckett's own thought was Fritz Mauthner. Certainly Mauthner's nominalism represented one of the earliest and most influential forms of postfoundationalism Beckett encountered. When the latter read *Beiträge zu einer Kritik der Sprache*, he copied out a lengthy quotation from the last section of the work in which Mauthner compares 'all the concepts or words of human thought' to 'mere ejaculations of air on the part of a human voice.'[11] *Company*, I shall argue, consistently treats speech not as a foundational reality, but as a mere ejaculation of air. It will be my claim that Beckett's story deliberately and scrupulously constructs all the old paradigms – an originary voice, a conscious present, a remembered past – but then proceeds to disassemble and disable those paradigms, to empty out both the Cartesian and Proustian self. If the narrative appears to emerge out of speech, it quickly yields to its opposite and other, a form of de-essentialized writing.

Company begins with what appears to be the self-immediacy and self-presence that characterize the 'inner speech' of consciousness: 'A voice comes to one in the dark.'[12] As Derrida has observed, Husserl treats the interior voice, the voice one hears speaking within, in precisely these terms: 'When I speak, it belongs to the phenomeno-logical essence of this operation that *I hear myself* [je m'entends] *at the same time* that I speak. The signifier animated by my breath and by the meaning-intention . . . is in absolute proximity to me.'[13] As a result, 'pure auto-affection, the operation of hearing oneself speak seems to reduce even the inward surface of one's own body; in its phenomenal being it seems capable of dispensing with this exteriority within interiority' (*SP*, 79). Carrying this argument to its logical conclusion, the voice becomes identified with consciousness, even equated with it: 'the voice *is* consciousness' (*SP*, 80). And yet, like the horse-leech's daughter, *Company* is a closed system: what it gives on the left-hand side of the speech–writing dichotomy, it takes back on the right-hand side. Thus, the opening of the story, quoted in full, reads: 'A voice comes to one in the dark. Imagine' (3). What began as a simple constative – the description of an event within the story – turns into a hortatory performative, urging that the reader imagine the event. In this instance, 'imagine' is exactly what we as readers must do, since *Company* confronts us with what is demonstrably *not* a voice but a text. Obviously there is nothing remarkable in such a situation – all fiction demands that we conjure up what is not there – but Beckett underscores this fact, insisting that we notice it, when he uses a visual metaphor ('imagine') to elicit an auditory phenomenon (speech), when he asks us, in effect, to hear with our eyes. In the very next paragraph that voice, already grown tenuous, becomes even less immediate, less palpable, as it slips further into the realm of supposition: 'That then is the *hypothetical proposition*. To one on his back in the dark a voice tells of a past' (3–4, my emphasis).

What is most striking about *Company,* and certainly of the greatest interest for the present discussion, is the story's double narrative. Like *Bleak House* – a text with which it is not often compared – *Company* offers us two distinct points of view: 'Use of the second person marks the voice. That of the third that cankerous other' (4). The story articulates itself into 59 sections, with the second-person narrative presenting what are purported to be memories from the past, the third-person narrative concentrating on the present.[14] Virtually every commentator assumes that because there are two distinct perspectives in *Company,* there are two distinct voices.[15] But this is to confuse a grammatical convention with a narrative reality, for Beckett's text is quite explicit: the voice is associated only with the second-person narrative, the 'cankerous other' with the third-person narrative.[16]

What is this insidious, this pathological, this cancer-like other? All that we know is that it stands outside and in opposition to the voice, that it is never identified with any source or site, that it assumes no character, acquires no style, and renders its utterances from some neutral and unimaginable space, seeming to hover beyond the narrative plane itself. These are precisely the terms that Barthes uses to describe *écriture*: 'writing is the destruction of every voice, of every point of origin. Writing is the neutral, composite, oblique space where our subject slips away, the negative where all identity is lost, starting with the very identity of the body of writing'; or: 'For [the scriptor] . . . the hand cut off from any voice, borne by a pure gesture of inscription (and not expression), traces a field without origin – or which, at least, has no other origin than language itself' ('Death of the Author' in *Image, Music, Text*, 142, 146). At the same time, we are told that this 'other' is 'cankerous,' an alterity that is also an exteriority, a malignancy that invades and subverts, that comes from without and attacks what lies within, functioning as an agent of what is diseased or unnatural. Such a characterization is repeatedly evoked in two of the most influential accounts of writing in the West. Plato, Derrida observes, 'maintains *both* the exteriority of writing *and* its power of maleficent penetration, its ability to affect or infect what lies deepest inside,' while Rousseau believes that 'speech being natural . . . writing is added to it, is adjoined, as an image or representation. In that sense, it is not natural . . . the [writerly] supplement is *exterior*, outside of the positivity to which it is super-added . . .'[17] As is perhaps by now clear, I want to propose that *Company* enacts the speech–writing dichotomy in the very structure of its storytelling, with the second-person narrative operating as an ever-receding, never-recoverable *parole*, and the third-person narrative operating as its opposite or 'cankerous other,' a form of Barthesian or Derridean *écriture*.

But if the two narratives are both built around, and designed to deconstruct, the speech–writing opposition, then how is this deconstruction handled in *Company*? According to the traditional conception of speech and writing, the voice is supposed to provide the unitary and coherent discourse necessary to establish a Cartesian first principle. In *Company* we encounter something markedly different, a locution without a location, a voice that is everywhere and no-where: 'The voice comes to him now from one quarter and now from another. Now faint from afar and now a murmur in his ear. In the course of a single sentence it may change place and tone' (9). More worrying still is the question of the voice's addressee: of whom and to whom does it speak? Section 8 explicitly raises the possibility that the utterance is not internal – not an instance of Husserlian *s'entendre parler* – but proceeds from 'another' (6). This speculation is dismissed on the grounds that 'Were it not of him to whom it is speaking . . . it would not speak in the second person but in the third' (7). But the third-person narrative immediately recognizes the fallacy in this logic ('So with what reason remains he reasons ill,' [7]), which ignores the obvious possibility that a first auditor might overhear the words of a speaker that were ad-dressed to a second auditor.[18] Section 28 provides a kind of summary view in which voice operates not as source but dissemination, not as identity but difference: 'Who asks in the end, Who asks? And in the end answers as above? And adds long after to himself, Unless another still. Nowhere to be found. Nowhere to be sought' (17).

Matters are, however, more complicated still. For the traditional role of speech is undermined not only by the mobility and plurality of the voice in *Company*, but also by the fact that this voice is repeatedly transformed into its writerly other. In other words, while the voice we encounter clearly does not function as a Cartesian *cogito*, even this highly suspect form of 'speech' has already been infected by the 'cankerous other' of writing. Hence, those moments in the text where the second-person narrative (associated with speech) is absorbed within, or framed by, the third-person narrative (associated with writing). Such a moment occurs, significantly, when the story's narrative structure is explained: 'Use of the second person marks the voice. That of the third that cankerous other. Could he speak to and of whom the voice speaks there would be a first. But he cannot. He shall not. You cannot. You shall not' (4). Here the erosion of narrative boundaries (*he* cannot/shall not becomes *you* cannot/shall not) has the effect of disabling those distinctions that are necessary for the speech–writing dichotomy. The privileged term (speech) is possible only if we can separate it from the unwanted exteriority represented by its opposite (writing), but if the two terms are transposable, if there is no difference between the originary term and its parasitical copy, between a narrative marked by 'you' and a narrative marked by 'he,' then the entire logic of the dichotomy collapses.

In *Company* Beckett helps precipitate this collapse by employing what I shall call a strategy of insidious citation. A section begins with or lapses into a second-person narrative (associated with voice), only to reveal that the 'you' we encounter is effectively in quotation marks, is being used as a form of citation *within* the third-person narrative (associated with writing). In such instances, writing engulfs speech. For example: '*Your* mind never active at any time is now even less than ever so. This is the type of assertion *he* does not question' (5, my emphasis). Or: 'Another trait the flat tone . . . For its affirmations. For its negations. For its interrogations. For its exclamations. For its imperations. Same flat tone. *You* were once. *You* were never. Were *you* ever? Oh never to have been! Be again' (13, my emphasis). This strategy is carried to an extreme when the narrative permits the impermissible, or better still 'speaks' the 'unspeakable,' by employing the first person, albeit citationally: 'To murmur, Yes I remember. What an addition to company that would be! A voice in the first person singular. Murmuring now and then, Yes I remember' (10). What must be underscored is that because these moments effectively occur within quotation marks – coming as conditionals or hypotheticals – we are meant to experience the distance separating them from the things they describe, meant to apprehend them as a type of mediated or secondary description. When we remember that the voice itself begins as an imagining or proposition, we start to appreciate the extent to which everything in *Company* resolves itself into a supplemental form of discourse, a kind of writing.

It, of course, goes without saying – I use this expression deliberately – that if the recovery of an originary voice through the second-person narrative is impossible, then the full accession to self-presence implied by a first-person narrative is unthinkable: 'You do not murmur in so many words, I know this doomed to fail and yet persist. No. For the first personal singular and a fortiori plural pronoun had never any place in your vocabulary' (45). Indeed, in *Company* the first-person singular or plural becomes the last person one is likely to meet: 'And whose voice asking this? . . . Nowhere to be found. Nowhere to be sought . . . Last person. I. Quick leave him' (16–17). As the first person here transmutes itself into last person, as 'I' becomes 'him,' as identity drifts into difference and similitude into otherness, we have entered into the unmistakably Derridean – and I would add Beckettian – world of *différance*. In this regard it is worth remembering what Derrida has said about his most famous neologism: that because *différance* can neither be heard (the ear does not register it as a unique sound) nor read (the eye does not recognize it as a legitimate word), it 'belongs neither to the voice, nor to writing,' but to the space 'between' ('Différance' in *Margins of Philosophy*, 5). How, then, do we speak or write about such a verbal aberration? How do we approach it in language?

As I have argued elsewhere, Derrida consistently associates *différance* with a figure of some importance to Beckett, one that carries us to the very limits of language, the figure of the unnamable (Begam, 1992). The verbal dislocations that occur in *Company* as the narrative attempts to work its way back through writing to the *s'entendre parler* of speech produce for Beckett the same outcome they do for Derrida: the appearance, however equivocal and fugitive, of the unnamable. Thus, if we return to the passage in which Beckett transforms the 'I' from first person to last person and quote it more fully, here is what we discover: 'Whose voice asking this? . . . Unless another still. Nowhere to be found. Nowhere to be sought. The unthinkable last of all. Unnamable. Last person. I. Quick leave him' (16–17). Or, consider the passage in which the narrative proposes naming the putative hearer of his disquisition 'H.' Enoch Brater has cannily pointed out the bilingual fun Beckett is having, since for the French speaker the 'H' can neither be said nor heard and therefore is 'no name' and has 'no being' (1994: 116). The narrative consequently abandons the attempt to 'name' the hearer: 'Then let him not be named H. Let him be again as he was. The hearer. Unnamable' (22–3). The last effort to identify hearer and speaker, to designate and differentiate them, involves considering and then rejecting two other letter-names, the familiar M and W: 'Is there anything to add to this esquisse? His unnamability. Even M must go. So W reminds himself of his creature as so far created. W? But W too is creature. Figment' (33).

Figment is an important word. For in the final analysis, *Company* represents not the emergence of an originary voice but the acknowledgment of invention, although even that cannot be located in terms of a beginning or an end: 'Yet another then. Of whom nothing. Devising figments to temper his nothingness . . . Devised deviser devising it all for company' (33). Beckett has carefully chosen his words: 'devise' from the Latin *dividere* meaning to separate, distribute, apportion, divide. But that is precisely what cannot be done: the classificatory divisions that make it possible to designate a primary speech and a secondary writing have completely dissolved. The suffixes in 'devised,' 'deviser,' and 'devising' telescope object into subject into verb, canceling in the process those discriminations that confer upon these words their semantic content. What remains is a series of fictions, a form of Proustian storytelling that simultaneously involves lying in both senses – on one's back and through one's teeth: 'For little by little as he lies the craving for company revives' (40); 'Or last if not least resort to ask himself what precisely he means when he speaks of himself loosely as lying' (41). It is not insignificant that the story ends with the reassertion of its own imaginary status: 'But with face upturned for good labour in vain at your fable. Till finally you hear how words are coming to an end. With every inane word a little nearer to the last. And how the fable too. The fable of one with you in the dark. The fable of one fabling of one with you in the dark . . . And you as you always were. . . . Alone' (46).

In a letter to Linda Ben-Zvi, Beckett summarized Mauthner's significance to him as follows: 'For me it came down to:/Thought words/

Words inane/Thought inane/Such was my levity' (Ben-Zvi, 1984: 66). In the conclusion to *Company*, Beckett's levity consists in playfully turning language inside out, stripping verbal reality to its roots, revealing that at its core 'every inane word' is 'empty' or 'void' (*inanis*), 'mere ejaculations of air' (ibid., 67). Such etymological unmasking is equally instructive when applied to a word like 'fable,' which derives, by way of *fabula*, from the Latin verb *for, fari*, meaning 'to speak' or 'to say.'[19] Hence, *Company* enacts the 'fable of one fabling,' the fabulous or incredible story of a speaking voice – not a *fons* but a *fans*, and most definitely without an *origo*. Even a stolidly Anglo-Saxon word like 'alone' yields surprising results, demonstrating how great is the internal distance separating *cogitans* from *cogitatum*. Thus, if 'alone' in its root meaning ('all one') suggests unity, an atonement of self, it simultaneously suggests its opposite, the tension between totality and singularity, between 'all' and 'one.' The solitude out of which 'company' is generated ends in a condition that is anything but singular. Indeed, as Pilling and Brater have shown, *Company* is one of Beckett's most plural works, a richly and densely allusive text in which an apparently solo performance is played to the 'accompaniment' of the Bible, Shakespeare, Milton, and Joyce, not to mention Beckett's own *oeuvre*.[20] It is no accident that the allusive 'voices' we hear 'echoing' through *Company* are entirely textual, instances not of *parole* but *écriture*. The 'company that Beckett keeps' is to be found among writers writing.

III

If the argument I have been advancing is to carry weight, then it should apply to those other works by Beckett where voice is at stake. It will be particularly useful to examine a selection of his writings for radio and stage from roughly the 1960s and 1970s. During this period, Beckett experimented extensively with the idea of voice and presence, or voice-as-presence, producing a number of works specifically devoted to this issue. The 1960s and 1970s are significant insofar as they represent a turn away from fiction. I would like to suggest that Beckett's creative activity during this time helped prepare the way for *Company*, published in 1980. Four radio plays are of particular interest: *Embers, Rough for Radio II, Words and Music*, and *Cascando*.[21]

Embers begins with one of Beckett's favorite words, 'on,' which through its punning play on the Greek introduces the idea of an absent 'being,' alongside the attempt to recover the memory of a

dead father.[22] Plato famously argued in the *Phaedrus* that what as-
sures the legitimacy and truth of *logos* or speech is precisely the
authorizing 'presence' of the father.[23] Yet here the attempt to recover an authenticating and originary voice is in vain. Henry invokes
the spirit of his father ('Who is beside me now? . . . My father, back
from the dead,' 93), but if the ghost of this latter-day Elsinore walks,
it does not talk ('To answer me? . . . No, he doesn't answer me,' 93),
implying that Henry – like the radio audience – is cut off from the
voice he summons, bereft of any connecting link, ontologically
orphaned.[24] The story Henry tells focuses on the attempt to recover
what has been lost. Bolton summons a doctor friend named Holloway
in the middle of the night, but when the latter appears, prepared to
administer a sedative, Bolton can only reply 'Please! PLEASE!' (96).
We do not learn the cause of Bolton's distress, despite the fact that
the dying embers before which he stands suggest a repressed or
occluded memory. That memory is, however, never revealed, and
by the story's close the 'embers' have grown 'cold' (104). The end
of the radio play answers its beginning with the words, 'Not a
sound' (104). 'On' in the sense of 'being,' 'presence,' 'persistence' –
and the adjustment one makes to a radio – now gives way to 'off.'
Voice-as-presence is precisely what is not dramatized in *Embers*.
Henry does not hear 'inner voices,' but the sound of the sea; the
audience does not hear the character of Bolton, but Henry's representation of him. Beckett, so well attuned to his medium, understands
that radio by its very nature gives us not *parole* but *écriture*, the
electronic inscription that is the broadcast.[25]

Rough for Radio II presents a grisly version of the speech–writing
dichotomy, juxtaposing an enforced confession with a stenographic
transcription. The confession appears to include an autobiographi-
cal element, since Fox relates a story about 'saving' a mole, a variation
on Beckett's childhood memory of the hedgehog. Yet, however much
Beckett teases us with hints of self-revelation, Fox's testimony, like
Henry's inner voice or Bolton's occluded memory, remains unre-
covered and unrecoverable. Indeed, during the interrogation, the
name of Mauthner is invoked (116), and we are assured that 'what
counts is not so much the *thing*, in itself' but 'the word, the notion'
(120), a 'sign or set of words' (122). Two points are especially worth
remarking. First, although Fox lapses into the Romantic language of
the alter ego or *moi profond*, speaking of 'my brother inside me, my
old twin' (119), the idea of a 'deep self' is burlesqued when Maud
recommends that Fox deliver his 'double' through a Caesarian sec-

tion and then volunteers to nurse the newborn herself. Second, while the testimony elicited is supposed to produce a 'strictly literal' record (116), the Animator insists that the Stenographer append three words which were never spoken ('between two kisses,' 124), thereby corrupting the 'verbatim' transcript. Of course, the categorical distinction between speech and writing has already been eroded by the form of the radio play itself, which treats Fox's confession and the Stenographer's transcription as instances of both speech (we *hear* them over the radio) and writing (the broadcast means we are not dealing with a *living* voice).

Words and Music offers another example of a kind of compelled testimony. A character named Croak, referred to as 'my Lord,' thumps his club, while Words and Music perform what becomes a story of recollected love. Words' recitation, we soon realize, is an exercise not in communion but rote memory, monitored by Croak's falling club.[26] While the recitation ultimately evokes the faded image of Lily ('so wan and still so ravished away,' 132), we learn nothing about her or her significance for Croak. As is the case in so many of Beckett's works, we approach what seems to be a source or origin – here the 'wellhead' – only to have the play abruptly end without any revelation. Words and Music appear to function as the rational and emotional expressions of Croak's state of mind, but we never move beyond these expressions (Mauthner's 'word') to the thing itself.[27] Moreover, insofar as the play suggests that Words' script is just that – a rehearsed piece of material, an example of Platonic *hypomnēsis* or the 'bad memory' associated with writing – there is a dissociation between Croak as consciousness or memory (wellhead) and what are, effectively, the electronic transcriptions of his 'mind.'[28]

Cascando plays a variation on *Words and Music*, again employing three characters to represent the basic constituents of radio: Voice, Music, and Opener. The play centers on the story of Woburn, whom we follow through a series of 'falls' as he travels to the seashore and then sets out in a boat for an island. The falls obviously resonate with the title, which implies a marking – analogous to *crescendo* or *diminuendo* – in which the music does not wax or wane, but breaks down, collapses, fails to achieve closure. Of special interest is the refrain 'it's in his head,' repeated with certain variations by Voice (who relates the story of Woburn) and Opener (who turns Voice and Music on and off). As we soon discover, the 'it' refers to a 'voice': 'They said, It's his own, it's his voice, it's in his head' (142).

Once again, Beckett dismantles the idea of an originary speech, here by means of an ambiguous possessive ('his'), which renders the identity of the voice uncertain – a voice that can, with equal plausibility, be associated with Woburn (who is the subject of the narration), Voice (whose name indicates an act of locution), or even Opener (who, in reporting what 'they' said, would describe himself in the third person). Opener goes on to reject the rule of identity ('No resemblance. I answered . . .,' 142) by which we connect 'voice' with 'head,' speech with origin, but he himself begins to doubt the identity of his own voice ('And that . . . is that mine too?,' 142). The story of Woburn presses toward its conclusion, intimating that a double advent is before us, the arrival on the island and at Woburn: 'come on . . . Woburn . . . it's him . . . see him . . . say him' (143); and 'I'm there . . . nearly . . . Woburn . . . it's him . . .' (144). This epistemological *nostos* is, however, never achieved, as we connect with neither the island nor Woburn. The play ends precisely where *Embers* began, with a bilingual pun which transforms the Greek *on* ('being' or 'presence') into an exhortation to persist and a recommendation to stay tuned (keep it 'on'). Ontology has become grammatology; voice-as-presence has become an electronic inscription, which can be turned 'on' and 'off.'

IV

The dramatic works dating from roughly the 1960s and 1970s reveal the same preoccupation with the speech–writing dichotomy that we discovered in the radio plays. Obviously the dynamic of this dichotomy is substantially modified by a live performance, which involves actors who are present both in body and voice. The theater poses, in other words, a special challenge for a writer who seeks to deconstruct the metaphysics of presence, who seeks to derealize the essential facticity of the stage. Five plays are of particular concern to us: *Krapp's Last Tape, Not I, That Time, Footfalls,* and *Rockaby*.[29]

Krapp's Last Tape represents Beckett's earliest experiment in the mixed media of live and recorded voices. The play functions as a kind of cybernetic version of Proust, a *Recherche* with a rewind and fast-forward. But if the tape-recorder faithfully reproduces Krapp's voice – the 'living word' of his past self – we experience his speech, as Steven Connor has noted, as yet another piece of electronic writing, the inscription of voice on tape.[30] Krapp at 27–9 and Krapp at 39 serve not as examples of Platonic *mnēmē* or Proustian *mémoire*

involuntaire – memory as an 'unveiling' of 'presence' – but as mediated versions of the self, an inscribed and therefore transcribed
interiority. It is not surprising that the narrative trajectory of the
story converges not on revelation but omission, the undisclosed
epiphany of 'that memorable night in March, at the end of the
jetty' (60). Admittedly, the stage accomplishes what the radio cannot, literally thrusting Krapp before us, insisting on his corporeal
reality, his inert and undeniable 'thereness.' But the Krapp we witness operates much as Croak and Opener do, turning himself 'on'
and 'off' like a machine, attempting to recover an anterior self which
remains stubbornly obscure. Krapp at 39 remarks 'clear to me at
last that the dark I have always struggled to keep under is in reality
my most – (60), and if, as the interrupted passage seems to imply,
darkness alone grants access to 'authentic' being, then it is significant
that the entire stage is dark, with the notable exception of Krapp
himself. Beckett's hero can ultimately be known only as a secondary effect, a byproduct or waste product, a kind of scatography in
which identity consists not in the recovery of the self but its evacu-
ation, here represented by a voice that has fallen into writing.[31]

More than perhaps any other play, *Not I* seems to dramatize the
situation of the *s'entendre parler*. The old woman of the story, 'prac-
tically speechless' (219) her entire life, is one day struck with a
logorrhea that compels her to admit that the voice she hears is 'her
voice alone' (219). At the same time, the circuit of the *s'entendre
parler* appears to close insofar as the 'stream of words' is caught 'in
her ear' (220). S. E. Gontarski remarks, in his study of the 'Kilcool'
manuscript, an early version of *Not I*, that the work was originally
conceived around the emergence of an 'inner voice.'[32] What is more,
the dramatic setting, involving the disembodied Mouth and the
cloaked Auditor, appears to reproduce the condition of the old woman
in the story babbling to herself. Such, in any event, has been the
view taken in most of the commentary on *Not I*; indeed, even the
criticism that approaches the play from a poststructuralist perspective tends to assume that we are dealing with a form of interior
monologue.[33]

Yet if we precisely examine the ways in which Beckett has constructed his frame and story, we discover how thoroughly he
emphasizes an experience of disjunction. Steven Connor argues that
so far from staging the *s'entendre parler*, *Not I* breaks 'the circuit of
self-understanding' (1988: 164) on which it depends. Connor di-
rects our attention to the following passage:

> ... all that ... steady stream ... straining to hear ... make some-
> thing of it ... and her own thoughts ... make something of them ...
> all – ... what? ... the buzzing? ... yes ... all the time the buzzing ...
> so-called ... all that together ... imagine! ... whole body like
> gone ... just the mouth ... lips ... cheeks ... jaws ... never – ...
> what? ... tongue? ... yes ... lips ... cheeks ... jaws ... tongue ...
> never still a second ... mouth on fire ... stream of words ... in
> her ear ... practically in her ear ... not catching the half ... not
> the quarter ... no idea what she's saying ... imagine! ... no idea
> what's saying! ... and can't stop. ... (1988: 220)

The passage illustrates, Connor observes, the 'sense that language
cannot ever securely be imaged as residing within the body, or
coming from it, is enacted here in the play between different constituents of the body, lips, cheeks, jaws, tongue and ear, which refuse
to join in self-identity' (1988: 164). The essence of the *s'entendre
parler* depends on closing the distance between interiority and
exteriority, between the mental and the physical. The voice serves
as a kind of ideal mediator between these realms – much like the
Christian *logos* – with the breath functioning as the medium that
joins internal and external, subject and object. For Descartes the
'inner voice' of the *cogito* grants full access to the self because through
it we may *know* the self in the fullest sense – achieve its identity,
interrogate its character, recognize its nature. But notice that the
old woman described in *Not I* has 'no idea what she's saying,' no
understanding whatsoever, and that she registers only a small part
of the words she herself utters ('not catching the half ... not the
quarter'). In addition to the disarticulation of parts that Connor
identifies, the passage also reveals the failure of the self to grasp its
own interiority and identity. We might push the matter further and
argue that here Beckett stages not only the deconstruction of the
s'entendre parler, but the mad inversion of the Cartesian *cogito*. The
system of ironic substitutions that Beckett develops is especially
rich: the rationalist French philosopher becomes a half-mad Irish
crone; the withdrawal into the heated closet becomes an excursion
for gathering cow slips; and the epiphanic moment that leads to
apodictic knowledge becomes a dizzying *dérèglement* in which 'all
went out,' and she 'found herself in the dark' (216–17) with a 'buzzing'
in her skull (217). It is particularly noteworthy that this internal
disconnection is presented in terms of a Cartesian dualism, which
figures the body as a machine: 'Or the machine ... more likely the

machine . . . so disconnected . . . never got the message' (218).

This sense of disconnection is further dramatized by the framing device, in which Mouth and Auditor appear as distinct entities. What is more, Mouth speaks not in the first person but in the third person, telling the story not of herself but of another. Indeed, precisely what is suppressed throughout is the first-person position that would close the gap between subject and object, the word 'I' appearing only once in the entire work and then in the title after a negation. What we are left with is an emptying out of the *cogito*, an admission not of self-knowledge but of self-ignorance. Although *Not I* does not present a metaphor for writing – Krapp's electronic inscription on the tape – it does something more radical and, finally, more unsettling. It demonstrates the extent to which the supplemental logic of writing has already entered into what appears to be the full presence of speech. The 'inner voice' of the *cogito* is here staged *sous rature*, an 'I' that has been crossed out by its own negation.

That Time has been described by Beckett as the 'brother to *Not I*' (Knowlson, 1996: 531). Again, Beckett disassembles the *s'entendre parler* by separating vocalization from audition in what purports to be an instance of interior monologue. Yet here he deepens the sense of internal dissociation by breaking up the 'monologue' into three different voices, A, B and C, each associated with different ages (Knowlson, 1996: 532). Substantively, the three stories all deal with the theme that dominated *Company*: the inability to bridge gaps, close distances, establish contact. In the case of the youngest voice, B, we learn of a series of meetings between lovers where contact is never established. They are described as sitting on the opposite ends of a stone, 'murmur[ing]' vows to each other but 'not touching' (228), as 'never turned' to each other (231), as stretched out 'parallel' in the sand (231). Meanwhile B sits at a window, struggling to 'keep the void out' (230) until he finally permits it to envelop him like 'a great shroud billowing in' (234). A's story involves the failure to establish contact with a past self and more specifically the failure to recover a childhood memory of 'hiding' in an abandoned spot, referred to as 'the ruin' (228). As an adult, he attempts to return physically to the spot, first by taking a bus ('to catch the eleven,' 231) which he learns is no longer in service, and then by going to the train station ('the Great Southern and Eastern,' 231) which is now closed ('boarded up . . . and the colonnade crumbing away,' 231). The endeavor to trace a line of continuity to a previous self, to integrate present and past, produces an experience of dislocation and dissolution, a moment of the kind of anticognition we encountered in *Not I* ('not knowing where you were or when you were or what,' 232). Finally, C's story deals with the inability to establish a sense of identity or integrity of the self. The major event described by C involves viewing a painting in the National Portrait Gallery in London, which had the effect of changing him profoundly ('never the same,' 230). C explicitly connects his life- transforming experience with the issue of self-identity: 'when you started not knowing who you were from Adam ... no notion who it was saying what you were saying whose skull you were clapped up in ...' (231). The refrain of C's monologue – that he was 'never the same' – implies that his underlying problem grows out of an inability to achieve an enduring sense of integrity, to be the 'same' through time and space. The concluding image of his monologue – the reduction of his existence to a room filled with dust – represents a radical grinding down of self that recalls Murphy's third zone: 'whole place suddenly full of dust when you opened your eyes from floor to ceiling nothing only dust and not a sound only what was it it said come and gone was that it something like that come and gone come and gone no one come and gone in no time gone in no time' (235).[34]

It should also be stressed that the originary experience the play describes – the child sitting alone in the ruins talking to himself (*s'entendant parler*) (230) – is reproduced in the supplemental experience the audience witnesses: an old man 'talking to himself.' Yet it is crucial that the old man does not actually talk to himself, that the voice we hear is not the 'living word' but the 'dead letter,' a temporally dislocated recording which issues not from 'this time' but 'that time.' What the play finally demonstrates is that 'this time' is always 'that time,' that a corrosive distantiation lies at the very heart of the Husserlian *Punkt*, that the mere act of apprehending a present moment renders it past, as consciousness inexorably transforms immediacy into mediacy.[35] Even the boy sitting alone in the ruins – image of a wasted Proustian garden – speaks in alien voices, voices that were not his own but 'made up' (230).

Footfalls presents another act of disembodied locution, but although here the unseen voice does not belong to the character before us on stage, the play is nevertheless concerned with precisely those issues that are crucial to the *s'entendre parler*. Hence, May's pacing, described as 'revolving it all ... in [her] poor mind' (240), metaphorically represents the movement of consciousness about itself, a kind of peripatetic *cogito*, while the insistence that she *hear* her footfalls becomes the sign and proof of her own presence: 'May: I mean, Mother, that I must hear the feet, however faint they fall. The mother: The motion alone is not enough? May: No, Mother, the motion alone is not enough' (241). Ontological verification is very much at stake in this play. Voice tells a story concerning an old Mrs. Winter and her daughter Amy – obvious stand-ins for the mother and May – and when the mother asks the daughter if she observed – 'anything . . . strange at Evensong?' (243), the latter offers the startling reply that she was not there: 'Mrs. W: Not there? Amy: Not there. Mrs. W: But I heard you respond' (243).[36] The mother in Voice's story repeats to Amy what Voice has said to May: 'Will you never have done . . . revolving it all . . . In your poor mind' (243). It is revealing that Voice has begun to function as a form of secondary inscription, telling a story that fictionally represents her own relation with her daughter. Morever, the story deliberately marks itself as a constructed narrative, complete with asides to the 'reader' ('as the reader will remember,' 242, 243) and reported dialogue. Voice, in other words, operates as a kind of writing, both in the sense that it parasitically feeds on the situation of the dramatic frame, doubling the story of May and her Mother, and also in the sense that 'speech' acknowledges its own 'writerly' constructedness. The 'footfalls' of the title are themselves the acoustic traces of presence, yet as we know from Beckett's biography, they represent the 'presence' not of the daughter but of the mother, and in this play it is precisely the mother (origin, speech, foundation) who has been transformed into her opposite or other (copy, writing, contingency).

Toward the end of his career with *Rockaby*, Beckett returns to a familiar image from the beginning of his career: a solitary figure in a rocking chair. The young man has been replaced by an old woman, nakedness by Victorian splendor, but the situation remains essentially unchanged. The rocking chair serves as Beckett's parodic reworking of Descartes, a mobilized *poêle* in which one carries on a sedentary conversation with the self. The split between body and mind, between exteriority and interiority, is represented by W (the seated woman) and V (her voice). Given the traditional speech–writing dichotomy, V should stand for the fully incarnated presence of consciousness, but Beckett, employing a now familiar strategy, renders her as a recorded or electronic text. Of course, W has no more 'presence' than V, operating as Opener did in *Cascando* or Croak in *Words and Music* – i.e. someone who activates the taped recording with the repeated invocation of 'More.' Significantly, the rocking figure seeks to retrieve a sense of self-identity and self-presence by searching 'high and low/for another/another like herself' (275). In finding such another, she hopes 'to see' and to 'be seen' (279), to achieve the reciprocal knowledge that ideally occurs when the *cogito* examines itself. As was the case in *Footfalls*, the effort at locating the self, at recovering an originary presence, is linked to the mother. So it is that V speaks of sitting in the chair where her mother sat, of being dressed as her mother was, in short of identifying with her (280). Yet 'in the end' the mother 'came off her head' (i.e., was 'off her rocker'), another one of Beckett's satiric inversions of the Cartesian moment as the basis of rational discourse.

It is also very much to Beckett's purposes that the subject of V's discourse is death. Derrida has written in several places about *écriture* as a form of thanatography or death-writing. Insofar as writing has traditionally been associated with waste, dross, expulsion, poison, violence, and the 'dead letter,' it has been regarded as the 'place of death.'[37] But just as importantly, writing is affiliated with death because the latter can only be narrated retrospectively, from a position of alienation, a position outside the self. As the old woman rocks herself into oblivion, bringing her 'long day' to its 'close,' she cannot directly grasp the moment of her own death, but must use those devices of writing – repetition and displacement – here literalized by the activity of rocking, to describe what she herself can neither comprehend nor experience ('rock her off/rock her off,' 282).

V

The survey I have performed in the foregoing pages is necessarily limited in scope, but it tells a remarkably consistent story: again and again, speech yields to writing, foundations give way to contingency. While Beckett's dismantling of voice-as-presence is revealing in itself, enabling us to situate his work in terms of such debates as modernity vs. postmodernity or humanism vs. antihumanism, it also helps explain – I want to suggest in closing – two of the most striking features of his career: his unprecedented interest in moving across genres and between languages.

Robbe-Grillet famously remarked in an essay on *Waiting for Godot* that Beckett's play dramatized Heideggerian *Dasein*, the existential reality of 'being there.'[38] Certainly the theater 'makes present' in a way that fiction cannot. But Beckett's dramatic works – including

Godot, which is about a character who is *not* there – effectively empty out the generic expectations of the stage. This emptying out or *askesis* is especially pronounced in those works where the question of voice (as *ousia, eidos,* or *cogito*) is under examination. In other words, to reverse Brater's formulation, in Beckett's plays we discover not the drama in the text, but the text in the drama, the writing in the speech. It is not surprising, then, that Beckett's interest in deconstructing voice-as-presence inevitably leads him to the generic intersection where this issue most urgently presents itself, the intersection between stage and page, between theater and fiction.

As a corollary, I would argue that Beckett's oscillations between English and French – not to mention his excursions into German – represent a similar interest in moving beyond linguistic foundationalism. After a certain point in Beckett's development, it becomes difficult to discuss his works in terms of 'originals' and 'translations,' a 'mother' tongue and an 'other' tongue. Mary Lydon develops this view in her essay 'The Mother-Tongue,' where she argues, with characteristic eloquence and insight, that we should begin to read Beckett outside a simple English–French binary.[39] I find Lydon's own suggestion – that Beckett's linguistic vagrancy is intimately bound up with his Irishness – both persuasive and salutary. I would also urge, however, that Beckett's wanderings across languages, his sense of linguistic homelessness and exile, serve to underscore his postfoundationalism, which assumes that there are no originary languages, no final vocabularies, no natural or mother tongues.

More than any other writer in the twentieth century, perhaps in history, Beckett has patiently and persistently undermined the idea of foundations, first principles, the thing-itself. In so doing, he has explored the economy of what Derrida calls the 'fonds sans fond,' the fund or surplus without bottom, which 'keeps itself forever in reserve even though it has no fundamental profundity nor ultimate locality' (Derrida, 'Plato's Pharmacy,' in *Dissemination*, 127–8). The 'ejaculations of air' that have issued from Beckett's own depthless reserve are at once base (unwelcome in polite society) and baseless (lacking in ground or limit), a fundamentalism without the foundationalism. In the world of Beckett's antimetaphysics, the fundamental sounds we hear are best summarized by Sainte-Beuve's remark: 'Nothing so resembles a swelling as a hollow.'

Notes

1   In one of the standard discussions of foundationalism, Jonathan Dancy writes 'C. I. Lewis, the most eminent classical foundationalist of the [twentieth] century, held that "unless something is certain, nothing else is even probable"' (1985: 54).

2   The classic statement of Nietzsche's position is to be found in his often cited, 'On Truth and Lies in a Nonmoral Sense': 'What then is truth? A movable host of metaphors, metonymies, and anthropomorphisms: in short, a sum of human relations which have been poetically and rhetorically intensified, transferred, and embellished, and which, after long usage, seem to a people to be fixed, canonical, and binding' (1979: 84). Although the essay was written in 1873, it was not published until after Nietzsche's death. Among the writings that did appear during Nietzsche's life, Gianni Vattimo identifies elements of postfoundationalism in as early a work as *Human, All Too Human* (1878); see Vattimo, *The End of Modernity*, 166–7.

3   Studies that have read Beckett alongside philosophy are too numerous to cite in full, but among these are Begam, *Samuel Beckett and the End of Modernity*; Butler, *Samuel Beckett and the Meaning of Being*; Cohn, *Samuel Beckett: The Comic Gamut*; Connor, *Samuel Beckett: Repetition, Theory and Text*; Henning, *Beckett's Critical Complicity*; Hesla, *The Shape of Chaos*; Hill, *Beckett's Fiction*; Kenner, *Samuel Beckett: A Critical Study*; Locatelli, *Unwording the World*; Moorjani, *Abysmal Games in the Novels of Samuel Beckett*; Perloff, *Wittgenstein's Ladder*; Rabinovitz, *The Development of Samuel Beckett's Fiction*; and Trezise, *Into the Breach*.

4   See 'Samuel Beckett, Fritz Mauthner, and the Limits of Language' and 'Fritz Mauthner for Company.'

5   Derrida discusses Plato in 'Plato's Pharmacy' in *Dissemination*, Rousseau in *Of Grammatology*, and Husserl in *Speech and Phenomena*.

6   See, for example, Begam, Connor, Hill, Moorjani, and Trezise.

7   Like Brater, Abbott especially emphasizes the role of voice in Beckett's theater: 'Mikhail Bakhtin may or may not be right when he writes that "drama is by nature alien to genuine polyphony," but it would appear that theater's capacity to showcase a voice – or its tendency to make one voice dominate, as Bakhtin maintains is the case in Shakespeare's plays – may in fact have been part of what drew Beckett to the theater' (1996: 45). Regarding the modern/postmodern debate, Abbott treats Beckett as 'postmodern' in his deconstruction of plot (principally in his fiction) and 'modern' in his reconstruction of character (principally in his drama): 'If [my] assessment is correct, then the kind of persistence I have been featuring in Beckett himself, as in his characters and voices, is a different kind of onwardness from that discussed in the first part of this chapter, which, being a trope, was entirely a matter of language and therefore necessarily (and vitally) hollow at its core. Important as this insight is, a view of Beckett which features primarily the Beckett of linguistic and tropological subversion may fail to account for the intense earnestness that distinguishes him from so many of his postmodern contemporaries' (50).

8 For a discussion of 'The Voice VERBATIM,' see Krance, 'Beckett's *Encores*' and Murphy's 'On First Looking Into Beckett's *The Voice*'; for critical responses to *Company*, see note 21 below.

9 See Nietzsche, 'Truth and Lies,' in *Philosophy and Truth*, and Derrida, 'White Mythology,' in *Margins of Philosophy*.

10 Obviously children have sensory experiences before they acquire language, but the kind of conceptual understanding that enables a child to construct categories like 'self' and 'world' depends on language.

11 Ben-Zvi, 'Fritz Mauthner For Company,' 67. In the same passage, Mauthner argues that the 'human brain' is closed off from 'reality' and 'consciousness' just 'as the surface of a stone is closed off from its chemistry' (67). Interestingly, Mauthner recognizes that such an assertion of contingency, is susceptible to its own contingency and he therefore begins the passage I have been citing by acknowledging that 'epistemological nominalism is not a world view that can be proved' (67). In so doing, he anticipates the pragmatism of a post–foundationalist like Rorty: 'To say that there is no such thing as intrinsic nature is not to say that the intrinsic nature of reality has turned out, surprisingly enough, to be extrinsic. It is to say that the term 'intrinsic nature' is one that it would pay us not to use, an expression which has caused more trouble than it is worth. To say that we should drop the idea of truth as out there waiting to be discovered is not to say that we have discovered that, out there, there is no truth'; Rorty, *Contingency, Irony, and Solidarity*, 8.

12 Beckett, *No How On: Company, Ill Seen Ill Said, Worstward Ho*, 3; further citations are noted parenthetically in the text.

13 Derrida, *Speech and Phenomena*, 77; further citations are noted parenthetically in the text as *SP*.

14 My count treats the last word of the story ('Alone.') as one of the 59 sections. The section demarcations are especially clear in the original single-volume Grove edition, which enlarges and places in bold the initial letter of each section.

15 While Ben-Zvi, Catanzaro, Jewinski, Krance, Levy, Locatelli, and Hardwerk offer interpretations of *Company* that are largely or primarily postfoundationalist, they all discuss the work in terms of two 'voices.' Hicks alone distinguishes between a third-person narrative and a third-person voice: 'the summary that markets *Company*, like the criticism that interprets it, tends to privilege two positions, that of the hearer and that of the second person voice, to the near exclusion of the third, the "other," whose third person discourse (not "voice") in fact dominates the text'; see 'Partial Interpretation and *Company*,' 313.

16 Narrative voice and narrative point of view are not one and the same, however much we may be tempted to identify the two on the model of an integrated consciousness. For an example of how voice and perspective can be separated, see James Naremore's analysis of Virginia Woolf in *The World Without a Self*.

17 The first quotation comes from 'Plato's Pharmacy' in *Dissemination*, 110; the second from *Of Grammatology*, 144–5. Derrida effectively cross-references the two passages when he compares Platonic writing to

Rousseauistic writing: 'The *pharmakon* is that dangerous supplement,' 'Plato's Pharmacy,' 110. It is worth remarking that while Rousseau tends to see writing as 'unnatural,' he makes clear in the 'Second Discourse' that 'natural man' is prelingusitic. Speech comes into being in primitive society, which Rousseau identifies with 'savage man'; see Rousseau, *The First and Second Discourses*, especially 119–23.

18   For readings that use this passage to identify voice with consciousness, see Locatelli, 173 and McCrudden, 49–50.

19   McCrudden also points out the etymological play with 'fable,' but his reading of its significance is markedly different from my own; see 'The Phenomenon of Voice in *Company*,' 59.

20   Pilling, 'Review Article: *Company* by Samuel Beckett'; Brater, *The Drama in the Text*, 112–15.

21   The composition dates for these works are: *Embers* (1959), *Rough for Radio II* (early 1960s), *Words and Music* (1961) and *Cascando* (1962).

22   Beckett studied Greek and would have been familiar with *on* ('being,' 'presence'), a term that is often used in philosophical contexts. For H. Porter Abbott's brilliant analysis of the trope of 'onwardness' in Beckett, see *Beckett Writing Beckett*, 32–42.

23   See for example section 275: 'Once a thing is put in writing, it rolls about all over the place, falling into the hands of those who have no concern with it just as easily as under the notice of those who comprehend; it has no notion of whom to address or whom to avoid. And when it is ill-treated or abused as illegitimate, it always needs its father to help it, being quite unable to protect itself'; *Phaedrus*, 69–70. For Derrida's discussion of the 'legitimacy' of speech, see 'The Father of the Logos' in 'Plato's Pharmacy,' 75–84.

24   *Embers* echoes not only the opening to *Hamlet* but also the 'Proteus' episode in *Ulysses*, which explores issues of epistemology and ontology, as Stephen strolls along Sandymount Strand listening to the 'wave speech' of the sea. That Joyce plays Stephen off against Hamlet is very much to Beckett's purposes. All quotations from the radio and stage plays come from *Collected Shorter Plays* and are parenthetically noted in the text.

25   Radio broadcasts, as well as tape recordings, function as kinds of 'writing' insofar as they literally reconfigure the voice, transcribe it in such a way that it becomes a form of secondary representation. That transcription is made electronically rather than scriptively, technologically rather than manually, but it is a transcription nevertheless and therefore carries with it all of the simulacral effects that Derrida attributes to writing.

26   When Croak arrives and announces that the theme is 'love,' Words simply repeats the set-piece on 'sloth,' substituting the word 'love' in appropriate places; at one point he catches himself failing to make the necessary substitution: 'Of all these movements then and who can number them and they are legion sloth is the LOVE is the most urgent . . .' (128).

27   In a paper delivered at the 1998 Conference of the Modern Language Association, Eric Prieto proposed a Schopenhauerian reading of *Words*

and Music – obviously very different from my own – in which Music functions as an expression of Will, which 'can communicate knowledge of the essential, noumenal realities' (2). I am grateful to Professor Prieto for having kindly made his paper available to me; it is adapted from a book manuscript entitled, *Listening In: Music, Mind and the Modernist Narrative.*

28 For the distinction between *mnēmē* and *hypomnēsis*, see 'Plato's Pharmacy,' 110–12.

29 The dates of composition for these plays are: *Krapp's Last Tape* (1958), *Not I* (1972), *That Time* (1974), *Footfalls* (1975), *Rockaby* (1980).

30 *Samuel Beckett*, 127–8. Connor is the only commentator I know of who treats the tape-recording as a form of writing.

31 On the relation between writing and Beckett's 'wordshit,' see Abbott, *Beckett Writing Beckett*, especially 63–7; for a politicized account of Beckett's 'excremental vision,' see Lloyd, *Anomalous States*, 41–58.

32 Gontarski refers to an 'inner voice' at various points; see *The Intent of Undoing in Samuel Beckett's Texts*, especially 132–3, 139.

33 See, for example, Mary Catanzaro's article, which offers a largely Lacanian reading of *Not I*, but which identifies the spoken text of Beckett's play with 'the realm of the inner voice' (37).

34 'a missile without provenance or target, caught up in a tumult of non-Newtonian motion . . . more and more in the dark, in the willessness, a mote in its absolute freedom'; see *Murphy*, 112–13.

35 For a discussion of the Husserlian *Punkt*, see Derrida, *Speech and Phenomena*, 60–9.

36 'Amy,' as critics have noted, is an anagram for 'May.'

37 See 'Plato's Pharmacy,' 91–3 and *Writing and Difference*, 182–4.

38 'Samuel Beckett, or Presence on the Stage' in Robbe-Grillet, *For a New Novel*.

39 See chapter 14 in Lydon, *Skirting the Issue: Essays in Literary Theory*. Lydon's use of 'mother tongue' is quite different from my own; she writes, 'as I evoke it here, the mother tongue, though properly archaic, carries no connotation of a full speech, of a recoverable maternal presence' (232).

References

Abbott, H. Porter (1996) *Beckett Writing Beckett: The Author in the Autograph.* Ithaca: Cornell University Press.

Barthes, Roland (1977) *Image, Music, Text.* Trans. Stephen Heath. New York: Hill and Wang.

Beckett, Samuel (1957) *Murphy.* New York: Grove Press.

—— (1959) *The Unnamable.* New York: Grove Press.

—— (1976) *Disjecta: Miscellaneous Writings and a Dramatic Fragment.* Ed. Ruby Cohn. New York: Grove Press.

—— (1984) *Collected Shorter Plays.* New York: Grove Press.

—— (1996) *No How On: Company, Ill See Ill Said, Worstward Ho.* New York: Grove Press.

Begam, Richard (1992) 'Splitting the *Différance*: Beckett, Derrida and the Unnamable.' *Modern Fiction Studies* 38(4): 873–92.

—— (1996) *Samuel Beckett and the End of Modernity*. Stanford: Stanford University Press.

Ben-Zvi, Linda (1980) 'Samuel Beckett, Fritz Mauthner, and the Limits of Language.' *PMLA* 95: 183–200.

—— (1984) 'Fritz Mauthner for Company.' *Journal of Beckett Studies* 9: 65–88.

Brater, Enoch (1994) *The Drama in the Text: Beckett's Late Fiction*. New York: Oxford University Press.

Butler, Lance St. John (1984) *Samuel Beckett and the Meaning of Being: A Study in Ontological Parable*. London: Macmillan.

Catanzaro, Mary F. (1980) 'Recontextualizing the Self: The Voice as Subject in Beckett's *Not I*.' *South Central Review* 7(1): 36–49.

—— (1989) 'The Voice of Absent Love in *Krapp's Last Tape* and *Company*.' *Modern Drama* 32(3): 401–12.

Cohn, Ruby (1962) *Samuel Beckett: The Comic Gamut*. New Brunswick, NJ: Rutgers University Press.

Connor, Steven (1988) *Samuel Beckett: Repetition, Theory and Text*. Oxford: Blackwell.

Dancy, J. (1985) *Introduction to Contemporary Epistemology*. Oxford: Blackwell.

Derrida, Jacques (1973) *Speech and Phenomena*. Trans. David B. Allison. Evanston, IL: Northwestern University Press.

—— (1974) *Of Grammatology*. Trans. Gayatri Chakravorty Spivak. Baltimore: Johns Hopkins University Press.

—— (1978) *Writing and Difference*. Trans. Alan Bass. Chicago: University of Chicago Press.

—— (1981) *Dissemination*. Trans. B. Johnson. Chicago: University of Chicago Press.

—— (1982) *Margins of Philosophy*. Trans. Alan Bass. Chicago: University of Chicago Press.

Descartes, René (1985) *The Philosophical Writings of Descartes*, vol 1. Eds. and trans. John Cottingham, Robert Stoohoff, and Dugald Murdoch. Cambridge: Cambridge University Press.

Gontarski, S. E. (1985) *The Intent of Undoing in Samuel Beckett's Dramatic Texts*. Bloomington, IN: Indiana University Press.

Handwerk, Gary (1992) 'Alone with Beckett's *Company*.' *Journal of Beckett Studies* 2(1): 65–82.

Henning, Sylvie Debevec (1988) *Beckett's Critical Complicity: Carnival, Contestation, and Tradition*. Lexington: University Press of Kentucky.

Hicks, Jim (1993) 'Partial Interpretation and *Company*: Beckett, Foucault, et al. and the Author Question.' *Studies in Twentieth-Century Literature* 17(2): 309–23.

Hill, Leslie (1990) *Beckett's Fiction: In Different Words*. Cambridge: Cambridge University Press.

Jewinski, Ed (1990) 'Beckett's *Company*, Post-structuralism, and *Mimetalogique*.' In *Rethinking Beckett: A Collection of Critical Essays*. Eds. Lance St. John Butler and Robin J. Davis. New York: St. Martin's Press.

Kenner, Hugh (1961) *Samuel Beckett: A Critical Study*. Berkeley: University of California Press.

Knowlson, James (1996) *Damned to Fame: The Life of Samuel Beckett*. New York: Simon & Schuster.

Krance, Charles (1990) 'Beckett's *Encores*: Textual Genesis as *Still*-Life Performance.' *Essays in Theatre* 8(2): 121–6.

Levy, Eric P. (1982) '"Company": The Mirror of Beckettian Mimesis.' *Journal of Beckett Studies* 8: 95–104.

Lloyd, David (1993) *Anomalous States: Irish Writing and the Post-Colonial Moment*. Durham, NC: Duke University Press.

Lydon, Mary (1995) *Skirting the Issue: Essays in Literary Theory*. Madison, WI: University of Wisconsin Press.

Locatelli, Carla (1990) *Unwording the World: Samuel Beckett's Prose After the Nobel Prize*. Philadelphia: University of Pennsylvania.

McCrudden, I. C. (1994) 'The Phenomenon of Voice in *Company*: Listening to the "I."' *Constructions* 9: 47–60.

Moorjani, Angela B. (1982) *Abysmal Games in the Novels of Samuel Beckett*. Chapel Hill: North Carolina Studies in the Romance Languages and Literatures, University of North Carolina Press.

Murphy, P. J. (1992) 'On First Looking Into Beckett's *The Voice*.' In *The Ideal Core of the Onion*. Eds. John Pilling and Mary Bryden. Reading: Beckett International Foundation.

Naremore, James (1973) *The World Without a Self: Virginia Woolf and the Novel*. New Haven: Yale University Press.

Nietzsche, F. (1979) 'On Truth and Lies in a Nonmoral Sense.' In *Philosophy and Truth: Selections from Nietzsche's Notebooks of the Early 1870s*. Ed. and trans. D. Breazeale. Atlantic Highlands, NJ: Humanities Press.

—— (1986) *Human, All Too Human: A Book for Free Spirits*. Trans. R. J. Hollingdale. Cambridge: Cambridge University Press.

Perloff, Marjorie (1996) *Wittgenstein's Ladder: Poetic Language and the Strangeness of the Ordinary*. Chicago: University of Chicago Press.

Pilling, J. (1982) 'Review Article: *Company* by Samuel Beckett.' *Journal of Beckett Studies* 7: 127–31.

Plato (1956) *Phaedrus*. Trans. W. C. Helmbold and W. G. Rabinowitz. New York: Macmillan.

Prieto, Eric (1998) 'Music and Mimesis in Beckett's *Cascando* and *Words and Music*.' Paper presented at the annual meeting of the Modern Language Association, San Francisco, Dec.

Rabinovitz, Rubin (1984) *The Development of Samuel Beckett's Fiction*. Urbana: University of Illinois Press.

Robbe-Grillet, Alain (1965) *For a New Novel: Essays on Fiction*. Trans. Richard Howard. New York: Grove Press.

Rorty, Richard (1989) *Contingency, Irony, and Solidarity*. Cambridge: Cambridge University Press.

Rousseau, Jean-Jacques (1964) *The First and Second Discourses*. Ed. Roger D Masters. Trans. John D. and Judith R. Masters. New York: St. Martin's Press.

Sellars, Wilfrid (1991) *Science, Perception and Reality*. Atascadero, CA: Ridgeview Publishing.

Trezise, Thomas (1990) *Into the Breach: Samuel Beckett and the Ends of Literature*. Princeton: Princeton University Press.

Vattimo, G. (1991) *The End of Modernity: Nihilism and Hermeneutics in Postmodern Culture*. Trans. J. R. Snyder. Baltimore: Johns Hopkins Press.

2
Beckett in the Wilderness: Writing about (Not) Writing about Beckett

Robert Eaglestone

'How could I write, sign, countersign performatively texts which "respond" to Beckett? How could I avoid the platitude of a supposed academic metalanguage? It is very hard.'

Jacques Derrida (1992)

'I do not deny that there are differences . . . between philosophy and literature . . . I am suggesting that we do not understand these differences.'

Stanley Cavell (1976)

'Literary commentary may cross the line and become as demanding as literature: it is an unpredictable or unstable genre that cannot be subordinated, a priori to its referential or commentating function.'

Geoffrey Hartman (1980)

Introduction: Beckett and the basic concepts of criticism

In *Being and Time*, Heidegger writes that the

real movement of the sciences [*wissenschaft* – sciences in the sense of 'branches of human knowledge'] takes place when their basic concepts undergo a more or less radical revision which is transparent to itself. The level which a science has reached is determined by how far it is *capable* of a crisis in its basic concepts.

He goes on to discuss a range of sciences and argues that each has (or had, by 1927) reached a crisis in its foundations: in mathematics, in the controversy over the reality of the object of mathematics; in physics, over relativity; in biology over 'vitalism'. In the human sciences, too, Heidegger identifies a crisis of foundations: 'the history of literature' he writes 'is to become the history of problems' (Heidegger 1962).

In this chapter, I will suggest that thinking about Beckett's work highlights problems in 'thinking about literature' (a field broader than 'English', perhaps: 'literature science' or 'thinking about literature'?). This means that thinking about Beckett's work is a very useful way to judge the capability for crisis of 'thinking about literature' and so, in turn, judge its 'real movement'. This is not because I think that any work by Beckett is a unique case – any more than any work of literature is unique or not unique – but because his works do clearly test the limits of our ideas about what literature is and the what foundations of 'thinking about literature' should be. (I feel sure that these problems could be explored using the work of any writer, given enough analysis: but the liminal nature of Beckett's writing focuses the discussion much more). This chapter, then, is less on Beckett's work itself and more on the frameworks which allow us to understand Beckett's work: what I have called 'thinking about literature'.

I take 'thinking about literature' to be a form of thinking and writing that in general, *pace* Derrida, 'is structurally philosophical', either explicitly or implicitly, and bears some relation to texts it calls 'literature' (in fact, naming them 'literary' may make up part of its structure) (Derrida, 1992: 53). 'Explicitly' here might mean something like: how 'thinking about literature' makes, or fails to make, sense of our lives, or how it clearly uses metaphysical assumptions. 'Implicitly' might mean something like: how forms of criticism that rely on, for example, discussions of form, politics or the history of performance turn out to make and to rely on deeper assumptions, usually thought of as being within the province of philosophy. However, it is not at all clear that these can be effectively separated, even for the sake of argument. Incidentally, it is not just thinkers in the European tradition like Derrida who argue this: in a discussion of Nussbaum, Hilary Putnam argues that the 'work of fiction must not be confused with the "commentary" and it is the commentary that is . . . a work of . . . philosophy' (Putnam, 1983: 199). Here again, the idea that 'thinking about literature' will always fall into the philosophical emerges, which in turn problematizes precisely the relation between the two discourses. I am, very briefly, going to look at five different ways of understanding the relationship between the literary and the philosophical. Each of these ways will incorporate Beckett's work in a range of ways, and each, in turn, will offer a version of how far 'thinking about literature' is 'capable of a crisis in its basic concepts'.

1. Literature as entertainment, philosophy as the work

Despite Aristotle's implicit 'defence of poetry' in the *Poetics*, the *locus classicus* for beginning to discuss the relationship between literature and philosophy has been the *Republic*. Reason demands, as Socrates reminds us, that poetry is banished from the state. The only art should be that which 'like the breezes from some healthy country' moulds the Guardians 'into sympathy and conformity with what is rational and right' (Plato, 1955: 195). Of course, even though Plato's position is one which has been attacked ever since, it still remains powerful. This philosophical distaste for literature as anything other than dubious entertainment was increased by the movement of 'analytic philosophy': one example here is Russell on Tolstoy. Russell admires him not for his 'philosophy': this he judges as weak and explicitly snipes at him and it in four places in his magisterial *History of Western Philosophy*. But Russell does admit to admiring Tolstoy as a writer when he forgets to theorize and just writes and feels:

> [W]hat is valuable in Tolstoi, to my mind, is his power of right ethical judgements, and his perceptions of concrete facts: his theories are, of course, completely worthless. It is the saddest misfortune of the human race that he has so little powers of reasoning. (Russell, 1998: 195)

This has set the tone for much analytic philosophy, despite its reflections on aesthetics.

One more contemporary example, from many, will be enough to illustrate this. In a collection of conversations with philosophers, Bryan Magee meets Iris Murdoch to discuss philosophy and literature. Magee has a preamble: philosophy 'is not, as such, a branch of literature: its quality and importance rest on quite other considerations than literary and aesthetic values. If a philosopher writes well, that's a bonus' (Magee, 1978: 264). Then, to Murdoch, he asks a leading question: '[W]hen you are writing a novel on the one hand and philosophy on the other, are you conscious that these two are racially different kinds of writing?' To which she has to reply:

> Yes I am. Philosophy aims to clarify and to explain, it states and attempts to solve very difficult highly technical problems and the writer must be subservient to this aim ... literature entertains, it does many things, and philosophy does one thing. (Magee, 1978: 264)

These seem very clear-cut distinctions. However, a sceptical mind might ask: why the need to make such clear divisions if the division was not blurred in the first place? Moreover, Murdoch's reference to Isaiah Berlin's famous essay on Tolstoy and History, 'The Fox and the Hedgehog' – the 'fox knows may things, but the hedgehog knows one big thing' – complicates matters (Berlin, 1998: 436). As Bernard Williams states in his memorial address for Isaiah Berlin, it was not that his work was not philosophical, it just was not philosophy as it was recognized in Oxford at the time, and part of the aim of Berlin's essay is precisely to question these boundaries by revealing the tensions between Tolstoy's world-view and his strengths as a writer, and implicitly, it seems to me, to question these boundaries. A reference to this is not merely to a way of making categories for thinking, but a reference to precisely the tension that Magee and Murdoch are trying to pass over.

The upshot of this division between the philosophical and the literary, for this for 'thinking about literature', is that, as Stein Haugom Olsen claims, 'style, content and structure are the subjects of literary criticism, and it is difficult to see what else it can be about' (Olsen, 1987: 3). However, as I have already suggested, this division is not as clear-cut as it might appear. There seem to be four ways of questioning this analytic and commercial division, at least in the case of Beckett.

2. Literature as philosophy

This first is to argue – *contra* the analytic position – that literature simply is part of philosophy, that it does the work of philosophy, if perhaps 'in a different key'. What does the 'work of philosophy' consist of? For Richard Rorty, it consists in making us less cruel by persuading us to become postmetaphysical liberal ironists. Literature has a role to play in this:

> [F]iction like that of Dickens, Olive Schreiner, or Richard Wright gives us the details about kinds of suffering endured by people to whom we had previously not attended. Fiction like that of Choderlos de Laclos, Henry James, or Nabakov gives us the details about what sorts of cruelty we ourselves are capable of, and thereby lets us redescribe ourselves. This is why the novel, the movies, and the TV programme have, gradually but steadily, replaced the sermon and the treatise as the principle vehicles of moral change and progress. (Rorty, 1989: xvi)

Rorty goes further in suggesting that not only does literature do the work of philosophy, it does it better than philosophy does: he offers, for example, 'Dickens as a sort of anti-Heidegger' and, in a world where only one or the other could be saved, Rorty writes that 'I should much prefer that they preserve Dickens' (Rorty, 1991a: 68). Rorty, of course, draws on the Pragmatism of James and on what he describes as the 'radical holism common to Wittgenstein, Quine, Dewey, Davidson and Derrida' (Rorty, 1991a: 130). Yet, perhaps oddly, he suggests that that literature and the philosophical position to which he allies it are 'in the service of democratic politics – as a contribution to the attempt to achieve what Rawls calls "reflective equilibrium" between our instinctive reactions to contemporary problems and the general principles on which we have been reared' (Rorty, 1989: 196).

For Martha Nussbaum, too, literature is a form of philosophy and central to philosophy's work. In her essay on Beckett, for example, she writes that her project to investigate the dialogue between philosophy and literature on the question 'how should one live?'

> takes its bearings from Henry James's claim that that the novelist's art performs a practical task, the task in assisting us in pursuit of that question by expressing a 'projected morality' and an active 'sense of life', and also from Proust's claim that it is only in a text having narrative form that certain essential truths about human life can be appropriately expressed and examined. At its core is the claim that literary form and human content are inseparable. (Nussbaum, 1990: 289)

Like Wayne Booth, Nussbaum, draws on the neo-Aristotelian project whose most convincing advocate in philosophy is perhaps Alastair MacIntyre: her claims stem from, or at least are a piece with, the arguments in *After Virtue* which stress that:

> man is in his actions, as well as in his fictions, essentially a story-telling animal . . . I can only answer the question 'What am I to do?' if I can answer the prior question 'Of what stories do I find myself a part?' . . . telling stories has a key part in educating us into the virtues. (MacIntyre, 1985: 216)

(In turn, it might be possible to trace the intellectual history of this to the movement of the Catholic church back to Thomism – and so Aristotelianism – after the first Vatican council.) Nussbaum too, finds the idea of Rawls' 'reflective equilibrium' very appealing. For Nussbaum, perception of suffering is a crucial part of the task of philosophy: we should aim to 'to make ourselves people "on whom nothing is lost"'. (Nussbaum, 1990: 169; James, 1934: 149). She adopts Rawls, and renegotiates him to produce the idea of 'perceptive equilibrium', the:

> ability to see and care for particulars, not as representatives of the law, but as what they themselves are: to respond vigorously with senses and emotions before the new; to care deeply about chance happenings in the world, rather than to fortify ourselves against them; to wait for the outcome, and to be bewildered – to wait and float and to be actively passive. (Nussbaum, 1990: 75)

Roughly, then, and despite their very different (and sometimes contradictory) points of intellectual origin and overall trajectory, both Rorty and Nussbaum see literature as doing a central part of the work of philosophy: effectively, as part of philosophy. This is either because interpreting a 'tragedy is messier . . . than assessing a philosophical example . . . [and] To invite such material into the centre of an ethical . . . is . . . to add to its content a picture of reason's procedures and problems that could not be readily conveyed in any other form,' or, for both, because literature is more 'democratic' than philosophy as traditionally understood: thus, the convergence for both in the work of Rawls (Nussbaum, 1986: 14).

I have discussed the problems with Nussbaum's understanding of literature elsewhere: despite their differences, Rorty's approach shares some similar difficulties. Both pass over the issue of textuality by seeming to assume an unmediated relation to the text: as Richard Wollheim argues, commenting on Nussbaum, 'the most powerful considerations for thinking that literature is an essential element in the formation of moral philosophy also show how crucial it is to have commentary as well' (Wollheim, 1983: 189–90). They also offer a straightforward understanding of the idea of reading (that, for example, it involves identification, the need for surprise and emotional response). Rorty's position is slightly more complex, but he too rejects 'the literariness of language' in his essay on Paul de Man (Rorty, 1991b: 132).

These two contrasting approaches (the neo-Aristotleian, the neo-pragmatist) both view literature as a key part of their projects: for each, the literary becomes the philosophical. If this is the case, then to write on 'Beckett and Philosophy' means that there is very little friction between the two: that one really is the other and all that is required is a commentary on how Beckett simply is philosophy or to show how Beckett – or any literature – can be reduced to philosophy. If this is the case with a writer like Beckett, then perhaps all of literary studies could easily collapse into an omnivorous discipline of philosophy.

3. Literature as a parody of philosophy

Another common view of the relation between the two areas is that literature can be – and Beckett is – a parody of philosophy, whether Cartesian (in the *Trilogy*, most famously) or other (Ullman, 1989: 158). Indeed, Beckett's 'first separately published work', the poem *Whoroscope* from 1930, concerns Descartes and (perhaps in an eggy nod to Swift's Lilliput) his preference for eggs 8–10 days old. If, as Cronin's biography suggests while giving the publication history, the poem is 'based on Descartes's life, not his theories', there is no 'philosophical' parody (Cronin, 1996: 116). However, just as the lobster's death and ensuing consumption at the end of 'Dante and the Lobster' stimulate thoughts of death, so the consumption of 'this abortion of a fledgling' by 'Descartes' are tied in with reflections on geometry and transubstantiation throughout the poem (Beckett, 1976: 84). There are other parallels or parodies: *Worstword Ho!* can easily be read as a parody of a phenomenological exploration of embodiment, for example.

Or another, perhaps more tendentious example: two men are talking in a public place, asking each other questions and discussing – either directly or indirectly – their ignorance, what they should be doing and the relationship of these to memory. Later they are joined in discussion by a third man and a slave boy. Questioning the slave boy, they get a development of what may – or may not be – universal truths. Dismissed from the conversation, the boy doesn't speak again. The conversation ends with the men deciding to leave, but not actually doing so. This is not, or not only, *Waiting for Godot*, but Plato's *Meno*.

But a parody is a parasite. Hillis Miller analyses the rhetorical significance of 'para' and argues that it is a doubly antithetical prefix, signifying proximity and distance, similarity and difference, interiority and exteriority: to 'parody' (from para + 'oide', or song) is to be implicated in and at an angle to the original discourse (Miller, 1979: 218–19). Of course, this difference needs to be thought out more clearly, but, to write roughly, a parody is part of philosophy. (And philosophers don't need poets to make them look ridiculous by imitation: in his *Dialogues Concerning Natural Religion*, David Hume parodies arguments by analogy, and, famously, Hegel parodies Kant, the swimming instructor who wants to know how to swim without getting wet) (Hume, 1980: Part 6). Parody comes down to 'literature as philosophy', and in turn reduces Beckett – and all literature if it is 'parodic' – to a footnote to, or at best, a humorous example of, philosophy.

4. Literature as an influence on philosophy

A third way of taking down these boundaries is to explore the way in which the literary has influenced philosophy: in the case of Beckett, this area is covered by, for example Richard Begam's work. For Begam, Beckett is a 'buried subtext . . . in French poststructuralism, the writer who spoke most resonantly to those thinkers in France who came after Sartre'. Expanding on work by Hill, Connor and Trezise, who read Beckett thought poststructuralism, Begam aims to 'read the discourse of poststructuralism through Beckett' (Begam, 1996: 11). Anthony Ullman's *Beckett and Poststructuralism* is also aware of this, and discusses the intersections of literary and philosophical ideas; Lance Butler sees Beckett as a 'deconstructionist *avant la lettre*' who fits the 'new paradigm of western consciousness . . . of postmodernism and poststructuralism' (Butler, 1999: 41).

All this begs two questions: first, is a literary influence separate from a wider cultural one? That is, is there anything specifically literary about this form of influence? Everyone is a child of their time. If literature has an influence on philosophy that is specifically different from, for example, a historical event, then what is it and how does it come about? Second, although it is fascinating and scholarly and important to trace these influences, is it necessarily illuminating? It reveals that significant figures have had ideas that influence each other, and that ideas often develop in parallel, but simply tracing the development of an idea is not necessarily the same as engaging with it. The study of how two contrasting discourses develop and cross-fertilize each other in many ways doesn't have to engage with the discourses *per se*. As Jonathan Rée points out, the history of philosophy 'is the curiously ritualised discipline that has managed to dominate academic philosophy ever since the eighteenth century, busying itself with canonical texts from the ancient Greeks to the present and forcing them into a narrative pattern with a beginning, a middle and an end' (Rée, 1999: 382). Like 'children playing with toy soldiers', its practitioners are concerned with assigning 'each philosopher to a unique place in a table of classification' (Rée, 1999: 382). And the same is often true, of course, of literary history. In this, Beckett's work and influence is no more than an exhibit to be filed away.

5. Just texts?

Finally, a fourth way of destroying this boundary would be to argue that the texts of literature and philosophy are just texts, and the genre distinctions we impose upon them are just that – violent impositions. Geoffrey Bennington states this position very clearly when he writes that 'there is no linear scale with a literary end and a philosophical end' (Bennington, 1988: 112). Of course, this is true in more than the banal sense that a philosophy book and a novel are both commonly called books and use language. Expanding Derrida's discussion in 'White Mythologies', it is possible to argue that both literature and philosophy often use, for example, narrative. In the case of novels, this is clear; in philosophy, it is more stealthy. *The Phenomenology of Spirit*, for example, is often compared to – or even described as – a *bildungsroman* (see, for example, Rée, 1987).

However, is this 'textualism', like Russell's turtles, the case 'all the way down'? Cavell's epigraph expresses a slightly different worry: 'I do not deny that there are differences ... between philosophy and literature or between philosophy and literary criticism; I am suggesting that we do not understand these differences' (Cavell, 1976: xviii). In reading 'philosophy' and reading 'literature' we have different criteria for arriving at conclusions – even postmodern temporary conclusions – and often have different aims for reading. This is not to say we can't read a novel 'philosophically' – indeed, I have been trying to ask how we might *not* read a work in this manner – or a work of philosophy 'poetically': it is just that I am not clear what these differences are. The difference may just be in the way we attend to texts. If there are just undifferentiated texts in a Borgesian library of Babel, why choose a philosophical way of attending (except through random whim) unless the text to which one attended had something specific to offer: and if it has something specific to offer, then there are not just undifferentiated texts. (All this shows is that we have worked from the presupposition that all writing is not 'undifferentiated text.')

Conclusion: Derrida's demanding dreams, crossing the line

Then we are left with one of two options. Either literature is one thing (foxy 'entertainment', knowing lots of things) and philosophy another (explanatory). Or, in different ways, literature turns out to be philosophy ('literature as philosophy'). Beckett's work – and the critical heritage of Beckett, the texts held together by the 'Beckett-naming function' – is a test case here. Either this work is philosophical or it is not. If it is philosophical, its literary nature disappears, and it may as well not have been written (for example, philosophy can explain our finitude better than Malone can). If it is literary, we cannot talk about it (but we do) (see Ricks, 1990). No wonder Derrida desperately dreams 'of a writing that would be neither philosophy or literature, nor even contaminated by one or the other' (Derrida, 1992: 73). What does this opposition reveal about the capability for 'thinking about literature' to be in crisis, about the 'history of problems'? I suggest that 'thinking about Beckett' is a way of beginning Derrida's dream (or at least, of falling asleep).

I suggest that the work of Beckett – again, as a test case – reveals a transformative moment, a 'real movement' in Heidegger's phrase, in 'thinking and writing about literature'. This movement has been discussed by Geoffrey Hartman in *Criticism in the Wilderness*, where he writes that literary 'commentary may cross the line and become as demanding as literature: it is an unpredictable or unstable genre that cannot be subordinated, a priori to its referential or commentating function' (Hartman, 1980: 201). In response to fears that 'the critical would jeopardize the creative spirit', thinking about literature was only 'acknowledged at the price of being denied literary status and assigned a clearly subordinate, service function' (Hartman, 1980: 212–13). In fact, for Hartman, thinking about literature is 'a genre, or a primary text' in its own right and the 'critical' writer is 'both an interpreter of texts and a self-interpreting producer of other texts' (Hartman, 1980: 6 and 162). Writers on Beckett are writers (in a full sense) 'after Beckett', not just chronologically, but in terms of their genre. However, the 'genre' of criticism is not a simple one: it turns out to be neither fully literary nor fully philosophical. Texts in genres share characteristics, and the 'critical genre' draws on both other works of 'criticism' and on other genres.

An example of this from outside the 'Beckett studies' world: Homi Bhabha has developed a great deal of his thought from a meditation on Salman Rushdie's novels.[1] In *The Location of Culture* the title of a key chapter, 'How Newness Enters the World', is taken from Rushdie, as are many of the essay's themes: Rushdie's work permeates his writing. But, and this is the crucial point, Rushdie's work doesn't just permeate Bhabha's at the level of commentary or ideas, but at the level of style. Just as Rushdie offers a polyglot postmodern performance, so Bhabha offers, as Bart Moore-Gilbert points out, a 'Babelian' one.[2] Moore-Gilbert goes on to describe Bhabha's 'characteristically teasing, evasive, even quasi-mystical style (or mystificatory)... designed to appeal to the reader's intuition... Bhabha often bends his sources – at times radically – to his own particular needs' (Moore-Gilbert, 1997: 115). This description would, of course, fit Rushdie too. Bhabha develops his writing both in the same genre as Rushdie's and in the same genre as 'thinking about literature'. I suggest that this same influence has worked on those 'thinkers about literature' who follow 'after Beckett'. Just as the events that are Rushdie's novels permeate Bhabha's work, the events that are Beckett's texts permeate Beckett criticism. And if Beckett's works are impossibilities, so, then, is criticism of Beckett. Paradoxically, not writing about Beckett's texts is the most responsive way of writing about his work. An awareness of this is precisely the capability for crisis of criticism – that Beckett just can't be written about. How much we can't talk is a sign of how criticism has developed.

Derrida, cited in the epigraph, hesitates to write on Beckett: Simon Critchley argues that the 'writings of Samuel Beckett seem to be particularly, perhaps uniquely, resistant to philosophical interpretation' (Critchley, 1997: 141). This essay has taken these claims seriously and explored why this is, not so much by looking at Beckett's work but at how literature and philosophy relate to each other, using Beckett as a test case. This has shown that, because the crisis 'thinking about literature' has opened up the literary to a new genre or at least a new way of thinking about itself, 'thinking about Beckett' will be as stuttering as Beckett's work appears to be, will be 'after Beckett'. This development in 'thinking about literature' accounts for the Beckettian trope in Beckett criticism that runs, with variations, like this: 'we cannot write on Beckett. We must write on'.

Notes

1 And Rushdie has returned the compliment: In *The Moor's Last Sigh*, Dr Zeenat Vakil, 'a brilliant young art theorist,' writes '*Imperso-Nation and Dis/Semi/Nation: Dialogics of Eclecticism and Interrogations of Authenticity in A. Z.* [the painter Auroura Zogoiby]' (Salman Rushdie, *The Moor's Last Sigh* (London: Vintage, 1996), p. 329). This is surely a backhanded reference to Bhabha's work.

2 Bart Moore-Gilbert, *Postcolonial Theory: Contexts, Practices, Politics* (London: Verso, 1997), p. 114: he takes the phrase from Homi Bhabha, *The Location of Culture* (London: Routledge, 1994), p. 135, and Bhabha in turn takes it from Derrida.

References

Beckett, Samuel (1976) *I can't go on, I'll go on: A Samuel Beckett Reader*, ed. Richard W. Seaver. New York: Grove Press.

Begam, Richard (1996) *Samuel Beckett and the End of Modernity*. Stanford: Stanford Univerity Press.

Bennington, Geoffrey (1988) 'Deconstruction and the Philosophers (The Very Idea).' *Oxford Literary Review* 10: 73–110.

Berlin, Isaiah (1998) *The Proper Study of Mankind*. London: Pimlico.

Bhabha, Homi (1994) *The Location of Culture*. London: Routledge.

Butler, Lance (1999) 'Samuel Beckett's End, or: The Perfect Future.' In *Beckett and Beyond*, ed. Bruce Stewart. Gerrards Cross: Colin Smith.

Cavell, Stanley (1976) *Must We Mean What We Say?* Cambridge: Cambridge University Press.

Critchley, Simon (1997) *Very Little . . . Almost Nothing*. London: Routledge.

Cronin, Anthony (1996) *Samuel Beckett: The Last Modernist*. London: Harper Collins.

Derrida, Jacques (1992) '"This Strange Institution Called Literature": An Interview with Jacques Derrida.' Trans. Geoffrey Bennington and Rachel Bowlby, in Jacques Derrida, *Acts of Literature*, ed. Derek Attridge. London: Routledge.

Hartman, Geoffrey (1980) *Criticism in the Wilderness*. London: Yale University Press.

Heidegger, Martin (1962) *Being and Time*, trans. John Macquarrie and Edward Robinson. Oxford: Blackwell.

Hume, David (1980) *Dialogues Concerning Natural Religion*, ed. Richard Popkin. Cambridge: Hackett.

James, Henry (1934) *The Art of the Novel*. New York: Scribner.

MacIntyre, Alasdair (1985) *After Virtue*, 2nd ed. London: Duckworth.

Magee, Bryan (1978) *Men of Ideas*. London: BBC.

Miller, J. Hillis (1979) 'The Critic as Host.' In *Deconstruction and Criticism*, Harold Bloom et al. eds. London: Routledge and Kegan Paul: 217–53.

Moore-Gilbert, Bart (1997) *Postcolonial Theory: Contexts, Practices, Politics*. London: Verso.

Nussbaum, Martha (1986) *The Fragility of Goodness*. Cambridge: Cambridge University Press.

Nussbaum, Martha (1990) *Love's Knowledge: Essays on Philosophy and Literature*. Oxford: Oxford University Press.

Olsen, Stein Haugom (1987) *The End of Literary Theory*. Cambridge: Cambridge University Press.

Plato, (1955) *The Republic*, trans. H. D. P. Lee. Harmondsworth: Penguin.

Putnam, Hilary (1983) 'Taking Rules Seriously – A Response to Martha Nussbaum.' *New Literary History* 15: 193–200.

Rée, Jonathan (1987) *Philosophical Tales: An Essay on Philosophy and Literature*. London: Methuen.

Rée, Jonathan (1999) *I See a Voice: Language, Deafness and the Senses – A Philosophical History*. London: Harper Collins.

Ricks, Christopher (1990) *Beckett's Dying Words*. Oxford: Clarendon Press.

Rorty, Richard (1989) *Contingency, Irony and Solidarity*. Cambridge: Cambridge University Press.

Rorty, Richard (1991a) 'Heidegger, Kundera, and Dickens.' In *Philosophical Papers*. Cambridge: Cambridge University Press, vol. 2: 66–82.

Rorty, Richard (1991b) 'De Man and the American Cultural Left.' In *Philosophical Papers*. Cambridge: Cambridge University Press, vol. 2: 129–39.

Rushdie, Salman (1996) *The Moor's Last Sigh*. London: Vintage.

Russell, Bertrand (1998) *Autobiography*. London: Routledge.

Ullman, Anthony (1989) *Beckett and Poststructuralism*. Cambridge: Cambridge University Press.

Wollheim, Richard (1983) 'Flawed Crystals: James's *The Golden Bowl* and the Plausibility of Literature as Moral Philosophy.' *New Literary History* 15: 185–91.

Part II
Beckett and French Thought

3
Cinders: Derrida with Beckett

Gary Banham

'A certain nihilism is both interior to metaphysics (the final fulfilment of metaphysics, Heidegger would say) and then, already, beyond. With Beckett in particular, the two possibilities are in the greatest possible proximity and competition. He is nihilist and he is not nihilist.'[1]

The above statement of Derrida's came in response to a question from Derek Attridge as to whether Beckett's writing was not already so 'self-deconstructive' that there was not much left to do. Both Attridge's question and Derrida's answer are intriguing indications of the stakes at issue in assessing how Derrida can be related to Beckett. Attridge's question contains within it a set of assumptions about the nature of Derrida's critical engagements, not least the idea that there is 'something' that he attempts to do. Were this assumption correct then there would be a great deal of difficulty in Derrida engaging at all with Beckett, as it is Beckett's engagement with 'nothing' that is precisely the indication of his writing. The problem of an engagement with Beckett's work is thus the problem which Heidegger described in *What is Metaphysics?* as the difficulty of engaging with nothing, not turning nothing into a something (Heidegger, 1993).

Far from Derrida's difficulty with Beckett being that he finds himself engaged on the positive project that would bar any possibility of relating to the nature of Beckett's work, he states instead in the interview with Attridge that he finds himself 'too close' to Beckett (Attridge, 1992: 60). This closeness will be investigated here in relation to Derrida's exploration of the 'cinder effect', of what 'remains' from 'ruin' which will be treated in proximity to the writing which we find in Beckett's *The Unnamable*. Through associating the works of Beckett and Derrida as bodies of writing which share in the engagement with the 'nothing' that brings both to the edge of nihilism, this chapter will draw out the nature of the difficulty with experiencing the effect of both these bodies of writing.

Beckett's trilogy of novels published in the early 1950s culminated in the publication of *The Unnamable*. The characters who existed in the earlier volumes *Molloy* and *Malone Dies* were treated in *The Unnamable* as the fictions they had always been. This undermining of the earlier volumes in the trilogy was connected to the elaborate presentation and dismissal of characters within *The Unnamable* itself. This culminates in the arrival of a voice which no longer has any identity attached to it at all:

> And there is nothing for it but to wait for the end, nothing but for the end to come, and at the end all will be the same, at the end at last perhaps all the same as before, as all that livelong time when there was nothing for it but to get to the end, or fly from it, or wait for it, trembling or not, resigned or not, the nuisance of doing over, and of being, same thing, for one who could never do, never be. (Beckett, 1958: 88)

Here the first substantive word is 'nothing', and whilst repetition is an explicit theme of this utterance, it is not a repetition of anything, as one 'could never do, never be'. The repetition of nothing by no one: this would be the most economical way of stating the 'theme' of *The Unnamable*.

How can such a writing take place at all and what is its effect? Writing of *The Unnamable*, Blanchot states:

> Perhaps we are not dealing with a book at all, but with something more than a book; perhaps we are approaching that movement from which all books derive, that point of origin where, doubtless, the work is lost, the point which always ruins the work, the point of perpetual unworkableness with which the work must maintain an increasingly *initial* relation or risk becoming nothing at all. (Blanchot, 1979: 120)

The question of the nature of works is raised by this work. It undoes the work it took to create it and abandons the notion that there is an experience other than that of the encounter with the nothing.

If nothing is not to be left alone, if the heart of the work which undoes its work is to reveal that which cannot be revealed and to engage with that which cannot be engaged as it is not a 'thing' at all, then Beckett's work must be a ruin in principle and thus be concerned to ensure its own failure. This suggests a connection with the work of Derrida, who has the same difficulty of ensuring that his works do not simply add to the mapping of entities but instead 'resist' incorporation into the metaphysical positing of beings. The 'place' where this is stated most vividly is in *Cinders*, a work characterized by plural voices, none of which has the authority of a central narrator, and which circle as incessantly as the 'voice' in *The Unnamable*.

> – I understand that the cinder is nothing that can be in the world, nothing that remains as an entity [*étant*]. It is the being [*l'être*], rather, that there is – this is a name of the being that there is there but which, giving itself (*es gibt ashes*), is nothing, remains beyond everything that is (*konis epekeina tes ousias*), remains unpronounceable in order to make saying possible although it is nothing. (Derrida, 1991: 73; see Banham, 1996)

The 'name' here given to the nothing is 'cinder'. The 'cinder' is not part of what can be placed, it lacks being and cannot be approached in words as it lacks the basic capacity to be expressed in any way other than a reference to the 'thereness' of appearances. This 'thereness' is not connected to the relation of beings to one another but is the 'placing' of them within the articulable realm of spacing itself. To trace spacing, to make the possibility of 'presence' appear as founded on nothing: this is the 'cinder effect' that Derrida explores.

If the 'voice' of *The Unnamable* is detached from any action, from any capacity to do anything other than speak in a vacuum about fiction, then this 'voice' exists in a realm of poverty. The poverty expressed within *The Unnamable* is given in the title of the work: the problem is that nothing cannot be named. To give names is to state that there is something in existence which is identifiable, open to view, and which appears when it appears as itself and not something else. With the experience of nothing there is no place to speak from, no one who can speak and no appearance of anything. We arrive then, in *The Unnamable*, at the very 'edge of language'.

Another writing of Derrida's that explores the 'edge of language' is *Sauf le nom (Post-Scriptum)*. Like *Cinders* this writing also circles round itself and it is also similar to *Cinders* in being cast in a plurivocal form.

> – 'At the edge of language' would then mean: 'at the edge as language', in the same and double movement: withdrawing [*dérobement*] and overflowing [*dérobement*]. But as the moment and the force, as the *movements* of the injunction take place *over the edge* [*par-dessus bord*], as they draw their energy *from having already taken place*, even if it is as a promise, the legible-illegible text, the theologico-negative maxim [*sentence*] remains as a *post-scriptum*. It is originarily a *post-scriptum*, it comes after the event . . . (Derrida, 1995: 60)

When we reach the 'edge of language' through the encounter with that which defies naming we find that language itself is an edge which cuts between the world and the one who speaks. This original cut is what Blanchot was referring to as the 'origin' of the work. At the 'origin' words stumble against that which calls them forth. If language is at such an edge then to engage with language is to be forced into a poverty which is original. This poverty consists in learning that the grounding of utterances is nothing. Before and after language is nothing. Language is after and in quest of nothing.

The waiting of which the 'voice' in *The Unnamable* speaks has no object. The 'voice' speaks of itself as incapable of renunciation and the finding of this incapacity is language.

> Yes, in my life, since we must call it so, there were three things, the inability to speak, the inability to be silent, and solitude, that's what I've tried to make the best of. (Beckett, 1958: 114)

The exploration of incapacity is connected to the problem of naming the basis on which naming stands. Just as language itself has no ground, so action requires something to focus it which would render it necessary to relate to a self as secure and stable. But if language itself is encountered in an original way as the 'post-scriptum' then it ceases to be possible to utilize it as a means to an end. The situation arises then which we could term an ethical suspension of the teleological. In this opening of language to its own disclosure the ethical encounter of being with its own lack of ground permits an exploration of nothing.

The granting of this opening by language has the effect of suspending the relation to action. In this suspension it becomes impossible to do anything except speak. And be silent. Which is to exist alone. But how to be alone when speaking involves an other to whom words are addressed? Does not the speaker of *The Unnamable* constantly invoke others who are there precisely to bear witness to his words? This is so, even though they are not 'there' at all but rather nowhere. The person who is not is spoken to by one who cannot speak in the silence which surrounds language as its ultimate base.

By contrast to the voice which seems to resound alone but requires and invents again and again, others who listen in Derrida's texts are constantly presented in plurivocal fashion. Another example of this is *A Silkworm of One's Own* from which we might 'cut' the following:

> Whilst in the language of rhetoric, a little like litotes, like extenuation or reticence, a diminution consists in saying less, sure, but with a view to *letting* more be understood.

> – But letting thus – and who lets what, lets who, be understood? – one can always speak of diminution *by diminution*. And, by this henceforth uncatchable stitching, still let rhetoric appropriate the truth of the verdict. (Derrida, 1996: 4–5)

Adding to the above the statement made by one of the interlocutors that there is here an attempt to 'diminish *ad infinitum*,' then this work again works its own undoing. The work of diminishing the infinite is itself an infinite task which given its incompletable nature demonstrates a failure in principle and inception to be its own basis. The failure of the attempt is inscribed in the exchange not least in the statement by one that an understanding will take place. The second speaker's questioning here touches precisely on the impossibility of the transaction which is engaged with by participating in the discussion.

Whether solitude or an infinite community of speakers is adopted as the method of addressing the 'edge' of language or rather the edge *as* language, matters little. Either way the work produced cuts itself. But this self-cutting, this severing of the work from itself, is a fracture which is original to the work of language and connects language not coincidentally to death. In the relation of language to life we find a cut between speech and action. In the relation of language to death we find the living proceeding by its own motion to its end. The end is infinite.

Between the opening of the *The Unnamable* and its conclusion words fill the void. What do these words do? They designate the opening of language to itself which opening occurs through the living death of the speaker/writer:

> perhaps that's what I am, the thing that divides the world in two, on the one side the outside, on the other the inside, that can be as thin as foil, I'm neither the one side nor the other, I'm in the middle, I'm the partition, I've two surfaces and no thickness, perhaps that's what I feel, myself vibrating, I'm the tympanum, on the one hand the mind, on the other the world, I don't belong to either, it's not to me they're talking . . . (Beckett, 1958: 100)

Between words and world there is the one on whom language bases itself. This one is termed the speaker/writer. This one is no one. But everyone is grounded here. The 'origin' of which Blanchot speaks is the space of the middle between words and world. This space opens and the divide or cut which is experienced through the word as creating the world speaks and says *I*.

The middle between the world and the word is broken. This breakage is the ground of experience but is not itself experienced as it is not available for a self but only the disintegration of selves can approach it. The breaking as the basis of experience: this is the 'cinder effect' discussed by Derrida.

> – Through the patient, tormenting, ironic return of the exegesis that leads to nothing and which the unsophisticated would find unseemly, would we be moulding the urn of a language for this cinder sentence, which he, he, has abandoned to its chance and to fate, a self-destructive virtue firing on its own right into the heart. (Derrida, 1991: 33)

The abandonment of nothing is what Heidegger characterized as the birth of metaphysics. To abandon nothing is to centre experience on something positive and assured, to find a ground in being for being. To seek after that which has been abandoned by philosophy is the suspensive task of entering the middle between words and world. Entering through the broken middle into the nothing.

The task of working to undo the work of making cannot be creating a new craft of holding language. We must rather be allowing the 'cut' of language to sink into us. The 'cinder sentence', *il y a là cendre*, finds its chance to be fateful. The fate of this sentence is tied to the deathly condition of language. But this condition is repeatable in the waiting which the 'voice' of *The Unnamable* describes. This repetition of the cinder sentence is the incessant finding of waste of effort to be integral to effort. If language is the urn of nothing then this shows us that to fail is to be and to be is to be on the way to nothing. The way is crossed by the non-way. This is the 'experience' of aporia.

> What am I to do, what shall I do, what should I do, in my situation, how proceed? By aporia pure and simple? Or by affirmations and negations invalidated as uttered, or sooner or later? Generally speaking. There must be other shifts. Otherwise it would be quite hopeless. But it is quite hopeless. I should mention before going any further, any further on, that I say aporia without knowing what it means. (Beckett, 1958: 7)

It is quite hopeless to attempt to avoid aporia. Avoiding would mean attempting not to engage aporia. If Derrida avoids directly addressing Beckett it is not because he can avoid aporia. The converse is the case. Derrida is aware that his path is entirely aporetic. The aporetic path followed by Derrida means he is always close, 'too close' to Beckett.

The 'voice' of *The Unnamable* declares that it does not know what aporia means. The meaning not being known could be settled by discovery if aporia was something. But aporia is nothing. The 'experience' of aporia is the experience of nothing. That is why it is 'quite hopeless'. If 'I' say aporia then 'I' say that there is a path which does not lead anywhere. This lack of 'place' which is involved with aporia's possibility marks aporia as impossible. The very nature of aporia is to escape meaning and this is its meaning.

If the 'voice' of *The Unnamable* begins its sojourn with impossibility then it will never end its journey. The diminution of the infinite is an infinite task. But this ensures that death does not interrupt language as language is the principle of death amongst the living.

Besides, *death* is always the name of a secret, since it signs the irreplaceable singularity. It puts forth the public name, the common name of a secret, the common name of the proper name without name. It is therefore always a shibboleth, for the manifest name of a secret is from the beginning a private name, so that language about death is nothing but the long history of a secret society, neither public nor private, semi-private, semi-public, on the border between the two, thus, also a sort of hidden religion of the *awaiting* (oneself as well as each other), with its ceremonies, cult, liturgy, or its Marranolike rituals (Derrida, 1993: 74).

The 'voice' of *The Unnamable* ventured the view that it was perhaps the middle, between the words and the world. This middle which arises from a cut is placed in this citation from Derrida's *Aporias* to be inhabited by death. Death is 'on the border' between the inner and outer, the same border that the 'I' of *The Unnamable* inhabits. The 'voice' of *The Unnamable* is the voice of death. Through language we meet death; it opens before us as that which we await and encounter through the nothing.

Derrida's *Aporias* takes us to this point only to begin multiplying questions. These questions touch precisely on the degree to which, on the crossed path, either Derrida or Beckett or both remain in the grip of the nihilism mentioned in the epigraph of this piece. To belong to nihilism is to uncover beneath metaphysics its underside which is, according to Heidegger, an abandonment of Being. The abandonment of questioning Being by substituting beings for Being has as its ultimate possibility the forgetting of Being in a new openness to nothing. Would this characterize the works of Derrida and Beckett and be their ultimate agreement?

The slippage of the 'voice' of *The Unnamable* from its place of utterance is integral to its utterance. This 'errancy' of speech in *The Unnamable* casts the 'voice' of this work outside itself. This 'thrown' nature of the voice prevents the voice from taking on the role of ultimate sayer of truth. For Derrida the approach to the question of waiting for death as the secret of language is followed by a sudden interrogation into this secrecy. Derrida questions himself:

> Who will guarantee that the name, the ability to name death (like that of naming the other, and it is the same) does not participate as much in the dissimulation of the 'as such' of death as in its revelation, and that language is not precisely the origin of the nontruth of death, and of the other? (Derrida, 1993: 76)

How could language enable us to know death 'as such'? Would this not be the nature of nihilism that it takes it that nothing can be known and hence that death is a solution to the problem of life?

If death was available 'as such' then death would not partake of the relation which we have been attempting to ascertain as integral to language, the relation to an original poverty. Death's 'as such' would be a new form of wealth, a further extension of the sway of positivity. Thus death would in fact function merely as another name and not for that which is unnamable save under the non-name of nothing. This is why Derrida turns away from the suggestion of Heidegger that being-towards-death is the waiting for something which will arrive, and instead follows the 'voice' of *The Unnamable* in assuming instead the relation to that which is not available as an occurrence due to the infinite nature of language.

> The ultimate aporia is the impossibility of the aporia *as such*. The reservoir of this statement seems to me incalculable. This statement is made with and reckons with the incalculable itself. (Derrida, 1993: 78)

The consequence of this statement is that nihilism is exposed as another name for the avoidance not, as Heidegger would suggest, of Being but rather of the poverty of 'original' experience. If metaphysics is understood in Heidegger's fashion as a series of names for Being, then it is not the term Being or any names given to it which matters but rather the act of nomination itself and the belief that what is named constitutes and controls the un-named. Returning to the 'origin' of language is to return to the repetition of the unnamable or, as Derrida terms it, 'the cinder effect'.

If nihilism is the attempt to name the unnamable with a term from positive science, then the return to the 'origin' of which Blanchot spoke cannot have as its basis a unitary sense. The 'origin' to which we are returned is presented by the 'voice' of *The Unnamable* as a repetition, the repetition of an awaiting for that which never arrives, as language never stops, but reaches out constantly further to its own edge, an edge which cuts.

> The undertaking is none of mine, if they want me to succeed I'll fail, and vice versa, so as not to be rid of my tormentors. Is there a single word of mine in all I say? No, I have no voice, in this matter I have none. That's one of the reasons why I confused myself with Worm. But I have no reasons either, no reason, I'm like Worm, without voice or reason, I'm Worm, no, if I were Worm I wouldn't know it, I wouldn't say it, I wouldn't

say anything, I'd be Worm. But I don't say anything, I don't know anything, these voices are not mine, nor these thoughts, but the voices and thoughts of the devils who beset me. (Beckett, 1958: 64)

As the 'voice' explores itself it finds itself to be constantly tangled in the impossibility of its own utterances, so that we are driven back to the situation which prevails in the polylogues composed by Derrida. There appears here to be only one voice which is bereft of company as part of its radical experience of poverty. But it is unclear that there are not in fact legions of voices or that the voice is not an impersonator of another.

Which aspect of the 'voice' is truer than the others? If there were a place for such truth, even in the figure of the devils here conjured with, then it would follow that there was a suitable name for the original experience of cutting which enabled it to be rendered as the object of a positive science. Then it would be a repetition not of the 'origin' but of the covering of this origin. The 'voice' therefore cannot know what it says or who is saying it, as the result of such knowledge would be to rob the work of its unwork and render it once again captured by the science of the positive.

If the 'voice' of *The Unnamable* is not captured in the trap of the ultimate naming machine then it must maintain its poverty. This requires the absence of reason and the impossibility of determination of whether identity is one or multiple or even possible. This is what is meant by the statement that the 'voice' does not want to be rid of its tormentors. Being tormented is integral to the poverty of the repetition of origin.

The 'voice' of *The Unnamable* states its privation precisely in the impossibility of naming itself. The question of naming and the loss thereof is the motif around which the 'voices' of *Sauf le nom (Post-Scriptum)* circle.

As if it was necessary both to save the name and to save everything except the name, *save the name* [sauf le nom], as if it was necessary to lose the name in order to save what bears the name, or that toward which one goes through the name. But to lose the name is not to attack it, to destroy or wound it. On the contrary, to lose the name is quite simply to respect it: as name. That is to say, to pronounce it, which comes down to traversing it towards the other, the other whom it names and who bears it. To

pronounce it without pronouncing it. To forget it by recalling it
(to oneself), which comes down to calling or recalling the other . . .
(Derrida, 1995: 58)

Here the 'experience' of aporia is explored through the relation to
the name. Can names be saved? What is it to relate to naming?
Another way of stating the arrival of nihilism is as a generalized
crisis of naming. In this situation no name seems right for anything, as all names come to have a generalized equivalence. How
in such a situation to save the name? The suggestion here is precise
and follows a pattern which is original and traditional at once. To
save through losing. Names are borne above all, in their most 'proper'
sense, by one whom they tell of. The one told of through the name
borne is a centre of experiences. But if experiences are crossed by
the aporia then this crossing entails a loss of self-identity. In the
'experience' of aporia the name flees in order for the opening of
world to its own nothingness to occur.

This opening is the moment at which an ethics is possible. In the
loss of name is the respect accorded to the singularity named. The
one calls to the other through the one losing itself and being in-
vaded at its heart by alterity. The name for alterity is selfhood, the
name for naming is expressed in the relation to self as other.

The 'cut' of language into the world is given in the experience of
dispossession as original. This dispossession is the self's loss of itself
through relationship to itself.

> There were four or five of them at me, they called that present-
> ing their report. One in particular, Basil I think he was called,
> filled me with hatred. Without opening their mouth, fastening
> on me his eyes like cinders with all their seeing, he changed me
> a little more each time into what he wanted me to be. Is he still
> glaring at me from the shadows? Is he still usurping my name,
> the one they foisted on me, up there in their world, patiently,
> from season to season? (Beckett, 1958: 14)

Here the 'voice' of *The Unnamable* presents naming as doubly usurped:
in an 'original' way as the name never belonged to the one who
was given it, and secondarily through the 'stealing' of the name by
another. These two usurpations are related to examinations by others
who we have reason to suspect do not exist, but since the 'voice' (if
it is always the same, which we have seen reason to doubt) has

doubtful claims to being believed, the impression of fiction attaching to the examination could itself be false. Whether it is false to believe that the examination is fictional or a fiction to think the examination false there is in either case a theft. The theft concerns the possibility of naming being adequate to what is named and thus relates naming as an event no longer plausible.

The figure of 'Basil' glares out of the shadows, which latter, since the writing of Plato's *Republic*, have always represented a place of illusion. From this doxal realm 'Basil' sees with eyes which are 'like cinders', *il y a là cendre*. What would there be to inspire hatred in the relation to the cinder?

> – The sentence says what it will have been, from the moment it gives itself up to itself, giving itself as its own proper name, the consumed (and consummate) art of the secret: of knowing how to keep itself from showing. (Derrida, 1991: 35)

The cinder effect names a self-giving. To give oneself to the name of the self is to give oneself to the other. This giving occurs secretly and we have already encountered another name for the secret: death. But whilst death is the relation to the otherness of selfhood for Heidegger, it is not so for Derrida and Beckett. To keep from appearing the finality of a word, this is what is at work in the cinder. The eye of the cinder is the wound of language. This wound is incessant, unclosing, unavailable to resolution in death.

The cinder's interminable effect is one which can be hated and which all hate who live with names, but the 'voice' of *The Unnamable* states after naming the figure of Basil that it is in safety 'amusing myself wondering who can have dealt me these insignificant wounds' (Beckett, 1958: 14). The cut of language is deep and causes hatred and yet is also not of significance save to one who holds to selfhood, to naming as resolution, in short, to nihilism.

If Beckett's work does its unwork in constantly unravelling, then this task of the diminishment of work is itself infinite. But the infinite task is not one which one is called to as a heroic duty but simply the 'experience' of aporia as non-experience, the naming of self as other, the comprehension of nothingness as beyond the words for Being. If, as Derrida suggests in the epigraph to this piece, Beckett is nihilist and not nihilist, then the 'not' is what enables the works signed by Beckett to be available for a non-nihilism. Through the entry into nothing, the non-work works silence in order to begin to speak of its lack of possibility of speaking. In this opening to the language of 'origin' deconstruction takes place, in the place named by the self.

> Unless this time it's the real silence at last. (Beckett, 1958: 111)

The 'real' silence never comes because it has already gone. The absoluteness of 'original' experience lies in its repetition, this repetition is the 'self-deconstruction' which Attridge named as the signature of the work of Beckett.

Notes

1 Derek Attridge (1989) 'This Strange Institution Called Literature: An Interview with Jacques Derrida', in Derrida (1992) *Acts of Literature*, ed. and trans. D. Attridge (Routledge: New York and London), p. 66. For a response to the statements made by Derrida about Beckett in this interview that takes a very different course to this one, see Royle (1995), ch. 8. For a different account of how Derrida's works provide a way of reading *The Unnamable* see Begam (1996), ch. 6.

References

Attridge, Derek (1992) 'This Strange Institution Called Literature: An Interview with Jacques Derrida'. Trans. Geoffrey Bennington and Rachel Bowlby. In J. Derrida, *Acts of Literature*, ed. D. Attridge. London & New York: Routledge.

Banham, G. (1996) 'The Terror of the Law: Judaism and International Institutions'. In J. Brannigan, R. Robbins and J. Wolfreys, eds, *Applying: To Derrida*. London: Macmillan; New York: St. Martin's Press.

Beckett, Samuel (1958) *The Unnamable*. London: Calder & Boyars.

Begam, Richard (1996) *Samuel Beckett and the End of Modernity*. Stanford: Stanford University Press.

Derrida, Jacques (1991) *Cinders*, trans. N. Lukacher. Lincoln and London: University of Nebraska Press.

Derrida, Jacques (1993) *Aporias*, trans. T. Dutoit. Stanford: Stanford University Press.

Derrida, Jacques (1995) '*Sauf le nom (Post-Scriptum)*', trans. J. P. Leavey, Jr. In Derrida, *On the Name*, ed. T. Dutoit. Stanford: Stanford University Press.

Derrida, Jacques (1996) 'A Silkworm of One's Own (Points of view stitched on the other veil)', trans. G. Bennington. *Oxford Literary Review* 18.

Heidegger, Martin (1993; first published 1929) 'What Is Metaphysics?' In Heidegger, *Basic Writings*, ed. David Farrell Krell. London and New York: Routledge.

Royle, Nicholas (1995) *After Derrida*. Manchester and New York: Manchester University Press.

4

The Role of the Dead Man in the Game of Writing: Beckett and Foucault

Thomas Hunkeler

Animated by a shuddering desire, Hölderlin's Empedocles throws himself into the fire of the Etna. And the poet adds: 'Yet still I hold you sacred [. . .], audaciously perishing' (Hölderlin, 1954: 56). Empedocles, the poetic philosopher, and Hölderlin, the philosophical poet: in more than one sense they herald the figures of Foucault and Beckett. Empedocles as the sacrifice of thought faced with the unthinkable; Hölderlin as the sacrifice of poetry faced with the Unnamable. Thought and poetry: confronted with their Other, whose name is also *madness*, they become sacrifice, offering themselves to what exceeds them, finishes and destroys them.

Foucault's thinking and Beckett's writing unfold as a enquiry into madness, a sacrificial opening towards what constitutes the hidden face of their undertaking, towards what is at the same time *its origin and its end*. In a sense, it is the experience of madness that *founds* the works of Beckett and Foucault, but it is precisely this foundation which in a paradoxical way also *ruins* every construction: 'In the happiness of the work, at the limit of its language, arises, in order to reduce it to silence and finish it, this Limit that the work was itself against everything that was not it. [. . .] What founded [the work] also ruins it' (Foucault, 1994a: 198). Foucault speaks of Hölderlin's work in general; but the Limit he talks about appears most of all in the different stages of the *Empedocles* drama: Empedocles as the 'Chosen One' whom Foucault describes as a figure that fades away when 'the area of a language lost at its utmost borders opens up, where it is most foreign to itself, the area of the signs that do not signify' (201). The lyricism of the latter Hölderlin opens towards madness in just the way Empedocles throws himself into the volcano, in a movement of challenge and dereliction, of almost Nietzschean pride and utmost modesty.

Foucault characterizes the beginning of the 1960s, when he wrote these lines, by what he calls the 'eternal debate between reason and madness' (Foucault, 1994a: 168). In the last pages of *Madness and Civilization*, Foucault defines madness in its most general form as the *absence* of a work, as a *silence* or a *break*, but also and more surprisingly as the *truth* of a work which designs its outer contour or its Limit. To write the history of madness as Foucault does it means to capture the original split that makes the work possible; but it also means to see in a work its own absence which makes it impossible as a total work. In Foucault's eyes, a work is always an *experience* in the Bataillian sense of the term, an experience that leads to a place of loss, of nonsense. Foucault is interested in the 'presence of madness in literature' (168) as he sees it at work in Blanchot, Roussel or Artaud, in Nietzsche, Van Gogh or Hölderlin. But what about Beckett? Is he also part of this family of writers who are not in front of madness, but on the verge of it, simultaneously inside and outside?

Probably not. Beckett's name does not appear on the lists of 'maudits' writers and thinkers Foucault likes to compile; and it does not appear very often in Foucault's writings in general. Nevertheless, it would be premature to conclude that Beckett's work did not have an influence on Foucault. In each of the few references Foucault makes to Beckett, he attributes a crucial position to him: that of a break with a certain past, of a new starting point for a fundamentally *different* kind of discourse. Twice, Foucault insists in interviews[1] that *Waiting for Godot* (1953) was a break with the Marxism, phenomenology and existentialism that was not only his background, but also that of a whole generation immediately after the war. But more importantly, Foucault quotes Beckett in two of his most important texts to introduce and support his own case: in 'What is an Author?' (1969)[2] and in 'The Discourse on Language' (1970), his inaugural discourse at the Collège de France. In both texts, Foucault tries to redirect his thinking towards a more explicit and more concrete analysis of the relations of power that govern every discourse. On the one hand, this redirection implies a questioning of the notion of an author as a particularly striking example of the tendency towards individualization that still very much pervades social sciences; on the other hand, it opens up his predominantly historical thinking towards the domain of politics, by focusing on the strategies of delimitation and exclusion society uses to keep discourse under control. In this light, Foucault's use of Beckett makes sense: the passages[3] from *Texts for Nothing* and the *Unnamable* that Foucault quotes – indicating the author's name in 1969, but not in 1970 – allow him to open up a space by giving a voice to the 'desire' of the one who is supposed to submit himself to the order of discourse but hesitates:

> At the moment of speaking, I would like to have perceived a nameless voice, long proceding me, leaving me merely to enmesh myself in it, taking up its cadence, and to lodge myself, when no one was looking, in its interstices as if it had paused an instant, in suspense, to beckon to me. (Foucault, 1986: 148)

A rather provocative inaugural statement from a newly elected professor of the Collège de France. More to the point, however, Foucault chooses to speak through Beckett's voice here – but not without modifying it first. His slightly altered Beckett quote emphasizes mainly the impossibility to express, against Beckett's own conviction that the 'impossibility to express' is always accompanied by the 'obligation to express' (Beckett, 1984: 139). The same applies to the way Foucault treats Beckett in 'What is an Author?' Here, the quote is exact, but Foucault neglects to comment on anything but the 'indifference' which is 'one of the fundamental ethical principles of contemporary writing' (Foucault, 1979: 141) for him. He fails to take into account that the quote from Beckett ('What does it matter who is speaking, someone said what does it matter who is speaking') not only *rejects* the notions of an author and of authority, but also and at the same time desperately *seeks* the speaker who produces the discourse. Foucault's reading of this passage and of Beckett in general is problematic precisely because it tries to erase this tension in Beckett's entire work.

In order to understand Foucault's partial (and very probably voluntary) blindness, it is necessary to analyse the way Foucault reads Beckett. His reading is to a large extent influenced and conditioned by Blanchot's (mis)reading (in the Bloomian sense; cf. Bloom, 1973) of Beckett. In 1966, Foucault had written an important essay on Blanchot,[4] and he always acknowledged the important and lasting influence this writer had on him. Indeed, Blanchot's opening question in his influential study 'Where now? Who now?' ('Où maintenant? Qui maintenant?') was 'Who speaks in Samuel Beckett's books?' (Blanchot, 1959: 308). But he dismissed this question immediately afterwards by focusing not on the 'I' but only on its erring voice, without beginning or end, on what he calls the impersonal obsession or 'la parole neutre'. 'The essence of language is the visible erasure of the speaker', Foucault says (1994a: 537), paraphrasing Blanchot and in the belief that he is also paraphrasing Beckett.[5] But he neglects the resistance that Beckett's text puts up to each appropriation, to every reading that tries to reduce its singularity.

'The danger is in the neatness of identifications' wrote Beckett in 1929 in the opening lines of his essay on Joyce (Beckett, 1984: 19). This warning is particularly useful for those who study the way Blanchot or Foucault have appropriated Beckett. If the subject is indeed a 'grammatical fold' (*un pli grammatical*) in the 'continuous dripping of language' (Foucault, 1994a, 537), such an appropriation is valuable and legitimate; but the question is if the Beckettian subject resigns itself to being *only this*. But such an affirmation is based on a profound misunderstanding of the structure of the Beckettian text. Back to Foucault's quote at the beginning of 'What is an Author?': 'What does it matter who is speaking, someone said what does it matter who is speaking.' The first statement 'what does it matter who is speaking' is reinterpreted from a statement of truth to a simple assertion by what follows: '*someone said* what does it matter who is speaking'. This statement is itself, as a result of the repetitive and deceptive structure of the text, reinterpreted as a recognition ('this assertion is itself produced by yet another speaker'), but most of all as a doubt ('what do I know about the speaker who produces all these statements, what do I know about the value of these statements'). The breach that opens up between the statement and its speaker(s) questions every notion of authority, originality or truth; up to this point, Blanchot's and Foucault's reading of Beckett is unproblematic. Their reading starts to diverge from its object when the 'incompatibility [...] between the appearance of language in its essence and consciousness in its identity' (Foucault, 1994a: 520) is treated as an experience in the strong, Bataillian sense of the word, as the passage to some kind of madness, and ultimately to truth. This experience is controlled and suspended in Beckett, but in Foucault's writings, it is treated as the joyful acceptance of the loss of subjectivity, turning into an idealized vision of madness that many critics blamed him for, into the erasure of man in a close future 'like a face of sand on the seashore'. In other words: to the Irish writer, the experience of madness remains a purely literary experience, without any privileged access to truth. In Foucault's eyes, the transition from the *oeuvre* to madness is a *qualitative* leap exemplified in Hölderlin, Nerval or Van Gogh, a leap that transgresses each time the boundaries between work and life, between representation and presence. In Beckett's view it is only a *quantitative* leap inside representation, from one level of representation to another. In his work, madness seizes only the characters; every time a narrator (or the 'author') is affected, he is lowered to the level of the characters by yet another narrator who appears behind him. Against Foucault's *abyss of madness*, Beckett proposes the *madness of the abyss*; against the *different* discourse madness promises, he proposes *other* discourses that try to control, without much success, the madness that catches them one after the other.

Beckett's work shares with Foucault's a nostalgic, but nevertheless radical view of madness: think of *Murphy* or *Watt*. Another tendency they both have in common is the fact that in their work, madness is intrinsically related to language and to the relationship the subject tries to establish with and through language. But whereas in Foucault, the discourse allows the subject to gain its freedom by loosing itself, like in Mallarmé's 'elocutionary disappearance of the poet' ('disparition élocutoire du poète'), in Beckett's work the gap between the subject and its speech is the source of constant anxiety. In *Watt*, one of Beckett's most important texts – not because it allows us to understand the Beckettian secret (which doesn't exist anyway), but because it treats some of the problems that are bound to play an important role in the later texts in a very explicit and almost experimental way – one of the most remarkable scenes is the visit of the Galls who come to tune the piano. During this scene, Watt is confronted with what the narrator calls the 'fragility of outer meaning', as the whole scene ceases 'very soon to signify for Watt a piano tuned, an obscure family and professional relation, [. . .] and so on' (Beckett, 1970: 73). But two questions nevertheless remain: 'But what was this pursuit of meaning, in this indifference to meaning? And to what did it tend? These are delicate questions' (75).

Beckett not merely confronts his character with an attack of madness to make him experience his limits. As a matter of fact, the Beckettian subject, of which the character is just one aspect, is not only the victim of this crisis, but also its witness, and even its executioner. According to Alain Badiou (1995: 35–8), the Beckettian subject is triple: it consists simultaneously of the *subject of passivity*, the *subject of enunciation* and the *subject of the question*. Of these three aspects, the third obviously cannot be found in Foucault's analysis of Beckett. The subject of the question is most radically opposed to the indifference that marks Watt as a character, and also, but to a lesser degree, the narrator. The 'blank indifference' ('blanche indifférence') Foucault sees at work in Beckett's 'what does it matter who is speaking' is only one aspect of the problem; it is accompanied by the *question* in the sense of inquiry or even torture. As Badiou points out:

> If, when you count the subject of enunciation, the subject of passivity and the subject of the question as one, the question itself vanishes as it returns into the indifference of being, you have counted wrong. (Badiou, 1995: 37)

It is astonishing that the author of *Discipline and Punish* seems to have been blind to the dimension of torture in the Beckettian work, even if it is true that the references to Beckett date back to a period when Foucault was not yet as interested in the political dimensions of discourse as in the 1970s. Contrary to what has been said (see for instance Guest, 1996), then, it is not the Foucaldian perspective that gives Beckett's work a political dimension it does not have; it is the Beckettian work that might have contributed to shape Foucault's attention to what Mallarmé or Blanchot neglect: the *resistance* of a subject towards a discourse it is unable either to refuse or to accept as its own.

In spite of its openly programmatical character, Foucault's *Discourse on Language* consists less of an outlook on works to come than of an assessment of things accomplished. Its emphasis is on the functioning and the genealogy of discourse and refers mostly to texts already written such as *Madness and Civilization* (1961), *The Order of Things* (1966) or *The Archaeology of Knowledge* (1969) – to books that belong to the history of science and tend to put their author and his position towards the discourses he talks about between brackets. Nevertheless, Foucault starts his *Discourse on Language* with some thoughts about the position he himself has in the discourse he is supposed to give. Foucault distinguishes two possible attitudes in this situation: the acceptance of 'the order of discourse', which implies also the acceptance of a beginning inside an area delimited by the institution; and the desire not to begin, but to slip into a discourse already present, like a 'happy wreck' (Foucault, 1986: 149) floating on the river of discourse. But he refuses to choose among those two options; or rather, he chooses them both by beginning a discourse which refuses what every beginning implies: a foundation. Beckett's voice that Foucault quotes confronts the notion of a *beginning* with the notion of a *continuation*; it also sets up an interiority against the exteriority of official speech, an interiority not of course in the sense of an appropriated or personal voice, but rather in the sense of a voice that encompasses and includes also the one who is speaking – what Foucault calls in his essay on Blanchot the 'thought from outside' ('pensée du dehors'), but what I would rather like to call in Beckett's case the 'writing of the inside'. As he sees himself obliged to take position towards his own discourse, Foucault appropriates this Beckettian subject, which is at the same time *outside* (as an origin) and *inside* its discourse, at the same time subject and object. By resisting the arrogance of official discourse and the temptation of impersonality, Foucault succeeds in finding a third place in discourse: the interstices, the gaps, what he calls 'the point of the possible disappearance' (Foucault, 1971: 8) of discourse. I would suggest calling this place the 'area of resistance'.

Resistance, first of all, against Foucault's own thinking, since it confronts the 'blank indifference' of language in its being with the simple fact that – as Yves Bonnefoy said in his own inaugural discourse for the Collège de France in 1981, and with a little sideswipe against Foucault – 'it is a fact that we say *I* when we speak, in the urgency of the days, in the midst of a condition and a place which remain, *whatever their pretence or their lack of being*, a reality and an absolute' (Bonnefoy, 1999: 21). Indeed, the problem that concerns Foucault at the time of 'The Discourse on Language', and that becomes more and more insistent with his activity in the GIP (Information Group on Prisons), is his own place inside the discourses by which society tries to control the problem of transgression. As Bonnefoy points out, faced with something intolerable in a concrete situation, we have to find out 'how this force that we are can, *against the drifting off of words*, affirm itself *nonetheless* as an origin' (22). In an interview in 1971, Foucault himself is quite clear about this: 'Some time ago, I myself worked on subjects as abstract and as far removed from us as the history of science. Today, I would definitely like to get out of it.' (Foucault, 1994b: 203)

What does this will to get out of a certain kind of discourse – scientific, academic or even philosophical – mean? Above all, this step signifies the rediscovery – beyond all shattered illusions of the Cartesian Ego – of another kind of subjectivity, a simple voice rather than an individual, that shows its capacity to *resist from inside* against a discourse through which it is always already constructed. For Foucault, to say 'I' doesn't mean to rediscover Sartre's 'engagement' with its humanistic load and with the subject as a foundational category; it means to give a voice to those who don't have one, and who until then were only the object of the discourse of society: the prisoners, the madmen. In *Madness and Civilization*, Foucault had tried to map out the archaeology of silence that falls upon madness; with his activity as a member of the GIP, he now tries to move from the study of silence to the practice of a voice of which he knows perfectly well that it will never really be the voice of those it sets out to defend. Nevertheless, by putting forth his own voice and his position of power as a professor in one of the most prestigious institutions of his country, Foucault accepts the challenge to speak for those who have neither voice nor power; by saying 'I' where, two years earlier, he would have said 'they'.

The relationship between the subject and the discourse it produces is crucial for any writer. In Beckett's work, questions such as 'what is the word' or 'how to say "I"' are intimately linked, and it has been said that Beckett found his voice only in 1946 when he moved from a third-person narrator as in *Murphy*, *Watt* or *Mercier and Camier* to a first-person narrator as in *Molloy*, *Malone Dies* or *The Unnamable*. This viewpoint is nevertheless an oversimplification, as an analysis of Beckett's early texts shows. Already in 1929, in his first published piece of writing, the short story 'Assumption', Beckett had chosen to confront two modes of expression: his protagonist's, who 'could have shouted and could not' (Beckett, 1995: 3), and the one of the 'Woman' with her 'clear, steady speech' (5), who tries unsuccessfully to save the protagonist before he is eventually 'swept away by a great storm of sound' (7). 'Assumption' confronts two types of language, but also two possible attitudes towards language: the mystic passivity in front of an elementary, powerful phenomenon, and the rational utilization of a simple instrument. The title of the short story shows clearly which of these two Beckett preferred.

In a 1937 letter to a German friend, Beckett speaks again, and in a less idealistic way, of the different attitudes a writer can adopt towards language. In this astonishingly openhearted letter, he defines in a very clear way his own position towards language:

> Let us hope the time will come, thank God that in certain circles it has already come, when language is most efficiently used where it is being most efficiently misused. As we cannot eliminate language all at once, we should at least leave nothing undone that might contribute to its falling into disrepute. To bore one hole after another in it, until what lurks behind it – be it something or nothing – begins to seep through; I cannot imagine a higher goal for a writer today. (Beckett, 1984: 171–2)

In these lines, Beckett describes his attitude towards language as it characterizes the texts after the war: a resistance from within. 'Represent this mocking attitude *towards the word, through words*' (172; emphasis mine): this is Beckett's task as he sees it in 1937, a task he uses to distinguish himself from Joyce ('apotheosis of the word') and Gertrude Stein ('still in love with her vehicle'). The so-called 'literature of the unword' that Beckett announces in his letter may need 'some form of Nominalist irony' (173); but it should not simply be a language game. The goal of his attempt is first and foremost aesthetic, says Beckett at the end of his letter: 'an assault against words in the name of beauty' (173).

Some years later, after the war, the issue will become not only aesthetic, but also ethical. In a little piece written for the Irish radio and entitled 'The Capital of the Ruins', Beckett describes the town of Saint-Lô, which had been totally destroyed in the war and was now supported by the Irish Red Cross. An almost hopeless task, with problems 'so arduous and elusive that [they] literally *ceased to be formulable*' (Beckett, 1990: 24–5; emphasis mine), writes Beckett, and he concludes:

> Some of those who were in Saint-Lô will come home realising that they got at least as good as they gave, that they got indeed what they could hardly give, a vision and sense of *a time-honoured conception of humanity in ruins*, and perhaps even an inkling of *the terms in which our condition is to be thought again*. These will have been in France. (27–8; emphasis mine)

This is not only praise for the Irish supporting those who don't have anything, but an effort to think and to speak faced with a foreign reality. By formulating 'the simple and necessary and yet so unattainable proposition that their way of being we, was not our way and that our way of being they, was not their way' (25), Beckett chooses the uncomfortable place of someone who is simultaneously inside and outside: confronted with a misery which is not that of the 'I' but of a collective 'we' of which the 'I' becomes the speaker. Still, we are far away from Sartre's 'engagement' with its pathos. What these lines announce is not a new humanity or a new humanism, but only man, 'incapable of recovering his own existence, never really present': man as Alain Robbe-Grillet (1961: 96) saw him in *Waiting for Godot* in 1953; man as he appeared to the young Michel Foucault, shattering once and for all his existentialist illusions.

'I shall soon be quite dead at last in spite of all' (Beckett, 1956: 7). 'I don't know when I died' (Beckett, 1995: 61). It has been said that Beckett's writing comes from beyond the grave; but in reality, his writing is placed not beyond or on this side of death, but at the exact place of death itself, where consciousness starts to fail. Foucault calls this situation 'the role of the dead man in the game of writing' (1979: 143): the moment when the individual character of the writing subject fades away to leave behind the 'singularity of its absence'. In Beckett's work, the disappearance of the author is never confirmed, since it tends to expand and to drag on through the whole book. 'Chronicle of a death foretold' in the case of *Malone Dies*; 'Memoirs from beyond the grave' in the case of the short story 'The Calmative'; the disappearance of a stable subjectivity (character, narrator or author) is precisely what drives Beckett to write: the void that doesn't give its sense but its movement to writing; a paradoxical movement that consists of the desperate effort to stop. Write in order not to write anymore, in order not to have to play this game anymore.

But writing is not a game unless we take this term in its Bataillian sense, as a Nietzschean kind of risky game, as a 'suspension of being beyond itself, on the verge of nothingness' (Bataille, 1973: 44). Writing is, and Foucault knows it very well, linked to the sacrifice of the author's life, and to the decision (if there is a decision) to make of death the paradoxical foundation of a work that lives at the same time through and against death.

'Und immer ins Ungebundene gehet eine Sehnsucht.' In 1932, Beckett quotes this verse by Hölderlin in a passage of his first novel *Dream of Fair to Middling Women* (Beckett, 1993: 138), and puts it in relation with his own aesthetic ideas. Even at this early stage of his writing, Beckett wants to supplant words by silence, continuity by discontinuity and unity by multiplicity: an ambitious programme that will only be realized years later, with *Molloy* and its 'sequels'. However, his juvenile passion for Hölderlin has left more than just some intertextual traces in his work. It is in Hölderlin's poetry that Beckett discovered the idea to *accommodate in the work* what threatens it, the idea to sacrifice the said to the unsaid and the nameable to the unnamable; in Hölderlin's poetry, which Foucault once described as revealing 'what no language could have said outside of the abyss in which it falls, what no fall could have shown if it wasn't at the same time an access to the summit' (Foucault, 1994a: 192). The abyss as the paradoxical summit: this is what Beckett had in mind when he quoted, at the end of *Watt* and in a fragmentary way, these lines from Hölderlin (1954: 65): ' . . . hurtled from boulder to boulder / down through the years to . . ' (' . . . von Klippe zu Klippe geworfen / Endlos in . . . hinab').[6]

Notes

1 'Archaeology of a Passion' (1983) and 'Le style de l'histoire'. In Foucault, 1994d: 608 and 650.
2 The same quote appears in fact already at the end of 'Réponse à une question' (1968). In Foucault, 1994a: 695.
3 Beckett, 1958: 129 and 1953: 213.
4 'La pensée du dehors'. In Foucault, 1994a: 518–39.
5 On the importance of paraphrase in Blanchot's criticism, see de Man, 1983: 60–78.
6 I would like to thank Marco Früh and David Houston Jones for their precious help with the translation and the English quotations.

References

Badiou, Alain (1995) *Beckett. L'increvable désir* (Paris: Hachette).
Bataille, Georges (1954) *L'expérience intérieure* (Paris: Gallimard).
Bataille, Georges (1973) 'Sur Nietzsche'. In *Georges Bataille, Oeuvres complètes tome VI* (Paris: Gallimard).
Beckett, Samuel (1953) *L'Innommable* (Paris: Minuit).
Beckett, Samuel (1956) *Malone Dies* (New York: Grove Press).
Beckett, Samuel (1957) *Murphy* (New York: Grove Press).
Beckett, Samuel (1958) *Nouvelles et Textes pour rien* (Paris: Minuit).
Beckett, Samuel (1970) *Watt* (New York: Grove Press).
Beckett, Samuel (1984) *Disjecta: Miscellaneous Writings and a Dramatic Fragment*, ed. Ruby Cohn (New York: Grove Press).
Beckett, Samuel (1990) *As the Story Was Told: Uncollected and Late Prose* (London: Calder).

Beckett, Samuel (1993) *Dream of Fair to Middling Women* (London: Calder).
Beckett, Samuel (1995) *The Complete Short Prose 1929–1989* (New York: Grove Press).
Blanchot, Maurice (1959) *Le livre à venir* (Paris: Gallimard).
Bloom, Harold (1973) *The Anxiety of Influence: A Theory of Poetry* (London: Oxford University Press).
Bonnefoy, Yves (1999) *Lieux et destins de l'image* (Paris: Seuil).
De Man, Paul (1983) *Blindness and Insight: Essays in the Rhetoric of Contemporary Criticism* (Minneapolis: University of Minnesota Press).
Foucault, Michel (1972) *Histoire de la folie à l'âge classique* (Paris: Gallimard). First published in 1961 as *Folie et déraison* (Paris: Plon). English translation: *Madness and Civilization* (New York, 1965).
Foucault, Michel (1963) *Raymond Roussel* (Paris: Gallimard). English translation: *Death and the Labyrinth* (New York, 1986).
Foucault, Michel (1966) *Les mots et les choses* (Paris: Gallimard). English translation: *The Order of Things* (New York, 1970).
Foucault, Michel (1969) *L'archéologie du savoir* (Paris: Gallimard). English translation: *The Archaeology of Knowledge* (New York, 1972).
Foucault, Michel (1971) *L'ordre du discours* (Paris: Gallimard).
Foucault, Michel (1979) 'What is an Author?' In Josué Harari (ed.), *Textual Strategies: Perspectives in Post-Structuralist Criticism* (Ithaca: Cornell University Press). For the slightly different French version, see Foucault, 1994a: 789–821.
Foucault, Michel (1986) 'The Discourse on Language'. In Hazard Adams and Leroy Searle (eds), *Critical Theory since 1965* (Tallahassee: University Press of Florida). English translation of Foucault, 1971.
Foucault, Michel (1994a–d) *Dits et écrits*, tomes I à IV (Paris: Gallimard).
Gros, Frédéric (1997) *Foucault et la folie* (Paris: Presses Universitaires de France).
Guest, Michael (1996) 'Beckett and Foucault: Some Affinities'. *Central Japan English Studies* 15: 55–68.
Hölderlin, Friedrich (1954) *Selected Poems*. Trans. J. B. Leishman (London: Hogarth Press).
Hölderlin, Friedrich (1984) *Hölderlin*. Ausgewählt von Peter Härtling (Köln: Kiepenheuer und Witsch).
Miller, James (1993) *The Passion of Michel Foucault* (New York: Simon and Schuster).
Robbe-Grillet, Alain (1961) *Pour un nouveau roman* (Paris: Minuit).

5
Deleuze Reading Beckett

Mary Bryden

Reading Beckett was for Deleuze a kind of recognition. In a filmed interview in 1988 (Deleuze, 1996),[1] he stated that his response to Beckett had been immediate and instinctive, unlike his interest in Robbe-Grillet, which had taken several years to develop. Earlier in that same series of interviews, he had asserted, unusually, that few authors had ever made him laugh more than Kafka and Beckett.[2] Beckett's name does indeed feature among the many literary authors cited in Deleuze and Guattari's two-volume *Capitalisme et Schizophrénie*. Deleuze's interest in Beckett did not, however, originate with his collaboration with Félix Guattari; Beckett is cited from time to time in his earlier solo works.

Deleuze's response to Beckett was a committed and distinctive one, and one based entirely on reading, in the first instance, and only latterly on viewing by television. One might have expected the two authors to have met at some point. Both were based in Paris, shared a publisher, Jérôme Lindon, of Editions de Minuit, and enjoyed heightened prominence at a similar time. The Deleuze/ Guattari interaction, which was to produce the two volumes of *Capitalisme et Schizophrénie* in 1972 and 1980, began in earnest just after the upheaval of the May 1968 uprisings in Paris: during those years, Beckett was awarded the Nobel Prize for Literature, and directed some high-profile productions of his plays. And yet, some ten years later, André Bernold, who knew both Deleuze and Beckett, found himself describing to Beckett the appearance, character and teaching style of Deleuze.[3]

For Deleuze, literature was something of a *voyage immobile*. Never an enthusiast of live theatre, he found unappealing the prospect of spending an entire evening on a sometimes uncomfortable seat, watching a performance with its own unstoppable momentum.[4] Thus, his writing does not extend to commentary upon the plays with which Beckett is most frequently associated, including *Waiting for Godot, Endgame, Happy Days, Krapp's Last Tape, Play,* or *Not I.* Instead, his references are primarily to the early part of Beckett's output, notably the novels.

Nevertheless, in 1992, within a few years of the deaths of both Guattari and Beckett, Deleuze devoted an important new text to four television plays by Beckett. In his later years, Deleuze had become fascinated with the idea of what he called the *épuration* of a writer: a purging or purificatory process in which a writer or artist in old age may produce works which are much more reduced and sober than earlier work.[5] The increasing sparseness and brevity of Beckett's later writing exemplifies this process at work, as does Deleuze's own commentary upon it, which has a spare, distilled quality, and was to be one of his last texts before his suicide in 1995. Titled *L'Epuisé,* it acts as a kind of 'postface' to the translation into French, by Edith Fournier, of *Quad, Ghost Trio, . . . but the clouds . . . ,* and *Nacht und Träume.*

Given his preference for armchair consumption, it is understandable that Deleuze should have gravitated towards television drama rather than stage drama. It is also consistent with his abiding interest in film, which produced two volumes on the cinema in 1983 and 1985.[6] Watching a television play, particularly on video, is an entirely different experience from watching it in the theatre. Its requirements for sound, lighting, camera position and montage bring it into close harmony with those associated with the cinematic genre, even though, as Steven Connor rightly points out: '[Beckett's] writing for television [. . .] retains and even highlights many of the features of the stage play – the single unchanging set, for instance, and the restriction of TV's mobility of viewpoint' (Connor, 1988: 149). From Beckett's point of view, a recorded (as opposed to live) television play offers the opportunity to control and to fine-tune each detail of the performative event. The result is an image which is static in *con*ception but non-static in *per*ception. From Deleuze's point of view, the television play, while retaining its affiliations with the theatre, has the advantage of lending itself to greater viewer control, for it can be analysed wholly, or in segments, sequentially, or interleavingly. Being accessible to scrutiny and rescrutiny, the medium offers the prospect of a more sustained encounter between Deleuze and Beckett than had been the case with the stage drama.

Given, then, its status as the only Deleuzian text (excluding articles) devoted exclusively to Beckett, *L'Epuisé* will be the main focus of this essay. Within it, particular attention will be given to Deleuze's analysis of *Quad*. Despite its economy, *L'Epuisé* is a complex text; on successive readings, variant elements seem to come to the fore. Deleuze begins by defining the central concept of *épuisement*. As in its English equivalent, 'to exhaust', the verb *épuiser* can denote two separate states, one of which can be seen as resultant upon the other. 'Exhaustion' is an extreme word. A trial in which all or most resources have been deployed can be said to be 'comprehensive'. An 'exhaustive' trial is one in which all possibilitites have been drawn out (Latin: *exhaurire*, to draw out or drain out). The secondary meaning – extreme fatigue, or being at one's wits' end – incorporates the organic cost of that depletion.

In Beckett's world, as Deleuze points out, exhaustion often seems inherent in human existence, as expressed by the voice in the second *foirade*: 'J'ai renoncé avant de naître' [I gave up before birth] (Beckett, 1976: 38).[7] There are many examples in Beckett's *oeuvre* of the narrating voice being racked with fatigue. However, the state of *épuisement* which interests Deleuze is not so much that in which no energy remains, but that in which no possibility remains. As Deleuze aptly puts it: 'Le fatigué ne peut plus réaliser, mais l'épuisé ne peut plus possibiliser' [The fatigued cannot accomplish any more, but the exhausted cannot even conceive of accomplishing any more] (Deleuze, 1992: 57). Balzac could be said to be a great *réalisateur*: he plumbed his imagination, and drew from it all the required constituents for his composite scenes. Balzac is, wrote Beckett in *Dream of Fair to Middling Women*, 'absolute master of his material, he can do what he likes with it, he can foresee and calculate its least vicissitude' (Beckett, 1993: 119). By a cumulative process, Balzac selects certain elements and rejects others. *Epuisement*, on the other hand, proceeds in reverse direction: 'On combine l'ensemble des variables d'une situation, à condition de renoncer à tout ordre de préférence et à toute organisation de but, à toute signification' [One combines the set of variables of a situation, on the basis of excluding any preferred order, any organized goal, and any meaning] (Deleuze, 1992: 59). In other words, all available combinations are attempted, but in a context which is uncoupled from any numerical, motivational or symbolic significance.

The most celebrated example of this latter tendency is the episode of the sucking stones in *Molloy*. The initial poser faced by the narrator is that of sucking his hoard of 16 stones 'comme j'entendais le faire, c'est-à-dire l'une après l'autre jusqu'à l'épuisement du nombre' [in Beckett's English translation, 'one after the other until their number was exhausted'] (Beckett, 1951: 94). The climax of the account for Balzac would no doubt be the resolution of the dilemma, arrived at by reasoning. Beckett's narrator does derive momentary satisfaction from an apparently elegant, if not perfect, solution. However, the climax of the account for Beckett is not the solution but the suspension of the conditions prompting that solution. In the end, we are told: 'Mais au fond [. . .] cela m'était parfaitement égal aussi de sucer chaque fois une pierre différente ou toujours la même, fût-ce dans les siècles des siècles' [Deep down it was all the same to me whether I sucked a different stone each time or always the same stone, until the end of time] (Beckett, 1951: 99).

There is a curious blend here of matter and nothingness. The central problem appears to be a practical and visualizable one: how to distribute 16 pebbles around the pockets in such a manner as to ensure that each of the 16 pebbles is sucked in order, none more than once. One might assume that the imperative to do this is merely a whim, a desire, of psychological origin. Yet the narrator maintains that it was 'un besoin physique' [a bodily need] (Beckett, 1951: 99]. In pursuit of his goal, a weighty yet abstract momentum is built up as minerals encounter fabric in a relentless cycle of configurations. At the end, there is only one stone left, and even it soon fades away, either swallowed, lost, or passed on to a grateful recipient. And were there ever 16 in the first place? After all, the narrator introduces his story by the words 'J'avais *mettons* seize pierres' [I had *say* sixteen stones] (Beckett, 1951: 92; my italics). Indeed, the solution at which he arrives – not, he acknowledges, the only solution – is one which does not rely on multiples (four stones in four pockets), but on systematic circulation of an indeterminately-sized batch of stones.

This episode is an example of what Deleuze calls 'disjonctions incluses' [inclusive disjunctions] (Deleuze, 1992: 61), a recurrent characteristic of Beckett's writing in which distinctions are not resolved, but co-exist and remain in play. It is a process which Deleuze summed up many times in his writing by the words 'I would prefer not to', the sinisterly undismissive phrase used by the employee Bartleby, the eponymous character of Melville's disquieting short story, when asked to perform office duties which depart from his habitual ones. The multiplicatory activity which spins off, in that story, from this apparently non-excluding phrase finds many echoes in Beckett's writing. To consult Beckett's handwritten notebooks for the novel *Watt*, for example – the work which Deleuze calls 'le grand roman sériel' [the great serial novel] (Deleuze, 1992: 61) – is to ponder upon the nature of a mind which could be so continuously permutative and so debilitatingly resistant to conceptual closure. Preferences in Beckett are short-lived, and there is in any case neither a *deus ex machina* to implement them nor a *status quo* to provide stability by default. As Deleuze observes in a splendidly Beckettian play of cancellation and qualification: 'Dieu, l'ensemble du possible, se confond avec Rien, dont chaque chose est une modification' [God, the sum of possibilities, merges with Nothing, of which everything is a modification] (Deleuze, 1992: 60).

In his first volume on cinema, Deleuze had used the verb *épuiser*, in a less developed way, to describe nineteenth-century naturalism. Writing of Zola, Deleuze asserts: 'Dans chacun de ses livres, [Zola] décrit un milieu précis, mais aussi il l'*épuise* [italicized in the original] et le rend au monde originaire' [In each of his works, [Zola] describes a precise setting, but he also exhausts it and returns it to an original state] (Deleuze, 1983: 175). Deleuze is here maintaining that the strength of Zola's writing derives from a blend of determinacy and indeterminacy, i.e. the anatomization of a particular historical and geographical landscape, allied to an indeterminate space structured by desires and functions in which the characters are simply fragments or constituents.

In *L'Epuisé*, Deleuze takes that concept into a different domain. The determinacy which he discerns in Beckett's television plays relates not to a specific cultural or geographical space, but to the disposition of that space. In these plays, the dimensions of the space, and the relation and distance between its inhabiting features, are not incidentals. They *are* the text. Yet these are for the most part stark and clinical spaces, devoid of the trinkets and haberdashery which humans commonly use to domesticate their living space. Their windows have no views: they are simply lenses or apertures for light and shadow. In a play such as *Ghost Trio*, the glimpses of the given space are cued and regulated by the invisible woman's voice. Hence, while noting the precision of the chamber's specifications, Deleuze also notes that: 'Ce que nous voyons, au contraire, c'est seulement un espace quelconque' [What we see, on the contrary, is merely a random space] (Deleuze, 1992: 95). Unlike the carefully crafted or engrafted spaces laid out by Zola, these are primarily – as Deleuze is of course not the first to suggest – spaces of the mind, products of an inner need to invoke and convoke. They are particularized but not particular spaces.

What *is* particular in them is the intensity attaching to these spaces or to the images which arise within them. Referring to the woman's face which appears in . . . *but the clouds* . . ., Deleuze points out that such images, arising from the shadows of the psyche, must, having been summoned, irrevocably fade again to the shadows: 'L'image est un souffle, une haleine, mais expirante, en voie d'extinction. L'image est ce qui s'éteint, se consume, une chute. C'est une intensité pure' [The image is a whisper, a breath, but an expiring one, in the process of extinction. The image is that which fades, burns out, a falling. It's pure intensity] (Deleuze, 1992: 97). A similar intensity – what Deleuze calls 'une intensité déchirante' [a searing intensity] (Deleuze, 1992: 102) – attends the choreography of ministering hands seen by the Dreamer in *Nacht und Träume*, where the dissipating image seems to find continuance in the last seven bars of Schubert's music.

It is in these intensities, founded upon what Deleuze calls 'une obscure tension spirituelle' [an obscure spiritual tension] (Deleuze, 1992: 96), which structure the course of these television plays. Deleuze does, however, differentiate between the plays in terms of the vectors for those intensities. In order to do this, he finds it convenient to posit three different modes of Beckettian expression, which he calls Langue I, Langue II, and Langue III. (Deleuze, like Beckett, had a certain fondness for tripartite divisioning. Asked in an interview what his favourite foods were, he replied that there were three items: brains, marrow, and tongue. He added mischievously that these items could be associated with the Christian Trinity, the brains being God the Father; the marrow, a fleshy vegetable, being Jesus, the Word Made Flesh; and the tongue being the Holy Spirit, who is said to have descended in tongues of fire.)[8]

All three 'Langues', in Deleuze's schema, are capable of achieving the Beckettian 'épuisement du possible' in different ways. The first, Langue I, is what Deleuze calls 'cette langue atomique' [this atomic language] (Deleuze, 1992: 66). It is a language of enumeration, in which combinatory relations replace syntactical ones. This language is associated with the novels, culminating in *Watt*, where words proliferate in circles of permutation. In order to 'épuiser le possible' with words, however, the words themselves must be exhausted. Hence, Langue II is a kind of metalanguage: a language not of nouns or names, but of voices. These voices are the wavelengths for what Deleuze calls 'les corpuscules linguistiques' [linguistic corpuscles] (Deleuze, 1992: 66). Langue II can be seen at the end of *L'Innommable*, when silence intervenes not from simple fatigue but from the perplexities of how to find the last word, how to recognize that last word, and to whom to attribute that last word. Langue II brings into focus the whole question of subjectivity: not so much 'what is being said' as 'by what means and by whom are words being said'. The voices of that novel are drunk with language and drunk with the prospect of its cessation, like the alcoholic for whom, Deleuze once said, 'c'est le dernier verre qui compte' [It's the last glass that counts].[9] The dipsomaniac, he maintained, is always focused not on the intermediate glasses, but on the last glass of the day: that is, the last that it is in one's power to drink before collapse, until the next day. That is the goal of the alcoholic search for *épuisement*. Similarly, Beckett's narrators, even when spewing out tides of words, are in search of the last word.

However, a repetitive and linear search for the limit in a series is a dead end, since the series itself is extensible and permutable into other series. The only way to transcend this impasse, according to Deleuze, is to seek the limit at an intermediate point *within* the series, between two terms or two voices. This, then, is Langue III, which relates language not to its enumerative capacity or to the voices which emit these enumerations, but rather to moments of shift, hiatus or disruption. This non-linguistic, non-phonetic language is that of Image, an image which may be either visual or sonic. Such an image is like a refrain which is mobile through time and space. In this context, Deleuze uses the musical term *ritournelle*, to which he and Guattari had already made extensive reference in *Capitalisme et Schizophrénie*.

The *ritournelle* denotes a phase of transit through spaces. It is linked to a space, but it is always on the move. It might be the frogs' chorus in *Watt*, where each frog croaks its own cadences which blend into the general refrain, or it might be the woman's face in . . . *but the clouds*. . . . In each case, the image, independent of history, geography or of any of the other specifics which words and voices can rarely suppress, comes into play, not as an object but as a process within the consciousness. Being an image in transit, it is not a terminus, but may itself prompt other images, words, music or sound. Langue III is found above all, according to Deleuze, in Beckett's television plays, which are able to combine a pre-recorded voice with an image which is constantly reconstituting itself.

In addition to the intensities afforded by image, there is another vector for Langue III, referred to briefly earlier: that of space. The space is staked out by Beckett – whether it be a square (as in *Quad*), a circle (as in . . . *but the clouds* . . .), a rectangular room with corridor beyond (as in *Ghost Trio*), or a lighted seating area (as in *Nacht und Träume*). The space is measured, but it is not a site or location. It is, to use a phrase Deleuze uses elsewhere, in his writing on cinema, 'un espace pré-hodologique' [a pre-hodological space] (Deleuze, 1985: 264–5), a space which is not setting the scene, suggesting obstacles or outcomes, but is simply a space in which movement and/or stillness can occur. The space is there to be peopled, however sparsely, but not to exert an influence on the bodies which inhabit it. It is a space of potentiality, where its conjunction with moving bodies offers new avenues of *épuisement*. For Deleuze, the Beckettian space resembles the Beckettian image in that its importance lies not so much in its content as in the energy which it incarnates.

Of the four television plays under consideration, Deleuze is able to allocate two to the criterion of space, and two to image, although in all cases allied to other linguistic or sonic elements. Hence, *Quad* is said to be space with both silence and music; *Ghost Trio* is space with voice and music; . . . *but the clouds* . . . is image with voice and poem, and *Nacht und Träume* is image with silence, song and music. All exemplify Deleuze's Langue III category, in that, while not divorced from the linguistic, their energies are exercised and spent in directions which are not solely reliant upon words or voices.

It might be argued that Deleuze appears to be schematizing these plays to an unwarranted degree. Yet his analysis seems to me to be sufficiently nuanced to be able both to associate these plays and to see each one as distinct. Indeed, Deleuze does proceed to devote further discussion to each individual play in turn. He notes, for example, the ways in which *Ghost Trio* reproduces triadic patterns as it develops. Hence, in addition to Beethoven's Fifth Piano Trio (an aural trio), apprehended by the ear, there is the structural trio of space, voice and music. There are also the three main camera positions: the door on the east side, the pallet on the west side, and the north window. Moreover, the play itself is divided into pre-action, action and re-action.

Quad, on the other hand, as the title also indicates, is structured not on the figure three but on the figure four. It exemplifies persuasively Deleuze's analysis. *Quad* presents the viewer with a quadrilateral, tramped by four figures. Although identical in appearance and gait, they can be differentiated by the colour of the robe they wear and by the percussion instrument which accompanies their movements. However, as Deleuze points out, it is space, and not character or dress, which categorizes them: 'On peut toujours leur affecter une lumière, une couleur, une percussion, un bruit de pas qui les distinguent. Mais c'est une manière de les reconnaître; ils ne sont en eux-mêmes déterminés que spatialement' [One can always assign to them a light, a colour, a percussion, or a footfall to distinguish them. But this is only a way of recognizing them; in themselves, their specificity is merely spatial] (Deleuze, 1992: 80). What they are to the viewer depends on their order and their position in the total event. They are the incarnation *par excellence* of Deleuze's concept of the *ritournelle* or refrain, the music being provided by the rasp of their feet on the playing area. Serially, as they pace and disappear, in all possible permutations, through all segments of the quad, they provide a kind of musical canon. Inexorably, they execute to the point of *épuisement* all possible combinations, as Beckett indicates in his directions:

> Quatre solos possibles, tous ainsi épuisés.
> Six duos possibles, tous ainsi épuisés (dont deux par deux fois).
> Quatre trios possibles deux fois, tous ainsi épuisés.
> [Four possible solos all given.
> Six possible duos all given (two twice).
> Four possible trios all given twice].

> (Beckett, 1992: 10–11).

In alignment with the four players' exits and entrances, Beckett also planned to exploit four colours of lighting in all combinations, giving the direction: 'Toutes combinaisons possibles de lumières ainsi épuisées' [All possible light combinations given] (Beckett, 1992: 11). This was found in rehearsal to impart too much complexity to the event and was therefore abandoned, but it does demonstrate how Beckett wished to explore the process of *épuisement* on as many fronts as possible.

The most acute form of *épuisement* in the play is, however, the spatial one. According to Deleuze, it attaches to that central point of the square. The centre point offers an event-possibility: that of collision. It is, moreover, the *only* possible event on the onward-bound trajectory of the players.

Several years earlier, Deleuze had devoted an essay to the Italian dramatist, Carmelo Beno. As with *L'Epuisé*, it took the form of a 'postface' printed after a translation into French of the author's work: in this case, Bene's play *Richard III*. Taken as a whole, Deleuze's essay is somewhat disappointing in range and depth. Nevertheless, some of his remarks about Bene, and about theatre in general, have interest and applicability in the context of Beckett's own writing. Notably, Deleuze writes in that essay about the enormous energy and potentiality which attaches, not to the origin or terminus of a given line of trajectory, but to its central point: 'L'intéressant, c'est le milieu, ce qui se passe au milieu. Ce n'est pas par hasard que la plus grande vitesse est au milieu' [What is interesting is the middle, what happens in the middle. It's no accident that the greatest speed is in the middle] (Deleuze, 1979: 95). Deleuze aligns the extreme points of the line along which the organism travels with past and future, asserting that the middle is the place of potentiality, of *devenir*, of becoming. The central point is that of: 'le mouvement, la vitesse, le tourbillon. Le milieu n'est pas une moyenne, mais au contraire un excès. C'est par le milieu que les choses poussent' [movement, speed, swirl. The middle is not an average, but on the contrary an excess. It is by way of the middle that things grow] (Deleuze, 1979: 95).

Indeed, in *Quad*, that movement does resemble a little swirl or whirlpool in the flow of movement. Moreover, the heightened potentiality of the middle zone is emphasized by the percussive crescendo which accompanies the approach to the centre. Each time, the centre is avoided by what Deleuze describes, exhaustively, as 'ce léger décrochage central, ce déhanchement, cet écart, ce hiatus, cette ponctuation, cette syncope, rapide esquive ou petit saut' [this slight central stalling, this dislocation, this gap, this hiatus, this punctuation, this syncopation, rapid sidestep or little jump] (Deleuze, 1992: 83). This punctuation of the line is not, however, a mere avoidance of collision with other players, since the same interrupting movement is made when there is a solo player. As the players negotiate the space, the space remains in negotiation with them.

As a spatial drama, *Quad* has much in common with ballet. Beckett does of course specify that ballet training is desirable if the piece is to be executed smoothly. Beyond that, however, the piece resembles ballet, as Deleuze points out, in so far as its narrative relies not upon words or voices, but upon gesture and posture. In ballet, movement *means*, as also does the interruption of that movement. *Quad* is also, maintains Deleuze, akin to a piece of music, built upon

melodic and harmonic lines, in which there is a continual movement of echoes, intensities and dissonances.

Quad may therefore function as a kind of case study for the analysis
which Deleuze sets forth in *L'Epuisé*, since it exemplifies his working definition of *épuisement*, as given at the start of this essay. All
track combinations are included, some more than once; consequen-
tially, so too are the accompanying colours, and the accompanying
percussive combinations, from solo instrument to quartet. However,
while Beckett has ensured the procession of all available permutations, he is at pains to emphasize that these transactions have been
separated from any symbolic system of meaning. He demonstrates
this by his use of the word 'say' ('disons' in the French translation),
as in: 'Say 1 drum, 2 gong, 3 triangle, 4 wood block' (Beckett, 1984:
292). By using this term he signals that, while drum, gong, triangle
and wood block are candidate instruments, other percussive instruments might be used.

In the case of colour, a riot of signifying systems are available. In
the field of heraldry, for example, the colours used by Beckett in
the Stuttgart production[10] – white, yellow, blue and red – would
denote, respectively, innocence, faith, loyalty and magnanimity. In
terms of planetary symbolism, they would denote the Moon, the
Sun, Jupiter and Mars. Again, however, side-stepping the imposition
of unwanted hermeneutics, Beckett uses the word 'say' to indicate
the optionality of the colours. His stipulations are even more clear
in the production notebook for *Quad*, held in Reading University
Library (MS 2100), where Beckett writes under the heading of '<u>Colours</u>'
the clarification: 'No symbolic link colour-percussion'.

In *Quad*, we are given no meaning other than the bodies before
us, their sound and their interaction, or its avoidance. These are
clearly human beings before us, and thinking beings, whose position statements are made by their bodies. Their bodies are stealthy
and yet provocative. They provoke thought as well as providing
visual spectacle. As Deleuze observes in his second volume on
cinema: 'Non pas que le corps pense, mais, obstiné, têtu, il force à
penser, et force à penser ce qui se dérobe à la pensée, la vie' [Not
that the body thinks, but, obstinate, stubborn, it forces one to think,
and forces one to think about what escapes thought: i.e. life] (Deleuze,
1985: 246). In film, Deleuze points out, the body is primary; the
affective or physiological state of the person is mediated through
the postures and gestures of the body. Moreover, the body, in its
visible organicism, is constantly in transit: 'Le corps n'est jamais au

présent, il contient l'avant et l'après, la fatigue, l'attente. La fatigue, l'attente, même le désespoir sont les attitudes du corps' [The body is never in the present; it contains the before and after, fatigue, expectation. Fatigue, expectation, even despair are attitudes of the body] (Deleuze, 1985: 246). Although Deleuze does not discuss *Quad II* in *L'Epuisé*, it illustrates effectively his observation. Now drained of colour and percussion, the figures drag themselves round the square, accompanied only by the trudging shuffle of their feet. Seeing it, Beckett declared that *Quad II* was *Quad I* one hundred thousand years later. When viewed in sequence, *Quad II* makes apparent the physical cost of exhaustivity. It demonstrates *épuisement* in both its senses.

In his essay on Bene, Deleuze maintains that there are two essential elements in any work of art. He summarizes these as: 'la subordination de la forme à la vitesse, à la variation de vitesse' [the subordination of form to speed, to variation in speed], and 'la subordination du sujet à l'intensité' [the subordination of subject to intensity] (Deleuze, 1979: 114). Although he does not explicitly refer to these criteria in his later analysis of *Quad*, it seems that his response to *Quad* – a response which exhibits none of the puzzlement, boredom or irritation which some viewers demonstrate on watching the piece – derives from the perception that both of these criteria are fulfilled. Indeed, many viewers experience the demotion of subjectivity and narrative form in *Quad* as a diminishment, or as an unwarranted mystification. For Deleuze, it is these factors which constitute the uncanny strength of Beckett's writing.

Notes

1 See *L comme Littérature* in Deleuze, 1996.
2 See *I comme Idée* in Deleuze, 1996.
3 See André Bernold, *L'Amitié de Beckett* (Paris: Hermann, 1992), pp. 85–6.
4 See *C comme Culture* in Deleuze, 1996.
5 See *M comme Maladie in* Deleuze, 1996.
6 Gilles Deleuze, *Cinéma I: L'Image-Mouvement* (1983) and *Cinéma II: L'Image-Temps* (1985).
7 Beckett's texts will here be cited in the language of first composition. His own translation into English will be given where appropriate.
8 See *M comme Maladie* in Deleuze, 1996.
9 See *B comme Boisson* in Gilles Deleuze, 1996.
10 The Stuttgart television première, broadcast on 8 Oct. 1981, was broadcast on British television on 16 Dec. 1982.

References

Beckett, Samuel (1951) *Molloy*. Paris: Editions de Minuit.
Beckett, Samuel (1953) *L'Innommable*. Paris: Editions de Minuit.
Beckett, Samuel (1976) *Pour finir encore et autres Foirades*. Paris: Editions de Minuit.
Beckett, Samuel (1976) *Watt*. London: John Calder.
Beckett, Samuel (1979) *Molloy*. In *The Beckett Trilogy*. London: Picador.
Beckett, Samuel (1984) *Quad*. In *Collected Shorter Plays*. London: Faber.
Beckett, Samuel (1984) 'I Gave up Before Birth'. In *Collected Shorter Prose 1945–1980*. London: John Calder.
Beckett, Samuel (1992) *Quad et autres pièces pour la télévision* (printed with Gilles Deleuze, *L'Epuisé*). Paris: Editions de Minuit.
Beckett, Samuel (1993) *Dream of Fair to Middling Women*. London: John Calder.
Bernold, André (1992) *L'Amitié de Beckett*. Paris: Hermann.
Connor, Steven (1988) *Samuel Beckett: Repetition, Theory and Text*. Oxford: Blackwell.
Deleuze, Gilles (1983) *Cinéma I: L'Image-Mouvement*. Paris: Editions de Minuit.
Deleuze, Gilles (1985) *Cinéma II: L'Image-Temps*. Paris: Editions de Minuit.
Deleuze, Gilles (1992) *L'Epuisé* (printed with Samuel Beckett, *Quad et autres pièces pour la télévision*). Paris: Editions de Minuit.
Deleuze, Gilles (1996) *L'Abécédaire* (edited videotape of filmed discussions between Deleuze and Claire Parnet, directed by Pierre-André Boutang, broadcast on Arte channel between 1994 and 1995). Vidéo Editions Montparnasse.
Deleuze, Gilles with Carmelo Bene (1979) *Superpositions*. Paris: Editions de Minuit.
Deleuze, Gilles with Félix Guattari (1972) *Capitalisme et Schizophrénie: L'Anti-Oedipe*. Paris: Editions de Minuit.
Deleuze, Gilles with Félix Guattari (1980) *Capitalisme et Schizophrénie: Mille Plateaux*. Paris: Editions de Minuit.

6
Beckett and Badiou

Andrew Gibson

This essay seeks to isolate what I take to be the four cardinal features of Badiou's work on Beckett. It arranges them in a logical and even chronological order which is partly implicit and partly explicit in Badiou's writings, but to which I have also added an outline or definition, and various, quite marked inflections. This seems to me to be important if Badiou's thought about Beckett is going to count elsewhere than in the world of contemporary French philosophy. Beckett's work occupies an important place in Badiou's philosophical system, but one that is none the less more than a little problematic if not obscure. The same cannot be said, for instance, of the work of Mallarmé, the other literary figure who is similarly significant for Badiou. Thus an effective and useful account of the relationship between Badiou's work and Beckett's does not require a wholesale translation of Badiou's philosophical system into Beckett studies. The need is rather for a specific, carefully considered elaboration of certain of the terms of that system on the basis of as full a knowledge as possible of what they mean within it. This is partly the case because, as I shall indicate later, in at least one crucial respect, Badiou's reading of Beckett seems to be at an angle to or atypical of his system. All the same, that reading is potentially very important for Beckett studies. It is important because it points in a quite different direction to the postmodern, poststructuralist and deconstructive methodologies that have been most significant for the Beckett criticism of the past decade. But it does this without any lapse back into the foundationalism, representationalism or existential humanism that so dominated work on Beckett before the arrival of Connor and Trezise.[1] There has long been a widespread but often rather vague conviction of the ethical significance of Beckett's work. It is precisely an ethical turn in Beckett criticism that the 'different direction' indicated by Badiou makes possible. It also makes possible a significant political or, more strictly, ethico-political reading of Beckett.[2] There are more and more complex problems around these issues than I can broach in this essay. However, towards the end of it, I shall try to indicate one or two of the most crucial points of divergence between Badiou's work and what I shall call 'postmodern Beckett criticism', particularly as the latter is exemplified in Anthony Uhlmann's recent book.[3] Uhlmann will thus serve as my example of a direction in Beckett studies from which Badiou and any work that emerges from his must be precisely distinguished.

For Badiou, truth is neither relative, nor thinkable only in its historical determinations, nor linguistically constructed. It is rather both radical and rare. Being is only conceivable as a multiple. Ontology is always a science of the multiple, logically best left to mathematics. This conception of Being implies, on the one hand, a concept of *doxa*, on the other, a concept of emergence. *Doxa* (or what Badiou provocatively calls 'opinion') is precisely the familiar reduction of Being in its multiplicity to the terms of knowledge; or rather, it is reduction and repetition together, the hardened form of repeatable and repeated *savoir*. Whatever it may count for historically – in terms that, it goes without saying, are not to be slighted – philosophically, it counts for nothing. Yet there is also emergence or, in Badiou's terms, the event, which arrives both as a supplement to Being and a radical interruption of *doxa*. The event is the mode in which the new enters the world. It is precisely the condition of truth in its rarity. A truth will be an extension of or constructed on the basis of the event. As Badiou puts it, a truth develops as a *fidelity* to the event. It may be thought of as the continuing trace of 'la supplémentation événementielle'.[4] But if, for Badiou, truth is both radical and rare; if he associates it with emergence; if what is true is only what can neither be anticipated nor produced by prior forms; if truth is always a supplement to a given multiple, a break with an established order; then truth is distinct from knowledge. More precisely, in Badiou's Lacanian terms, it 'makes holes' in the orders of *savoir* and representation and is 'indiscernible' to them.[5] In other words, from the point of view of the situation it comes to supplement, truth is 'lessness'. A truth involves a reduction or diminution of or – to introduce the first of my four key terms – a *subtraction* from previous knowledge. Subtraction, writes

Badiou, is intrinsic to 'the action of a truth'. It is the means by which I can arrive at an apprehension of 'cela seul qui peut être connu en réel'.[6] That apprehension is produced by what Badiou calls 'une épuration de toute épaisseur qu'on puisse savoir'.[7] The *épuration* in question is part of the Beckettian project: on the very first page of his book on Beckett, Badiou suggests that thought is never properly subtracted from the spirit of its time save through 'un labeur constant et délicat'. It is clear that he conceives of Beckett as engaged in such a labour.[8] Badiou's Beckett is concerned with subtraction as a patient, disciplined, 'lessening' of *savoir* and *doxa*.[9] For Badiou, it would be crucial to register the active force of what Beckett told Janvier of '[mon] désir de m'appauvrir davantage'.[10] 'Appauvrissement' is the very condition of what Badiou calls the 'indiscernible'. It is the condition of the 'incalculability' of a truth, and thus of its newness (*E*, p. 31). In effect, in Badiou's terms, what Beckett was asserting to Janvier was his decision 'not to give up on his desire' ('Ne pas céder sur son désir', *E*, p. 43). This phrase of Lacan's has been crucial to Badiou. In the terms of *L'éthique*, *acharnement* – not giving up – means establishing and sustaining a relation to a given situation from the point of view of the event that arrived to interrupt it. This is what is involved in writing as subtraction.

Of course, it is not hard to conceive of Beckett's project in such terms. We may seem to be on familiar ground. The development of the work from at least *Watt* onwards can be plausibly described as involving a progressive diminution or elimination of artistic resources. This is most notably the case in the period running from *Watt* to the *Texts for Nothing*. (In view of what I am about to say, however, it is also important to underline the fact of there 'always being more'. This is most markedly evident after what might seem to be the *nec plus ultra* of subtraction, *Breath*.) Such a development would seem to promote or endorse a paradoxical concept of Beckett's art as an addition that aims to take away, as a movement of 'presencing' that, at the same time, 'makes holes' in what is already present. This concept is strikingly evident in that *locus classicus*, Beckett's letter to Axel Kaun, where the image employed is the same as Lacan's:

> As we cannot eliminate language all at once, we should at least leave nothing undone that might contribute to its falling into disrepute. To bore one hole after another in it, until what lurks behind it – be it something or nothing – begins to seep through; I cannot imagine a higher goal for a writer today.[11]

The 'language' in question is precisely orthodox or what Beckett calls 'official English', the language of *doxa*, and the 'goal' is close to the Unnamable's, if expressed in a less Célinian tone than his:

> Not to be able to open my mouth without proclaiming them, and our fellowship, that's what they imagine they'll have me reduced to. It's a poor trick that consists in ramming a set of words down your gullet on the principle that you can't bring them up without being branded as belonging to their breed. But I'll fix their gibberish for them.[12]

Badiou in fact insists that it is precisely unnamability – the unnamability of pure singularity – that sets a limit to subtraction.[13] Otherwise, however, there would appear to be no *necessary* limits to the latter. In this respect, thought itself can only be self-legislating. It is not *required* to be as it is.

Thus in Badiou's thought – and in Badiou's account of Beckett – the concept of subtraction is linked to a concept of an 'action restreinte' or 'ascèse méthodique'. It is necessary to distinguish the practice of subtraction from the violence of destruction or negation. In this context, it is important to note Badiou's insistence that Beckett's work is 'plus *pensé*' than is commonly believed.[14] 'Action restreinte' is a term that Badiou derives from Mallarmé. It designates a practice that may be aesthetic, as in the work of Mallarmé, Beckett and others, or philosophical, as in Plato, the Cartesian reduction or Husserlian *épochē*. It may be defined as the reduction of the complexity of experience to certain major functions or 'axiomatic terms'. These latter mark out the boundaries of what thought then proceeds to take as its sphere of operation. They are the markers or instruments of a thought or an art in its specificity as project or *tentative*. They determine the production of this specific thought or art as speculation or Mallarméan 'pure notion', as self-grounding or self-constituent. The poem or work cannot *be* general or refer to any generality.[15] In its singularity, it proffers not a *savoir* but a *pensée*. The structural features of that *pensée* are formulated, not in response to what is judged to be an 'exterior reality', but axiomatically. Nothing confirms the universe constituted by and as the work as having a right to exist. In this respect, the work is pure affirmation. This is what Badiou means by Beckett's concern with the 'generic'. Beckett's art is a reduction of experience to certain cardinal functions, to certain questions concerning them, and to certain responses to these questions. Badiou insists that the importance of the mathematization of logic has been that logic now appears only in local manifestations. The result is the production of worlds (of thought) within which *'la logique est une dimension interne'*.[16] It is precisely as a 'localized logic' that what Badiou calls Beckett's 'axiomatics of humanity' must be understood (*EG*, p. 332). Beckett sets out from 'existential axioms' that Badiou says are not reducible to universal ones. He 'decides an existence into being' and establishes its consistency only around this decision (*LPTL*, p. 127). He commits himself to treating in writing only themes apprehensible as 'essential determinations' (ibid., pp. 330–1). Such 'determinations' are not to be understood as objective essences nor as established in their right to existence. The Beckettian *tentative* proceeds axiomatically. It is ineluctably founded on a 'soit', 'mettons', 'disons', 'supposons que' or, in the final words of Beckett's 'Mirlitonnade' (which Badiou quotes), 'parlons-en' (*EG*, p. 329).

In Beckett, then, precisely, almost paradigmatically, Badiou discovers what he calls 'une pensée qui s'obtient dans le retrait, la défection, de tout ce qui supporte la faculté de connaître' (*QPP*, p. 220). Subtraction is not a nihilism. It is not a destructive process whose end is the void (as though that end could ever be reached). It is rather the inseparable condition of an intellectual or aesthetic practice that 'makes itself from the ground up'. Of course, 'action restreinte' is no more unitary or wholly consistent a principle in Beckett's work than is subtraction. There are comparatively 'wild' or 'unruly' works (like *Watt*) in which an 'action restreinte' is most clearly perceptible in localized form (above all, as permutation). But there are also works like *The Lost Ones* in which such 'action' becomes a governing principle and approaches an almost classical perfection. Nevertheless, alongside the 'progressive reduction' in Beckett's art from *Watt* to *Breath*, there is also another, quite distinct development. This runs from *Watt* through *How It Is* to *Quad* and beyond, if not 'sans hésitations ni repentirs'.[17] In certain works at least, 'action restreinte' is not merely a question of the occupation of particular sites and the performance of particular functions. It develops to a point where it has the force or scope of a general rule. The two developments are mutually reinforcing:

> There are many ways in which the thing I am trying in vain to say may be tried in vain to be said. I have experimented, as you know, under duress, through faintness of heart, through weakness of mind, with two or three hundred.[18]

Within this bleakly brilliant tissue of self-contradictions, Beckett indicates the paradoxical interinvolvement of a process of subtraction; an axiomatic principle ('predetermined vanity of the endeavour'); and a practice of 'action restreinte' manifesting itself in an extraordinary proliferation of 'localized logics' or 'experiments' in thought. But there is also more at issue in the passage in question. The lines just quoted open Beckett's last substantial contribution to the *Three Dialogues* with Georges Duthuit. The logic of this contribution is intensely sustained, but also turns over, like the Moebius strip:

> I know that all that is required now, in order to bring even this horrible matter to an acceptable conclusion, is to make of this submission, this admission, this fidelity to failure, a new occasion, a new term of relation . . . I know that my inability to do so places myself, and perhaps an innocent, in what I think is still called an unenviable situation, familiar to psychiatrists. For what is this coloured plane, that was not there before. I don't know what it is, having never seen anything like it before. It seems to have nothing to do with art, in any case, if my memories of art are correct. (*TD*, p. 145)

The passage announces the inevitability of failure. It proclaims Beckett's inability – as critic and as artist – to produce the 'new occasion'. But it does so only abruptly to testify to the van Velde painting as 'new occasion' itself. In its change in tone and address, the passage even labours to render such an experience of the painting.

It would seem, then, that the 'new occasion' can be formulated only in terms of a paradoxical, ironic logic. The principle is one of paradox as reticence or obliquity, an 'approach in reverse'. Wearily sceptical as to the point to any repetition of 'innovative' modernist practices, the passage none the less ends by twisting round into an affirmation of an instance of them. In other words, it moves from subtraction and 'action restreinte' to a concern with the possibility of the *event*. The event is the third of my four terms. My reading of the end of the third *Dialogue* is intended as a kind of miniaturization of Badiou's account of the history of Beckett's project. The concept of the event is crucial to that account. According to Badiou, after *Texts for Nothing* (1950), Beckett finally succumbs to a conviction of his own failure. He emerges from it only in *How It Is* (1960). This latter text constitutes a clear break, not only with the established themes of Beckett's work, but also with the more established Beckettian style and manner (*B*, pp. 11–12). With *Texts for Nothing*, it becomes clear that Beckett's art of subtraction or what Badiou calls his 'enquête sérieuse sur l'humanité pensante' has led him into an impasse (*B*, p. 11).[19] He must work his way out of the latter, by a labour turned towards a partial undoing of what the first labour has produced. Thus Beckett's work begins to open itself up to chance, the incident, 'brusques modifications du donnée' (*B*, p. 39). The Beckettian subject and the Beckettian text are exposed to alterity, though the process is uncertain, hesitant, very slow and given to backslidings (*B*, p. 38). The alterity in question is complex: the Beckettian subject opens up to the voice of the other, for instance, to the possibility of happiness, even to love, in what are often tiny ways. But above all, from 1960 onwards, both subject and text open up to the event. Crucially, Badiou understands the event in Beckett's work as '*adding*' itself to Being (*B*, p. 38, italics mine). After the long and patient labour of subtraction and within the discipline of an 'action restreinte', the event arrives as an addition or supplement.

Not surprisingly, perhaps, Badiou has grown more and more interested in Beckett's later work and, above all, in *Worstward Ho*. In 'Être, existence, pensée: prose et concept', this text functions almost as a résumé, even a mise-en-abîme of the Beckettian trajectory. For, in Badiou's terms, it traces the course of a long labour which ends at length in a cul-de-sac. This latter, however, is broken by a 'rupture événementielle'. Badiou understands this 'rupture' as having the status of the appearance of the constellation at the end of Mallarmé's *Coup de dés*:[20]

> Enough. Sudden enough. Sudden all far. No move and sudden all far. All least. Three pins. One pinhole. In dimmost dim. Vasts apart. At bounds of boundless void. Whence no farther. Best worse no farther. Nohow less. Nohow worse. Nohow naught. Nohow on. Said nohow on.[21]

In the key passage in his commentary on these lines, Badiou suggests that

> au moment où il n'y a plus à dire que la figure stable de l'être, alors surgit dans une soudaineté qui est une grâce sans concept une configuration d'ensemble dans laquelle on va pouvoir dire 'plus mèche encore' . . . Cependant, ce pouvoir-dire n'est plus un état de l'être, un exercice de l'empirer. C'est un événement . . . (*EEP*, p. 184)

The 'stable figure of being' is produced in the disciplined elaboration of an 'action restreinte'. The 'worsening' with which the text is so preoccupied is a consequence of subtraction. But as both procedures approach a limit-point, what emerges is a *pouvoir-dire*. Badiou understands this power as a question, not of will, conscious intention or rational choice, but of an *il arrive que* ... It is therefore what he calls 'a grace without concept'. The twist perceptible here, as at the end of the third *Dialogue*, is arguably intrinsic to Beckett's aesthetic logic. In Badiou's terms, the 'on' of *Worstward Ho* is not to be equated with any existential 'will to meaning'. It is rather the 'on' of saying reduced 'à la pureté de sa cessation possible' (p. 184), the bare, minimal reversal of the word 'no'. In other words, paradoxically, however uncertainly, the event becomes possible as a Beckettian process of repudiation, denial and *ascesis* moves towards its completion.

Yet this conception of the event in Beckett is austere and almost quietist in tendency. It is therefore curious, seen in relation to other aspects of Badiou's thought (which could certainly not be described as quietist). In *L'éthique*, Badiou describes the event as arriving as a supplement to a given situation. It constrains us to decide on a new way of being which the conservative principle would decree to be impossible. Badiou's major examples include the French Revolution, Schoenberg's twelve-tone system, Galilean physics, the encounter of Eloisa and Abelard. As Badiou conceives of it, the event in Beckett hardly appears to be of this order. More importantly, in *L'éthique*, any openness to the event is less significant than the decision to stay faithful to it, or what Badiou calls *fidelity*.[22] What matters is the intensity or persistence with which the subject continues to think a world according to what has happened to change it, to make it new. This diligent persistence or fidelity results in the 'construction' of a truth (*E*, p. 60). But Badiou appears to reverse this structure – the structure of the progress of a truth – in what he has to say of Beckett. For Beckettian fidelity appears to be rather to the *possibility* of the event than to any specifiable event in itself. The very concept of fidelity seems less relevant, here, than that of courage. Badiou has in fact increasingly adopted the latter word in his discussions of Beckett, most notably in 'Être, existence, pensée'. Badiou sees the early Beckett – Beckett before *How It Is* – as disposed to a belief in predestination (*B*, p. 40). He refers to this belief as *sourd*, deaf, unreceptive, closed in on itself. At length, however, Beckett moves beyond this early belief to an examination of the possible conditions of freedom, however aleatory and minimal they may appear to be (ibid). Increasingly, he asks the question of how we may hope that a truth will arrive (*B*, p. 46). This requires a practice of ascesis on the one hand, and vigilance on the other. The first is a practice of subtraction or stripping away, undertaken with what is, for Badiou, a kind of principled intransigence (*B*, p. 13). Beckett undertook this 'constant and delicate labour' without promises or guarantees, and with no certain knowledge of where it was tending. It led him into crisis and impasse. But it is also the very heart of the Beckettian lesson, which is a lesson in measure, exactitude and courage (*B*, p. 9). Equally, for Badiou's Beckett, attentiveness – attentiveness, that is, to the possibility of the most radical difference that is the event – is or becomes a principle. If, in Badiou's work, Beckett is sometimes shadowed by Mallarmé, at the end of 'Être, existence, pensée', Badiou also *opposes* the two, in what is apparently a decisive move, as Irish insomniac to French faun. For Mallarmé, it is always possible to break from the poetic endeavour, to relinquish the effort. It is possible to suspend activities, to cease to pose the poet's question. There is always the possibility of a grateful return to the indeterminacy from which the poetic endeavour sprang and will spring again. But there is no possibility of any such relaxation in Beckett. His work allows no significant place to any suspension of operations. He is intransigent, not only in his asceticism, but in his injunction to watchfulness (*EEP*, p. 187).

Oddly, then, Badiou manages to make Beckett both vital and central and yet, at the same time, incidental to the mainstream of his own thought. For his Beckett both listens out for and works to identify the event, and yet follows a trajectory that is apparently not determined by it. The obvious point of contrast, here, would be another key figure for Badiou, St Paul. For if, on the one hand, St Paul explores the question of the law that might structure 'un sujet dépourvu de toute identité', on the other, that subject is 'suspendu à un événement', the only proof of which is that a subject declares it.[23] In 'Art et philosophie', Badiou describes a work or works of art as constructing a particular truth in a 'dimension postévénementielle' (*AP*, p. 25). For Badiou, the work or *oeuvre* as series is provoked by and a protracted response to the event. But the Beckettian series rather moves laboriously *towards* the event, adumbrates it or occasionally testifies to it, above all, in *Worstward Ho*. This may seem to suggest that the condition of Beckett's art is a liminal one. But the concept of liminality diminishes the importance of the way in which the Beckettian work *works*. A more appropriate metaphor than the threshold might be the negative that stays un-developed. But this, again, is too static and too simple. The extraordinary implication of Badiou's work on Beckett is that Beckett's art is neither a representation, nor an expression, nor an indica-tion of a truth. It is rather a disposition, a way of waiting for a truth, of clearing the ground for it, even conjuring its arrival. Badiou leads me to think of Beckett's art as both a preliminary or prelude and a strikingly vigorous 'action'; as a process of scratching away or scratching out, and a formulation of provisional frames that are both skeletal, and extremely precise. By implication, the process in question is also an ethico-political practice. Subtraction, 'action restreinte', courage or persistence, all conceived of in relation to the possibility of the event: in Badiou's account of it, the four car-dinal features of Beckett's work are the coordinates of an ethico-political formulation. Taken together, they constitute a co-herent, ethico-political aesthetic.

To conceive of Beckett in such terms, however, is to depart from the emphases currently dominant in the more advanced Beckett criticism. Over the past decade, in a number of distinguished and theoretically sophisticated studies, various Beckettians – Connor, Trezise, Hill, Locatelli, Begam – have insistently articulated Beckett in postmodern or poststructuralist terms.[24] But those terms are not Badiou's, as I will briefly show with particular reference to the most recent contribution to this line of thought, Anthony Uhlmann's *Beckett and Poststructuralism*. In the first instance, the 'postmodern Beckettians' assume the priority for Beckett of a general economy. In Trezise's phrase, this latter 'produces the world and exceeds it' as a 'strangeness constitutive of all familiarity' (*IB*, p. 29). Uhlmann, whose book is chiefly Deleuzean, assumes precisely the priority of a general economy in arguing that, 'like Deleuze', Beckett 'seems to posit a univocity of being in his writings' (*BP*, p. 110). Not only is this to identify Beckett with what Badiou sees as most problematic in Deleuzean philosophy.[25] It is also to identify him with a con-cern with the general rather than the *generic*. It is the generic or 'action restreinte' that, for Badiou, is Beckett's more pressing con-cern. 'Generic writing' is a project that must be conceived, not in relation to what 'comes before' it, but as developing in relation to a principle of limitation or – better – determination. It is therefore also a mode of action. Secondly, the general economy may be con-ceived of as a shuttling movement of differentiation which is itself without differentiation. As Hill puts the point, it 'enables difference as such – which cannot exist "as such" – to be articulated, while at the same time rendering [difference] perpetually unstable and precarious' (*BF*, p. 9). But this 'movement' cannot be thought save from *within* differentiation. The 'outside' is also an inside. The general economy that traverses a restricted economy is also reduced within it. Thus if Beckett's art struggles towards what is prior to or outside or a condition of sense and meaning, that struggle can never be completed. This, again, is the case with Beckett in Uhlmann's account of him: Uhlmann draws on Deleuze's concept of 'inclusive disjunction' to suggest the 'oscillation' in which, he claims, Beckett is trapped (*BP*, p. 96). Such is the case, for instance, with *Molloy*, which 'even as it tears the surface of words in sabotaging the world of order . . . still constitutes a relation' (*BP*, p. 83). From Badiou's point of view, however, such a conception of Beckett erases the difference between destruction and the discipline of subtraction. It also severely underestimates the power of subtraction as a mode of resistance to the 'relation' to a given 'world of order'.

Thirdly: for Badiou, after the long and patient labour of subtraction, there is the possibility of the event, as addition or supplement. The event has no such status in the work of the 'postmodern Beckettians'. It is either neglected or banalized. From Badiou's perspective, the neglect is surely due to the extent to which the critics have insistently placed language at the very centre of Beckett's concerns. What is always in question, even if subjected to the most radical questioning, is a concept of truth as correspondence, and therefore the relationship between truth and language. But, for Badiou, truth is rather a question of an axiom or decision understood as consequent upon an event. Language comes after, has a secondary or subordinate function, precisely as a concern with the 'nomination' of the event. The event – at least, in Badiou's more crucial conception of it – is not 'mundane'.[26] It is the condition of truth in its rarity. For the Deleuzean Uhlmann, by contrast, the event is everywhere, as a function of becoming itself.[27] Finally: the principal concerns of recent Beckett criticism have put linguistic and epistemological concerns to the fore. By contrast, Badiou's principal concern is ethics. The 'postmodern Beckettians' have either not been much concerned with the description of a Beckettian ethics, or have described it rather oddly. Uhlmann ascribes to Beckett a Deleuzean ethics 'outside the system of judgement'. But however 'desubjectified', can an '"ethical practice" of seeking bodies which suit and avoiding bodies which do not suit your own' really be Beckett's (*BP*, p. 124)? Can it even be properly distinguished from bourgeois prudence and self-interest? As articulated by Badiou, Beckett's ethics is also an ethico-politics, and one with considerable resonance and power, particularly at the current time. Here, Badiou's account of the political implications of the Beckettian aesthetic needs to be brought into contact with Adorno's. Simon Critchley has recently reminded us of the importance of Adorno's reading of Beckett: Beckett's work is distinguished by a kind of 'weak messianic power'.[28] He chooses a *via negativa* for his messianism because he is scrupulous in his refusal of discredited positivities, as the latter conspire, in Adorno's phrase, 'with all extant meanness and finally with the destructive principle'.[29] At this moment, the most significant issues in Beckett studies are just beginning to congeal around the questions raised by Badiou on the one hand, and Adorno and Critchley on the other. This is the case, not least, with the relationship between Beckett's work and the 'extant meanness' of contemporary politics and political culture, what Badiou calls our *abjection contemporaine*.

Notes

1 See Steven Connor, *Samuel Beckett: Repetition, Theory and Text* (Oxford: Blackwell, 1988), hereafter *SB*; and Thomas Trezise, *Into the Breach: Samuel Beckett and the Ends of Literature* (Princeton, NJ: Princeton University Press, 1990), hereafter *IB*.

2 For the distinction I would want to maintain between political and ethico-political work, see my *Postmodernity, Ethics and the Novel* (London: Routledge, 1999), hereafter *PEN*; p. 4.

3 Anthony Uhlmann, *Beckett and Poststructuralism* (Cambridge: Cambridge University Press, 1999), hereafter *BP*.

4 Badiou, *L'éthique: essai sur la conscience du mal* (Paris: Hatier, 1993), hereafter *E*; p. 38.

5 *E*, p. 39; and *Le nombre et les nombres* (Paris: Seuil, 1990), p. 276, n. 2.

6 'Conférence sur la soustraction', *Conditions* (Paris: Seuil, 1992), hereafter *C*, pp. 179–95, p. 179.

7 Badiou, *L'être et l'événement* (Paris: Seuil, 1989), p. 472.

8 *Beckett* (Paris: Hachette, 1995), hereafter *B*; p. 5.

9 It is precisely this production of 'holes' in *doxa* that Badiou sees as a crucial part of the task of art. Art is a question posed to 'opinion', above all, perhaps, in contemporary culture: for 'la question d'aujourd'hui est celle-ci, et nulle autre: y a-t-il autre chose que de l'opinion, c-est-à-dire, on pardonnera (ou non) la provocation, y a-t-il autre choses que nos "démocraties"?' 'Art et philosophie', hereafter *AP*, in *Petit manuel d'inesthétique* (Paris: Seuil, 1998), hereafter *PM*, p. 29. This illustrates the political dimension to Badiou's aesthetics at its simplest. In particular,

he is specifying the mode in which art addresses one of his principal targets, the culture of the social-democratic phase of neo-liberalism (or 'Blaijorism', as the economists have started to call it). It is possible to place Beckett's work in relation to the specific constructions and distributions of 'opinion' in contemporary culture in a way that brings out its considerable political force. This may even be why Beckett is currently attracting so much attention from a younger generation of British and Irish intellectuals, a generation for whom we have in some sense 'finished with Marxism'.

10 Ludovic Janvier, *Samuel Beckett par lui-même* (Paris: Seuil, 1969), p. 18.

11 'German Letter of 1937', *Disjecta: Miscellaneous Writings and a Dramatic Fragment* (London: John Calder, 1983), hereafter *D*; pp. 170–3, p. 172.

12 *The Unnamable*, in *The Beckett Trilogy* (London: Picador, 1978), p. 298. A more extensive discussion of this passage in relation to my point, of course, would have to take the full measure of the irony implied in its tone.

13 See *CS*, p. 195: 'Soustraire est ce dont procède toute vérité. Mais la soustraction est ce qui norme et borne, sous les espèces de l'innommable, le trajet soustractif'. This is crucial to Badiou's ethics, as the return to the theme of the unnamable in *L'éthique* makes clear. It is also crucial to Badiou's ethical account of Beckett at the end of 'Conférence sur la soustraction' (pp. 194–5). This passage is probably the most explicit and to my mind the most compelling indication in Badiou's work of the possibility of an ethical reading of Beckett.

14 Badiou, 'L'écriture du générique: Samuel Beckett', in *C*, pp. 329–66, p. 332.

15 Badiou, 'Que pense le poème?', hereafter *QPP*, in Roger-Pol Droit (ed.), *L'art est-il une connaissance?* (Paris: Le Monde, 1993), pp. 214–24, p. 214.

16 'Logique, philosophie, "tournant langagier"', hereafter *LPTL*, in Badiou, *Court traité d'ontologie transitoire* (Paris: Seuil, 1998), pp. 119–28, pp. 127–8.

17 See *B*, p. 39. Badiou is describing the process whereby, after *How It Is*, Beckett's work begins gradually to open up to chance and the event. But the sporadic, intermittent, irregular character of that movement as Badiou describes it is also that of other 'lines of development' in the Beckett *œuvre*.

18 'Three Dialogues', hereafter *TD*, in *D*, pp. 138–45, p. 144.

19 Briefly: the practice of subtraction produces a conception of being as indeterminate. But once Beckett had arrived at this conception – in Badiou's terms, once he had 'named' it as the *noir-gris* – he was thrown back on to an experience of subjectivity as the endless torture of the solipsistic *cogito* (*B*, p. 38). Within this polarized structure, the only movement possible was one of unceasing, sterile oscillation.

20 'Être, existence, pensée: prose et concept', hereafter *EEP*, in *PM*, pp. 137–87, pp. 182–5.

21 Beckett, *Worstward Ho* (London: John Calder, 1983), pp. 46–7. Badiou, of course, takes the French text as his example.

22 For a detailed elaboration of these points, see *E*, pp. 36–9.

23 Badiou, *Saint Paul: la fondation de l'universalisme* (Paris: Presses Universitaires de France, 1997), p. 6.
24 Connor, *SB*; Trezise, *IB*; Leslie Hill, *Beckett's Fiction: In Different Words* (Cambridge: Cambridge University Press, 1990), hereafter Hill, *BF*; Carla Locatelli, *Unwording the Word: Samuel Beckett's Prose Works After the Nobel Prize* (Philadelphia: University of Pennsylvania Press, 1990); and Richard Begam, *Samuel Beckett and the End of Modernity* (Stanford: Stanford University Press, 1996).
25 See Badiou, *Deleuze* (Paris: Hachette, 1997), for instance, at p. 69, where Badiou clearly specifies both the closeness of his philosophy to that of his former colleague at the Université de Paris VIII, and one or two crucial differences between them.
26 One problem with my own earlier account of Badiou and Beckett, *PEN*, pp. 146–56, is my failure to make this distinction clear. My account of the event in *Texts for Nothing* is concerned only with what I would currently refer to as the banalized version of it which, though present in Badiou's thought, is not the most significant one.
27 Actually, for a Deleuzean, Uhlmann makes surprisingly little use of the concept of the event. But it can hardly fail to be implicit in part at least of his case, notably, perhaps, in the sections on 'Haecceity' and 'The Order of Time' in the fourth chapter (pp. 120–30).
28 Simon Critchley, *Very Little ... Almost Nothing: Death, Philosophy, Literature* (London: Rouledge, 1997), p. 22; hereafter *VL*.
29 Quoted in Critchley, *VL*, p. 24.

References

Badiou, Alain (1989) *L'être et l'événement*. Paris: Seuil.
Badiou, Alain (1990) *Le nombre et les nombres*. Paris: Seuil.
Badiou, Alain (1992) 'Conférence sur la soustraction', and 'L'écriture du générique: Samuel Beckett'. In *Conditions*. Paris: Seuil.
Badiou, Alain (1993a) 'Que pense le poème?'. In Roger-Pol Droit (ed.), *L'art est-il une connaissance?* Paris: Le Monde.
Badiou, Alain (1993b) *L'éthique: essai sur la conscience du mal*. Paris: Hatier.
Badiou, Alain (1995) *Beckett*. Paris: Hachette.
Badiou, Alain (1997a) *Saint Paul: la fondation de l'universalisme*. Paris: Presses Universitaires de France.
Badiou, Alain (1997b) *Deleuze*. Paris: Hachette.
Badiou, Alain (1998a) *Court traité d'ontologie transitoire*. Paris: Seuil.
Badiou, Alain (1998b) 'Art et philosophie'. In *Petit manuel d'inesthétique*. Paris: Seuil.
Beckett, Samuel (1978) *The Unnamable*. In *The Beckett Trilogy*. London: Picador.
Beckett, Samuel (1983a) *Worstward Ho*. London: John Calder.
Beckett, Samuel (1983b) 'German Letter of 1937'. In *Disjecta: Miscellaneous Writings and a Dramatic Fragment*. London: John Calder.
Begam, Richard (1996) *Samuel Beckett and the End of Modernity*. Stanford: Stanford University Press.

Connor, Steven (1988) *Samuel Beckett: Repetition, Theory and Text*. Oxford: Blackwell.

Critchley, Simon (1997) *Very Little ... Almost Nothing: Death, Philosophy, Literature*. London: Routledge.

Gibson, Andrew (1999) *Postmodernity, Ethics and the Novel*. London: Routledge.

Hill, Leslie (1990) *Beckett's Fiction: In Different Words*. Cambridge: Cambridge University Press.

Janvier, Ludovic (1969) *Samuel Beckett par lui-même*. Paris: Seuil.

Locatelli, Carla (1990) *Unwording the Word: Samuel Beckett's Prose Works After the Nobel Prize*. Philadelphia: University of Pennsylvania Press.

Trezise, Thomas (1990) *Into the Breach: Samuel Beckett and the Ends of Literature*. Princeton, NJ: Princeton University Press.

Uhlmann, Anthony (1999) *Beckett and Poststructuralism*. Cambridge: Cambridge University Press.

7
The Body of Memory: Beckett and Merleau-Ponty

Ulrika Maude

In recent years, the body has become academic box office. Whether the focus has been on gender, sexuality, textuality or any other bodily construct, books on different aspects of the topic have flooded the market. One of the salient characteristics of these accounts of embodiment has been the mutation of the significance of the body into the problem of the body as signification. This trend has had its impact on Beckett Studies; in the last decade and a half, several fine works on Beckett's relation to the above aspects have appeared in print.

What has been written about less, however, is the persistence with which Beckett explores the very basics of bodily existence, those conditions that are already in swing before culture lays its mark on embodied identity. If, as is sometimes suggested, it is the material body that forms the ultimate foundation of identity, by constituting that self that is both singular and, in its perpetual complexity and mutability, always plural and indecipherable, then it is Beckett more than any other writer who deals with this predicament in his work.

Despite the transcendentalist claims of early Beckett criticism, it is now widely concurred that the Beckettian characters' experience of the world is a markedly physical, bodily experience. Whether we are dealing with the prose or the drama, it seems to be the body, rather than the cogito, that gives the characters assurance of their existence. In *Company*, the narrated character is lying on his back in the dark, listening to a voice. The figure is aware of this 'by the pressure on his hind parts and by how the dark changes when he shuts his eyes and again when he opens them again' (Beckett, 1992b: 5). His existence, in other words, is determined and even brought about by tactile, visual and acoustic sensations. In *Footfalls*, we learn, through the female voice that narrates May's childhood conversation with her mother, that it is not enough for May merely to feel her existence through motion; May also needs to *hear* she exists, however faint the feet fall. When May, a moment earlier in the play, addresses her mother, the conversation not surprisingly centres around the mother's bodily needs: 'Would you like me to inject you again? [...] Would you like me to change your position again? [...] Straighten your pillows? Change your drawsheet? Pass you the bedpan? The warmingpan? Dress your sores? Sponge you down?' (Beckett, 1990: 400). Much of the dramatic tension in Beckett's drama, as Pierre Chabert has pointed out, stems less from the psychological conflicts of conventional theatre than from the starkly physical conflicts of bodily existence (Chabert, 1982: 25).

Many of the bodily experiences in Beckett, especially before the late prose, are brought to the reader's or spectator's attention through the characters' difficulties in motility, and the pain and discomfort thereby induced, or through the performing of normal bodily functions which seldom appear normal or unconditioned in Beckett. This said, however, we should not see Beckett's works as 'a portrait gallery of cripples,' but rather as one of the most serious efforts in literature to bring the body to the forefront (Chabert, 1982: 24).

There is, in other words, a distinction between being merely aware of the body, and between paying conscious attention to it. In literature, Beckett's work belongs to the latter, rather rare category, and his interest in Proust, in whose works bodily experiences also play a significant role, may in part stem from this factor. Deirdre Bair, in her biography of Beckett, discusses Beckett's interest in the French author Jules Renard, whose ability to study himself and in particular whose approach to 'natural functions' Beckett admired: 'He always speaks so well about chewing and pissing and that kind of thing,' Bair reports Beckett to have said to his friend Georges Pelorson, and points out the similarities between Renard's diaries, in which Beckett was particularly interested, and *Malone Dies* (Bair, 1990: 124–5).[1] In *How It Is*, Beckett's concern for the body is summed up in his narrator's mention of the great needs that will eventually fail him: 'the need to move on the need to shit and vomit and the other great needs all my great categories of being' (Beckett, 1996: 15).

In theory, Beckett's interest in the body and the physical world in general coincides with the trend in phenomenology, represented more by Heidegger and Merleau-Ponty than by Husserl and Sartre, that called for a reorientation from the transcendental to 'the phenomenology of everydayness'. Although Heidegger acknowledged the corporeality of our existence together with the important point of the body's temporality, it was, however, Merleau-Ponty who, with his theory of the incarnate subject, brought the body to the centre of philosophical interrogation.

In order to shed light on his theory of the incarnate subject, Merleau-Ponty, in *Phenomenology of Perception*, first published in 1945 and presumably written during the Second World War, introduces the phenomenon of the phantom limb. If the amputee is consciously aware of the loss of one of his limbs, Merleau-Ponty asks, why, as is well known, does he still feel pain in the missing limb, or even occasionally attempt to use it? More baffling still is the fact that an emotion or a circumstance similar to the one that caused the loss of the limb habitually creates a phantom limb in subjects who previously had no sensation of one (Merleau-Ponty, 1992: 76).

In order to find a solution to this fascinating paradox, and simultaneously to expose the inadequacy of both rational and empirical philosophy to address the problems of embodiment, Merleau-Ponty introduces the concept of the habitual body or body image, his idea of 'an organic thought through which the relation of the "psychic" to the "physiological" becomes conceivable' (Merleau-Ponty, 1992: 77). For although psychology at first glance would appear to offer the most obvious solution to the phantom limb, at least in the cases in which the personal emotions, history and memories of the patient function as the triggering element, it fails to explain the disappearance of the phantom limb when the nerves of the former limb leading to the brain are severed. Instead, then, what is needed is an explanation of how psychic factors and physiological conditions merge into one. For the phenomenon, as the above factors indicate, is neither the result of a mere *cogitatio* nor the simple result of objective causality.

The phantom limb appears to be connected to a refusal of mutilation, but bodily deficiency can only continue to be evaded if the subject is aware of the situations in which she or he faces a risk of having to encounter the disability, just as the subject of psychoanalysis, Merleau-Ponty adds, knows precisely what she or he does not want to face, otherwise the repressed issue could not be avoided with such success (Merleau-Ponty, 1992: 80). We refuse mutilation, says Merleau-Ponty, because part of us remains 'committed to a certain physical and inter-human world', and continues to tend towards this world despite disablement and handicaps (Merleau-Ponty, 1992: 81):

> To have a phantom arm is to remain open to all the actions of which the arm alone is capable; it is to retain the practical field which one enjoyed before mutilation. The body is the vehicle of being in the world, and having a body is, for a living creature, to be intervolved in a definite environment, to identify oneself with certain projects and be continually committed to them. (Merleau-Ponty, 1992: 81–2)

The world however, not only conceals but also reveals to the subject her/his deficiency, for we are conscious of the world through our bodies, and when our habitual world arouses in us intentions that we can no longer perform, by presenting to us objects which appear as utilizable to limbs that we no longer have, we become aware of our disability precisely to the degree that we are ignorant of it. We bury our intentions in objects, which however exist externally to our intentions, although they may exist for *us* only to the extent that they arouse in us volitions or thoughts (Merleau-Ponty, 1992: 82). Beckett shows an awareness of this fact in many of his works, although the relationship his characters have to intentionality is more complex than Merleau-Ponty's account of the matter. In *Malone Dies*, for instance, Malone's inventory of possessions includes '[o]ne boot, originally yellow, I forget for which foot' (Beckett, 1979: 229). Malone, of course, is incapable of walking. The recurring bicycles that the characters are unable to ride and the chairs that they can no longer sit on or the food their bodies no longer digest, function in a similar manner, accentuating the bodily disabilities of the characters. It is precisely through the contradiction between our intention on the one hand, and our actual ability on the other, that Merleau-Ponty comes to the conclusion that our bodies consist of two distinct layers: that of our habit-body and that of our actual, present body.

A phantom limb, therefore, is not a mere recollection but is, in fact, the same arm that has been lost to the subject, 'that same arm, lacerated by shell splinters, its visible substance burned or rotted somewhere, which appears to haunt the present body without being absorbed into it. The imaginary arm is, then, like repressed experience, a former present which cannot decide to recede into the past' (Merleau-Ponty, 1992: 85). We are dealing here with a bodily memory, an organic intelligence, whose applicability reaches far beyond the experiences of mutilation. We are dealing with a phenomenon akin to repression, in which a traumatic occurrence leaves the subject forever trapped in a past future which is no longer accessible to her/him. Merleau-Ponty says,

One present among all presents [...] acquires an exceptional value; it displaces the others and deprives them of their value as authentic presents. We continue to be the person who once entered on this adolescent affair, or the one who once lived in this parental universe. New perceptions, new emotions even, replace the old ones, but this process of renewal touches only the content of our experience and not its structure. Impersonal time continues its course, but personal time is arrested. (Merleau-Ponty, 1992: 83)

Through the two bodily layers, the habitual and the present body, the body is, in fact, the meeting place of the past, the present and the future, because it extends the past into the bodily present, simultaneously containing the outlines of the future that the body anticipates (Langer, 1989: 32). Bodily experience therefore cannot be reduced to introception occurring at a particular moment of the present. Neither is bodily temporality reducible to the order of objective time, as the experience of the phantom limb shows us.

According to Merleau-Ponty, the subject, 'at the dawn of perception,' begins to outline the '"indeterminate horizons" which signal the emergence of a world for us' (Langer, 1989: 46). The temporal structure of our body enables us to 'carry this primitive acquisition of horizons along, so that a more determinate world of objects can begin to exist' (Langer, 1989: 46). The world is therefore not ready-made but rather built up in a dialectical movement between the incarnate subject and the world. A case in point are habits: to learn to ride a bicycle or to play an instrument or to become accustomed to a particular item of clothing, 'is to be transplanted into them, or conversely, to incorporate them into the bulk of our own body' (Merleau-Ponty, 1992: 143). We are not dealing with intellectual analysis or with a mechanical recording of impressions but rather with the 'bodily comprehension of a motor significance,' a bodily knowledge which reveals the body as an expressive space, with a language of kinds of its own (Langer, 1989: 47). The body, says Merleau-Ponty, 'is our general medium for having a world' (Merleau-Ponty, 1992: 146). Through its different operations, whether they be merely life-sustaining, expressive in themselves, or whether 'the meaning aimed at cannot be achieved by the body's natural means' and acquires an instrument, our bodily experiences force us to 'acknowledge an imposition of meaning which is not the work of a universal constituting consciousness' (Merleau-Ponty, 1992: 146-7).

This is what Merleau-Ponty refers to as a 'a new meaning of the word "meaning"' (Merleau-Ponty, 1992: 146).

The notion of the habitual body or body image, then, is our intuitive sense of our bodies, which makes everyday functioning possible. It is the body's own sense of occupying space, without which the most simple actions would become impossible. Put in phenomenological terms, the present body functions as an object in an intentional act of consciousness, whereas the body image or the habitual body involves the idea of pre-intentionality (Gallagher, 1995: 226).

The bodily memory, habits and motor capacity that Merleau-Ponty discusses seem exceptionally relevant if we consider not only one particular piece of work by Beckett but the whole Beckettian canon. Indeed, in trying to recall individual features and events, especially in the different prose works by Beckett, the reader easily becomes uncertain and muddled up about characters, character-traits and events and their correspondence to particular works. Not only do certain character-traits, such as old age and decrepitude, repeat themselves throughout Beckett's works; other identifying markers such as great-coats, hats, boots, crutches, bicycles and stones, to mention but a few Beckettian props, are endemic to the works. Frequent, too, is the maiming of the body, which varies in degree from work to work. It is almost as if the whole Beckettian *oeuvre* had its own body image, into which certain articles of clothing and certain orthopaedic accessories were as a rule incorporated.

Merleau-Ponty's discussion of the body image and of bodily memory seems both strangely to coincide with and problematically to differ from Beckett's discussion of involuntary memory in his book on Proust, written in 1930 and published a year later. The stance Beckett takes towards habit forms the first problem, for the notion of habit has profoundly negative connotations in Beckett's *Proust*, due to the numbing effect habit has on perception. Habit, Beckett says, goes hand in hand with voluntary memory in Proust's work, which is an inadequate instrument of evocation, for it is a construct of the intellect; uniform, colourless, distanced; devoid of feelings of anxiety (Beckett, 1970: 32–3). Voluntary memory, in its bluntness, fails miserably to evoke the past, for we can only truly remember 'what has been registered by our extreme inattention' (Beckett, 1970: 31). By the latter, Beckett is referring to experiences that occur outside the realm of habit and conscious attention, those experiences, 'accumulated slyly and painfully and patiently,' that form 'the essence of ourselves' (Beckett, 1970: 31). Merleau-Ponty's habitual body or body image, however, in spite of the body's association with habit, is both constituted and functions in a pre-reflective realm, before the separation of subject and object; before, that is, the subject's entry into an objective, or what later theorists would call symbolic, realm. It is the present body for Merleau-Ponty, instead of the habitual one, that pertains to the realm of the objective world governed by the intellect. In phenomenological terms, it is the present body that functions as an intentional object, thereby rendering the difference between Merleau-Ponty and Beckett terminological rather than ideological.

Involuntary memory, says Beckett, cannot be evoked at will, but is 'provided by the physical world, by some immediate and fortuitous act of perception' (Beckett, 1970: 36). For Proust as for Beckett, it seems, this kind of memory alone can bring back the past in full. Here, however, we are faced with a second problem, for Beckett's account of the subject's relation to involuntary memory is itself contradictory. On the one hand Beckett seems to find in Proust's involuntary memory proof of the non-repeatability of the subject; on the other hand, involuntary memory seems to provide the very possibility of 'retrieving the past self as it was' (Connor, 1988: 47–8). The paradox here seems to be between a continuous and in some sense unified self and a deeper belief in the discontinuous nature of subjectivity, in the individual seen, as Beckett puts it, as 'a succession of individuals' (Beckett, 1970: 19).

If we return, once more, to Merleau-Ponty's discussion of the phantom limb, we find the conflict between the continuity and discontinuity of individuality in the very phenomenon of the phantom limb itself. The body, in Merleau-Ponty, functions as a register of experiences, carrying the past within it, and therefore providing the subject with a sense of continuity, while simultaneously, in its dynamic aspect, differing from that past. The phantom limb, therefore, functions as an involuntary memory of kinds, one that cannot be consciously willed away, but rather forms part of the essence of the incarnate subject's identity, while yet being lost on an objective, intentional level.

Merleau-Ponty himself discusses Proust's ideas of intellectual or voluntary memory, the mere description of the past, consisting only of characteristics rather than full structures of experience (Merleau-Ponty, 1992: 85–6). Authentic memory, Merleau-Ponty says, involves our bodies in a past experience, evokes in us emotions and sensations which we have difficulty in facing and yet are not willing to leave behind (Merleau-Ponty, 1992: 86). In Beckett's *Proust*, bodily perception, instead of isolated thought, is indeed the triggering factor of involuntary memory, for the first occurrence of it is brought about by the 'long-forgotten taste of a madeleine steeped in an infusion of tea' (Beckett, 1970: 34). Further examples given by Beckett include smells, noises, visual perceptions and even the action of stooping, a motor activity that the body is aware of essentially through the sense of touch (Beckett, 1970: 36–7).

Beckett's work itself abounds in examples of embodied memory, in characters caught in past experiences that keep re-emerging like phantoms throughout the canon. Memories in Beckett, just as in Proust, furthermore, are evoked through the whole gamut of the senses. *Krapp's Last Tape*, essentially a memory play, written in English in 1958, shall here serve as an example of the much wider functioning of embodied memory throughout Beckett's writing.

If, as has at times been suggested, the principal activity in *Krapp's Last Tape* is that of listening, then we should begin by noting that two different kinds of sound figure in the play. On the one hand we have the sounds that originate in the actual physical and temporal location of the stage, such as the clatter of the metal tins in which the tapes are kept; the thump of the dictionary and the ledger when they are banged on the table, 'the clink of the glass against the bottle' when Krapp goes backstage for a drink, and last but not least 'the noises of the body itself: Krapp's breath, panting slightly, [. . .] his shivers, the sounds of mastication, of throwing up, his sighs of satisfaction or coughing when he drinks; the sounds of Krapp moving on the stage' (Chabert, 1976: 57). The noises and sounds that have their origin in stage activities, in other words, function as markers of the present tense in the play. Krapp's past, on the other hand, is signalled by the voices and other sounds, such as the laughter, that we hear on the tapes. A sonorous tension is thus created between the present and the past, bringing not only Krapp, but the audience, too, to a close perceptual awareness of the different tenses in operation.

The different acoustic 'scenes' in *Krapp's Last Tape*, as Beckett acknowledged, engage both Krapp and the audience with varying degrees of intensity. In 'Suggestions for TV Krapp', Beckett refers to the episodes as having different 'listening values' that he grades 'Low', 'Intermediate' and 'High', the first being of little impact: 'All references to health and work' ('Suggestions for TV Krapp' is reproduced in Zilliacus, 1976: 204–5). These, it would be fair to say, belong to the realm of Beckett's own variant of 'voluntary memory'. In the case of the latter two categories, however, the playing, pausing, winding and changing of the tapes make not only Krapp re-experience his past, with all of the senses reactivated by the triggering effect of the voice; they also make it clear that if Beckett's audience is brought to the theatre as much to hear as to see, the missing visual imagery, notwithstanding, is provided by the act of listening. The oscillation of the different audio-temporal levels, in other words, serves not only to make Krapp relive his past in a peculiar form of time travel; the tapes also enable the audience, due to the visualizing quality of sound, to see the phantom of the younger Krapp on stage, side by side with the now decrepit Krapp.[2]

The voice on tape functions much like a conductor of perception, evoking the particular sensory experiences that prevail in each recollected memory. The famous scene in the hospital garden is a case in point: although Krapp does not initially remember the 'black ball' when he is reading the ledger, rather, as the stage directions have it, '*He raises his head, stares blankly front. Puzzled*', once he has listened to the tape, Krapp can again feel the ball in his hand, just as he vows on the tape he always will (Beckett, 1990: 217). The full impact of the memory of the mother's death is hence truly activated not by the written note on the ledger which does not result even in voluntary memory, nor even by the sound of Krapp's voice, but by the tactile sensation of the 'small, old, black, hard, solid rubber ball' that Krapp once clutched, and is thereafter left clutching, 'until [his] dying day' (Beckett, 1990: 220). It is almost as if it were the past body that summoned Krapp from the spaces and places he once occupied.

One of the most moving examples of embodied memory in Beckett is the lake scene in *Krapp's Last Tape*, which is repeated, with slight variations, three times in the play. The first time Krapp comes upon the recollection it is narrated in explicitly tactile terms: ' – my face in her breasts and my hand on her. We lay there without moving. But under us all moved, and moved us, gently, up and down, and from side to side' (Beckett, 1990: 220). The fact that Krapp is hard of hearing emphasizes the intensity with which he listens to the tape, his hand cupping his ear, his body 'bent or twisted over the machine' (Chabert, 1976: 51). The different effects the voice has on the present Krapp can be read across his face in a succession of expressions, almost as if it were the body that became 'the sensitive receptacle upon which the voice engraves itself' (Chabert, 1982: 28). Krapp's face is a blank of annoyance, but when the memories evoked by the voice cause a change in Krapp's level of attention, the mask of his face ruptures, 'his body unbends, unfolds, moves away from his listening posture, the trunk and face slowly lift, a relaxation is produced of hand and face' (Chabert, 1976: 52). The recorded voice transports Krapp through time and space to locations beyond the scope of the other senses, only to thrust these senses into action. Through the voice on tape, in other words, Krapp grows a phantom body. When Krapp relistens to the tape, the scene is experienced in terms of sight, sound, tactile sensations, the body in motion, rocked by the undulating water:

> – gooseberries, she said. I said again I thought it was hopeless and no good going on and she agreed, without opening her eyes. [. . .] I asked her to look at me and after a few moments [. . .] after a few moments she did, but the eyes just slits, because of the glare. I bent over to get them in the shadow and they opened. [. . .] Let me in. [. . .] We drifted among the flags and stuck. The way they went down, sighing, before the stem! [. . .] I lay down across her with my face in her breasts and my hand on her. We lay there without moving. But under us all moved, and moved us, gently, up and down, and from side to side. (Beckett, 1990: 223)

The distinction between the present Krapp and the past one both collapses and is simultaneously made more acute by the appending sense of loss that accompanies Krapp's recollections. The doubling of the body that the voice effects, in other words, far from freeing Krapp from the constraints of embodiment, serves only to make the predicament more severe. The boat scene ends the play, leaving the protagonist *'motionless staring before him'* (Beckett, 1990: 223). The tape winds on, establishing an uncanny continuity of movement between the rocking boat and the austere stage. Through the voiced bodies and the spooling tape recorder, in other words, Krapp is irrevocably linked to his losses.

In the section of *Phenomenology of Perception* dedicated to sexuality, Merleau-Ponty writes about a girl who, when forbidden to see her lover, suffers from insomnia and a loss of appetite, eventually losing her voice, much as if it had been severed from her body like a limb lost in an accident. The voice is not reawakened until the girl is left free to encounter her lover. Merleau-Ponty explains the loss of voice, which he compares to the manner in which 'certain insects sever one of their own legs,' by the fact that the significance of the interhuman world has been lost to the girl once the most fundamental of interhuman relationships is denied her (Merleau-Ponty, 1992: 163). The voice, devoid of its interhuman function, has lost its meaning. 'The memory of the voice is recovered when the body once more opens itself to others or to the past, when it opens the way to co-existence and once more [. . .] acquires significance beyond itself' (Merleau-Ponty, 1992: 165).

Something similar is at stake in *Krapp's Last Tape*, in which damage is registered in the voice itself. Krapp's present voice is described as 'cracked'; the importance of this detail is disclosed by the fact that Beckett wrote the play with Patrick Magee's voice in mind, after he had heard Magee reading passages of his prose on the BBC Third Programme in December 1957.[3] James Knowlson recounts how moved Beckett was 'by the cracked quality of Magee's distinctively Irish voice which seemed to capture a sense of deep world-weariness, sadness, ruination and regret' (Knowlson, 1996: 444).[4] In *A Cultural History of Ventriloquism*, Steven Connor discusses the manner in which our voices can function as 'a persona, a mask or a sounding screen' through which we project ourselves to the world (Connor, 2000: 5). He adds:

> At the same time, my voice is the advancement of a part of me, an uncovering by which I am exposed, exposed to the possibility of exposure. I am able to shelter behind my voice, only if my voice can be me. But it can be me only if it has something of my own ductility and sensitivity: only if it is subject to erosion and to harm. My voice can bray and buffet only because it can also flinch and wince. My voice can be a glove, or a wall, or a bruise, a patch of inflammation, a scar, or a wound. (Connor, 2000: 5)

When Krapp's younger voice is heard on tape, it is a '*Strong voice, rather pompous*', achingly different from the broken, at times raucous voice of the decrepit man on stage (Beckett, 1990: 217). The play of continuity, discontinuity and loss is acted out in the voices, distinctly other while irreducibly connected.

The theme of memory in *Krapp's Last Tape*, the temporal sedimentation of body upon body, other and yet same, that our existence in its discontinuous unity consists of, keeps recurring throughout the Beckettian canon, with slight, phantasmagorically fading and reappearing variations that verge on the boundary of existence and non-existence, much like the phantom-limb experiences in Merleau-Ponty's work. The above-quoted lake scene from *Krapp's Last Tape* that first occurs in *Dream of Fair to Middling Women*, is one of the fundamental memories in Beckett's work, together with the recurring scene in Beckett's prose of an old man and child plodding along a narrow country road: 'Nothing from pelves down. From napes up. Topless baseless hindtrunks. Legless plodding on. Left right unreceding on' (Beckett, 1992b: 126). Once the narratee has walked down the country road in his youth, he is left walking down it for ever, 'Sole sound in the silence your footfalls. [. . .] So many since dawn to add to yesterday's. To yesteryear's. To yesteryears'" (Beckett, 1992b: 11). Recollections like these keep emerging and waning like phantom limbs throughout the body of Beckett's writing.[5]

It is in the nature of memories, in the flow between past and present, to be incomplete, phantom-like, fragile. Memories in Beckett, however, have their own special air, which gives them their idiosyncratic quality. In *Not I*, Mouth has a sudden flash of feeling coming back, 'imagine! . . . feeling coming back! . . . starting at the top . . . then working down . . . the whole machine' (Beckett, 1990: 379–80). The unnamable, in the final part of the novel, experiences itself as an ear that grows itself a body. If we are, in the case of Mouth and the unnamable, dealing with actual phantom-limb experiences, what is distinctly Beckettian about the memories is the plainly corporeal nature of the recollections. Triggered not by mere intellectual memory but by the body's own recollection of sensory experience, the strange time and place sequences in works such as *Company*, the four novellas, *That Time* or any other Beckettian haunting of the present by the past, become explicable in so far as the past is sedimented in the body itself, in a perpetual present continuous tense that leaves what has once been experienced and what can never truly be left behind irreversibly echoing in the characters' bodies. The bodies in Beckett seem not only to exist in several tenses, but to have both a time-arresting stative aspect and an active, dynamic one that is almost time itself. It is as if the paradoxes present in Beckett's account of involuntary memory were in fact aspects of continuity and discontinuity embedded in the very notion of bodily existence.

The clash between the stative and the active corporeal aspects is one of the triggering factors of the negative bodily experiences that form such an important part of the Beckettian canon.[6] Our awareness of what we have been physically capable of in the past and of what we can no longer perform makes our bodies the focal point of our anxieties, causing us, at times, not to coincide with ourselves. In *Molloy*, the narrator, while lying in his mother's bed and narrating his quest for his mother, experiences his limbs as alien: 'when I see my hands, on the sheet, which they love to floccillate already, they are not mine, less than ever mine, I have no arms [. . .] And with my feet it's the same, sometimes, when I see them at the foot of the bed, one with toes, the other without' (Beckett, 1979: 61–2). The incapacitated limbs in their present aspect are no longer recognized as the same limbs that once enabled the riding of the bicycle that the body, in its habitual, stative aspect, still continues to consider within its reach. In the second act of *Happy Days* a reversal of this experience occurs, for Winnie, who is now buried up to her neck in the mound, mentions her arms and her breasts, and goes on to add, '[w]hat arms? – [w]hat breasts?', as if the current loss of these body parts rendered their existence in the past suspect, reducing them in effect to hallucinations, turning the habitual body itself in *Happy Days* into yet another example of phantom bodily experiences in the Beckettian canon (Beckett, 1990: 161). When the body is at one with itself, on a day on which we happen to play a musical instrument or to run or to dance or to perform any other motor activity particularly well, Gabriel Josipovici observes, 'we feel ourselves to be *more ourselves* than is normally the case, more actively part of the world' (Josipovici, 1996: 112). In the negative bodily experiences we so frequently encounter in Beckett, the habitual body, the body in its stative aspect, functions as a signifier that is out of sync with its signified.

In short, Beckett grounds the very basics of subjectivity, its enigmatic play of continuity and discontinuity, firmly in the body. Beckett's work finally coincides with Merleau-Ponty's precisely in its insistence on the body's unnegotiable irreducibility. Where Beckett differs from Merleau-Ponty, however, is in the avidity with which the latter finds in the body a new locus of meaning. While Beckett's work insists on grounding subjectivity in materiality, it radically departs from Merleau-Ponty's work in its stern refusal of all forms of transcendence. The affirmative nature of Merleau-Ponty's thinking is in conclusion lost in Beckett. The points of convergence are matched by a fundamental divergence. The connection between Beckett and Merleau-Ponty remains shimmering and fragile, not unlike the flickering phantoms we encounter in their works.

Notes

1 Bair quotes the following passage from Renard's diary, an entry of 7 April 1910, which, according to Bair, particularly impressed Beckett: 'Last time I wanted to get up. Dead Weight. A leg hangs outside. Then a trickle runs down my leg. I allow it to reach my heel before I make up my mind. It will dry in the sheets' (Bair, 1990: 124; Renard, 1964: 248). Anthony Cronin, in his Beckett biography, confirms Beckett's interest in Renard and gives an account of Beckett's having read the above passage to his friend Georges Pelorson twice in a row (Cronin, 1997: 148). James Knowlson, in his biography, mentions the great interest with which Beckett read 'the meticulous self-analysis of Jules Renard's *Journal intime*' (Knowlson, 1996: 126).

2 At times the audience is even presented with a *mise-en-abyme* effect, as when Krapp is listening to a passage in which a younger version of himself recites his experiences of listening to 'an old year': 'Hard to believe I was ever that young whelp. The voice! Jesus! And the aspirations! [*Brief laugh in which KRAPP joins.*] And the resolutions! [*Brief laugh of KRAPP alone*]' (Beckett, 1986: 218). Not only, in other words, do we have Krapp joining his middle-aged version in laughter over his younger self; we also have the young Krapp laughed at by the middle-aged Krapp, who in turn is laughed at by the old Krapp. The audience is thus faced with three protagonists, two of them phantoms. We have a habit of seeing what we hear, '[t]he ability to do so is part of our psychology; instinctively, we visualize sounds in terms of images. By contrast, we tend not to hear what we see' (Guralnick, 1996: xvi).

3 The BBC Third Programme, dedicated to music, drama and the arts, was inaugurated in 1946, to accompany the Home Programme and the Light Programme. In 1967, with the introduction of BBC Radio 1, the existing networks were renamed and the Third Programme became BBC Radio 3.

4 The working title Beckett gave *Krapp's Last Tape* was the 'Magee Monologue' (Knowlson, 1996: 444).

5 The passage from *Dream* I am referring to is the following:

> the thought or dream, sleeping and walking, in the morning dozing and the evening ditto, with the penny rapture, of the shining shore where underneath them the keel of their skiff would ground and grind and rasp and stay stuck for them, just the pair of them, to skip out on to the sand and gather reeds and bathe hands, faces and breasts and broach the foothills without any discussion, in the bright light with the keen music behind them – then that face and site preyed to such purpose on the poor fellow that he took steps to reintegrate the facts of the former and the skin of the zephyr, and so expelled her, for better or for worse, from his eye and mind. (Beckett, 1992a: 114)

6 Elaine Scarry, in her book on pain and its representation, points out the rarity with which physical suffering is depicted in literature, es-

pecially when compared to the consistency with which psychological suffering is represented in literary works (Scarry, 1985: 11).

References

Bair, Deirdre (1990) *Samuel Beckett: A Biography* (London: Vintage).

Beckett, Samuel (1970) *Proust/Three Dialogues* (London: Calder & Boyars).

Beckett, Samuel (1979) *The Beckett Trilogy: Molloy, Malone Dies, The Unnamable* (London: Picador).

Beckett, Samuel (1990) *The Complete Dramatic Works* (London: Faber and Faber).

Beckett, Samuel (1992a) *Dream of Fair to Middling Women* (Dublin: Black Cat Press).

Beckett, Samuel (1992b) *Nohow On: Company, Ill Seen Ill Said, Wostward Ho* (London: Calder).

Beckett, Samuel (1995) *Samuel Beckett: The Complete Short Prose.* Ed. S. E. Gontarski. (New York: Grove Press).

Beckett, Samuel (1996) *How It Is* (London: Calder).

Chabert, Pierre (1976) 'Beckett as Director'. *Gambit* 7(28): 41–63.

Chabert, Pierre (1982) 'The Body in Beckett's Theatre'. *Journal of Beckett Studies* 8: 23–8.

Connor, Steven (1988) *Samuel Beckett: Repetition, Theory and Text* (Oxford: Blackwell).

Connor, Steven. (2000) *A Cultural History of Ventriloquism* (Oxford: Oxford University Press).

Cronin, Anthony (1997) *Samuel Beckett: The Last Modernist* (London: Flamingo).

Gallagher, Shaun (1995) 'Body Schema and Intentionality'. In José Luis Bermúdez, Anthony Marcel and Naomi Elian (eds), *The Body and the Self* (Cambridge, MA: MIT Press).

Guralnick, Elissa S. (1996) *Sight Unseen: Beckett, Pinter, Stoppard, and Other Contemporary Dramatists on Radio* (Athens, OH: Ohio University Press).

Josipovici, Gabriel (1996) *Touch* (New Haven and London: Yale University Press).

Knowlson, James (1996) *Damned to Fame: The Life of Samuel Beckett* (London: Bloomsbury).

Langer, Monika M. (1989) *Merleau-Ponty's Phenomenology of Perception: A Guide and Commentary* (London: Macmillan).

Merleau-Ponty, Maurice (1992) *Phenomenology of Perception*. Trans. Colin Smith. (London: Routledge).

Scarry, Elaine (1985) *The Body in Pain: The Making and Unmaking of the World* (New York and Oxford: Oxford University Press).

The Journals of Jules Renard (1964) Ed. and trans. Louise Bogan and Elizabeth Roget (New York: George Braziller).

Zilliacus, Clas (1976) *Beckett and Broadcasting: A Study of the Works of Samuel Beckett for and in Radio and Television*. Acta Academiae Aboensis, Ser. A. Humanoira, vol. 51, no. 2 (Åbo, Finland: Åbo Akademi).

Part III
Beckett and German Thought

8
Trying (Not) to Understand: Adorno and the Work of Beckett

David Cunningham

> *Vladimir*: This is becoming really insignificant
> *Estragon*: Not enough

It will not be a question, in what follows, of seeking to read the work of Beckett *in terms of* that of Adorno (of reading these works, more or less playfully, as if they were tendentious thematizations of something called 'Adornian philosophy'), nor even, quite, of reading Beckett *through* Adorno (claiming, in some way, that a general and invariant interpretative framework or methodology available in Adorno's aesthetic theory is the most adequate, within an economy of competing frameworks, for elucidating the 'true' meaning of these works). Rather, it will be a question of asking, via Adorno, something like a prior question, of the form: how should one, or on what basis is it possible to, 'try' to read Beckett's work, philosophically? It is in the context of this question that the site of a philosophical engagement with Beckett's work will present itself here.

To ask such a question is to ask how one responds, philosophically, to the way in which these works 'work'; how philosophy might engage with what is 'at work' in them. The problems, in this regard, which would seem to be opened up by what is 'particularly' at work in Beckett's work, are suggested by Derrida in a 1989 interview with Derek Attridge:

> How could I write, sign, countersign performatively texts which 'respond' to Beckett? How could I avoid the platitude of a supposed academic metalanguage? It is very hard . . . The composition, the rhetoric, the construction and the rhythm of his works, even

the ones that seem the most 'decomposed,' that's what 'remains'
finally the most 'interesting,' that's the work, that's the signature,
this remainder which remains when the thematics is exhausted
(and also exhausted, by others, for a long time now, in other
modes). (Derrida, 1992: 60–1; see also, Critchley, 1997: 145–7)

'That's the work', says Derrida, following immediately, as if to explain such a designation more clearly, with 'that's the signature'.
What is 'at work' in Beckett's work would, then, Derrida implies, be
that which, precisely, makes it singular and particular. This, Derrida
goes on to suggest, is not to be found in those 'ideas' expressed or
illustrated thematically 'in' the work, but in that which 'remains'
after the ('exhausted') attempt at critically tracing such a thematics
would have taken place.

Writing on *Waiting For Godot*, Leo Bersani, in his extraordinary
book with Ulysse Dutoit, *Arts of Impoverishment: Beckett, Rothko, Resnais*,
suggests something not dissimilar:

> they [Vladimir and Estragon] are waiting for salvation. And if we
> like, we can think of that salvation in religious terms: it is God's
> coming that will save them. But such a reading certainly does
> not account for the originality of Beckett's play . . . It has . . . im-
> plicitly been recognized not only that the religious theme
> inadequately accounts for *Godot*, but that this theme may be present
> so that the thematic itself may be subordinated to different or-
> ders of meaning. (Bersani and Dutoit, 1993: 28)

The question of what this notion of 'different orders of meaning'
(and their relation to the philosophical) might entail is one I shall
return to below in the context of Adorno's aesthetic theory. Before
doing so, however, it is already possible, in this light, to propose,
following up Derrida's suggestion, that the strongest moments of
Adorno's engagement with Beckett's work might lie precisely in
their resistance to a straightforward interpretative attempt to locate
finally a series of philosophical ideas as *thematically* revealed within
these writings. As such, a central claim implicit in the piece that
follows will be that a rethinking of the relationship between Beckett
and philosophy must not simply be a question of, for example,
swapping an apparently 'outmoded' existentialist/Cartesian 'meaning', say, for a more 'up-to-date', but still tendentiously imposed,
deconstructive or psychoanalytic one. If a shift of philosophical

site has, inevitably, taken place, with regard to the way in which Beckett's work comes forth for 'us' in 'our time' – a shift which might well be broadly described in terms of a movement from existentialism to deconstruction – this must be seen as one which unsettles more than our conception of the thematics of this work.

I

In the draft introduction to his unfinished and monumental *Aesthetic Theory*, Adorno begins with a section entitled simply 'The Obsolescence of Traditional Aesthetics'. Citing the work of Benjamin, in particular, he asserts here the necessity, in the most powerful of modern approaches to art and literature, of taking into account 'a situation where consciousness no longer hopes that fundamental principles will lead to insight into the traditionally great questions of aesthetics, especially those of a metaphysical dimension, but instead seeks insights in spheres that formerly held the status of exempla' (Adorno, 1997: 333). As such, for Adorno, the historical task that philosophical aesthetics once took upon itself of providing a universal concept for 'art', and for aesthetic experience and judgement generally, is now at an end; replaced, precisely, by the need to attend to that which is particular: the 'signature' of the work, in its singularity, as Derrida says.

At the same time, Adorno's critique of traditional aesthetics can be seen as a part of a more general analysis of, what he famously calls, a logic of identity-thinking; a logic Adorno associates, in different ways, with metaphysical idealism, instrumental rationality and the fetishistic character of the commodity form as the repetition of the 'ever-always-the-same'. Aesthetics is implicated within such a logic in so far as it exemplifies philosophy's traditional striving for an absolute conceptual identity which would seek, with varying levels of violence or repression, to erase or subsume any moment of non-identity or otherness in its 'object'. The result of this is that the pursuit of a general concept of art, which would arrive at some identity within which all particular works might be fully incorporated (as simple 'exempla'), must now be abandoned as both unrealizable and undesirable. Instead any philosophical approach to the individual work would have be done with a responsiveness to its moment of *non-identity* which would, for Adorno, also include, crucially, its 'non-conceptual' status. In other words, the 'false' identity of traditional aesthetics is to be challenged by Adorno via a redefinition of aesthetic experience as, precisely, a certain experience of the 'non-identical'; an experience which stems from what Adorno regards as the non-subsumptive (because non-conceptual) character of the work of art. It is in this context that one would have to read Adorno when he states:

> Inherently every art work desires identity with itself, an identity that in empirical reality is violently forced on all objects as identity with the subject and thus travestied. Aesthetic identity (by contrast) seeks to aid the non-identical, which in reality is repressed by reality's compulsion to identity. (Adorno, 1997: 4)

If art, for Adorno, is not without its own moment of identification or rationalization (necessarily given that it is itself an organized construct and, as such, the product of a rational imposition of form), it can still be distinguished, by virtue of its 'separation from empirical reality' within modernity, from the repressive identification compulsion that rules this 'reality'.

The crux of this distinction, between repressive identification and aesthetic identity, lies in Adorno's exposition in *Aesthetic Theory* of the dialectic of mimesis and rationality in the work. His rather unorthodox use of the term 'mimesis' here has its origins in Benjamin's early writings on language and should be taken to refer less to 'imitation', as traditionally conceived, than to the desire for a non-violent affinity of subject with object. It is in this sense that art 'is a refuge for mimetic comportment' in which 'the subject exposes itself . . . to its other' (Adorno, 1997: 53). Of course, mimesis is not the only element in art in so far as it can only emerge through its dialectical relation to, what Adorno refers to as, rationality or construction. However, the utopian moment of the mimetic element in art is, for Adorno, indicated through what he regards as a kind of materialist prioritization of the object which distinguishes the work of art from the repressive identification of instrumental rationality. For Adorno, if art is 'entwined with rationalisation . . . [it] mobilizes technology in an opposite direction than does domination' (Adorno, 1997: 54). As Lambert Zuidervaart summarizes Adorno's point:

> Ordinary and scientific discourse cannot fully know the non-identical, because such discourse imposes identity without respecting nonidentical qualities. In virtue of their mimetic

character, art works honour the nonidentical, but only by flaunting discursive categories. (Zuidervaart, 1993: 144–5)

This claim is the basis for both Adorno's famous defence of autonomous art (as against Sartrean or Brechtian demands for its commitment), and his insistence upon the historical character of the work of art and of the aesthetic theory which would attempt to 'understand' it. It is in this sense that Adorno asserts the need for an aesthetic theory which could, as Zuidervaart expresses it, in some way bridge the gap between art and discourse and thus interpret what he calls the 'truth-content' of the art work.

It is in this context that one would have to read Adorno's dramatic assertion, in his one essay devoted to Beckett, 'Trying to Understand *Endgame*' ('Versuch, das Endspiel zu verstehen'), that one 'could almost say that the criterion of a philosophy whose hour has struck is that it prove equal to this challenge'; the challenge, that is, of 'trying to understand' the truth content of Beckett's work (Adorno, 1991: 244). As Simon Jarvis has suggested, this notion 'that works of art are constitutively in need of a philosophical interpretation of their "truth-content" . . . is an idea which can easily be misunderstood' (Jarvis, 1998: 104). It is, at any rate, already clear, however, that for Adorno the challenge Beckett's works make *to philosophy* (and, as such, its dramatic importance) lies not in the demand for the elucidation of some hidden metaphysical or political thematic present within them, but in the conjunction of these enigmatic modern works' 'difficulty' with the critical task of aiding 'the nonidentical, which in reality is repressed by reality's compulsion to identity'. The response of philosophy to such an art must, if nothing else, therefore, be constituted around a constant vigilance with regard to the danger of performing an unwitting act of repressive identification in the bringing of what is at work in these works into the realm of philosophical conceptuality (with its inherently identificatory character). The dilemma articulated by Derrida – 'How could I write, sign, countersign performatively texts which "respond" to Beckett? How could I avoid the platitude of a supposed academic metalanguage?' – is one which already lies at the heart of Adorno's decision to respond to the challenge of these works in, as he very deliberately phrases it, *trying* to understand them.

Anticipating the potential misunderstandings Jarvis refers to, Adorno is, thus, apparently very clear: 'interpretation of *Endgame* cannot pursue the chimerical aim of expressing the play's meaning in a form mediated by philosophy' (Adorno, 1991: 243). If, then, the understandings sought by traditional aesthetics (and, in a different but parallel way, by literary criticism), would always misunderstand what is at work in this work, in its singularity, how then *can* philosophy *try* to understand Beckett? What 'different orders of meaning', in the words of Bersani and Dutoit, are at stake here?

Everything hinges on this 'trying'. What qualification to understanding is insisted upon by Adorno here? The necessity of qualification is obvious: understanding belongs, customarily, to the concept's logic of identity. Yet at the same time it is, of course, unavoidable; certainly we cannot but identify in so far as we would think on art at all. How then to think and read, somehow, *differently*, in order to pursue an understanding of Beckett other to that which could only ever misunderstand what is at work in these works; a misunderstanding which would stem from a failure to respond, precisely, to the way in which the non-identical asserts 'itself' there? In a conventional attempt at understanding Beckett, 'something' always 'remains', and that remainder (that which is non-identical to the identity established by understanding), is all important: 'that's the work, that's the signature'.

II

As Zuidervaart summarizes the project of *Aesthetic Theory*, the 'interpretation of specific art works belongs to what Adorno conceives as the general task of contemporary aesthetics: to understand the apparent unintelligibility of modern works of art' (Zuidervaart, 1993: 146). It is in this sense that Beckett's work becomes something like exemplary for Adorno: 'Understanding it can mean only understanding its unintelligibility, concretely reconstructing the meaning of the fact that it has no meaning' (Adorno, 1991: 243). In fact, for Adorno, this just is the 'truth-content' of Beckett's art. As such, any approach to the essay on *Endgame* must be organized around this question of how the (philosophical) task of comprehending the incomprehensibility of Beckett's work can be understood and attempted.

Adorno begins the essay with a comparison; a comparison intended to mark out, in its difference, something of Beckett's particular 'signature' and its importance:

> Beckett's oeuvre has many things in common with Parisian existentialism . . . But whereas in Sartre the form – that of the *pièce à*

thèse – is somewhat traditional, by no means daring, and aimed at effect, the form overtakes what is expressed and changes it . . . For Beckett absurdity is no longer an 'existential situation' diluted to an idea and then illustrated. (Adorno, 1991: 241)

The importance, for philosophy, of attempting to 'interpret' Beckett's work is suggested, then, by virtue of a contrast to the forms of interpretation of meaning invited by what Adorno refers to as a 'degraded' conception of drama as 'a clattering machinery for the demonstration of worldviews', apparent in certain 'existentialist plays' (Adorno, 1991: 242). Beckett's work requires a different form of interpretation through an attention to different orders of meaning. Evidently, as Bersani and Dutoit suggest, the status of 'meaning', as used in relation to what is at work in Beckett's work, is crucial here.

As Adorno notes, 'applied to drama, the word "meaning" is ambiguous'. If, in Sartre, 'absurdity' is 'illustrated' as a thematic within the play (and, thus, invites a philosophical interpretation of its meaning in these terms), absurdity is, according to Adorno, set to work in a far more radical way in Beckett's drama whereby 'the determinate negation of content becomes its formal principle' (Adorno, 1997: 250). In other words, what for Adorno is most powerfully resisted in Beckett's work, as it is not in Sartre's, is turning 'meaninglessness' into a positive 'meaning' itself which can be thematized, and thus identified, within the play:

For Beckett absurdity is no longer an 'existential situation' diluted to an idea and then illustrated. In him literary method surrenders to absurdity without preconceived intentions. Absurdity is relieved of the doctrinal universality which in existentialism, the creed of the irreducibility of individual existence, linked it to the Western pathos of the universal and lasting. Beckett thereby dismisses existentialist conformity, the notion that one ought to be what one is, and with it the easy comprehensibility of presentation. (Adorno, 1991: 241)

This seems to suggest that the signature of what is, particularly, at work in these works ('that which remains'), is approachable, initially at least, through a question of form. (And isn't that what Derrida's choice of terminology would seem to suggest also?: 'The composition, the rhetoric, the construction and the rhythm of his works . . . this remainder which remains when the thematics is exhausted).' It is, Adorno appears to state, an attention to form which would provide the breach in any philosophical identification of Beckett and Sartre on the level of a thematic understanding. At the same time, this will, in turn, Adorno asserts, serve to show that the 'meaning' of Beckett's and Sartre's works are quite different: 'the form overtakes what is expressed and changes it'. This apparent primacy of form (as, perhaps, a different order of meaning), is also reiterated in the brief comments on *Endgame* in the final chapter of *Aesthetic Theory*, already partially quoted: '*Endgame* is neither a play about the atom bomb nor is it contentless; the determinate negation of its content becomes its formal principle and the negation of content altogether' (Adorno, 1997: 250). This is to say that, if Beckett's works negate content or meaning, thus achieving a kind of meaningless-ness, this must still take place through the formal principle of the work which situates its empirical elements within some 'meaning-ful configuration'; it is, as Adorno carefully phrases it, an 'organized meaninglessness' (Adorno, 1991: 242). Another earlier passage from *Aesthetic Theory* elaborates upon this:

> Beckett's plays are absurd not because of the absence of any mean-ing, for then they would be simply irrelevant, but because they put meaning on trial; they unfold its history. His work is ruled as much by an obsession with positive nothingness as by the obsession with a meaninglessness that has developed historically and is thus in a sense merited, though this meritedness in no way allows any positive meaning to be reclaimed. Nevertheless the emancipation of art works from their meaning becomes aes-thetically meaningful once this emancipation is realized in the aesthetic material . . . They enunciate their meaninglessness with the same determinacy as traditional art works enunciate their positive meaning. Today this is the capacity of art: through the consistent negation of meaning it does justice to the postulates that once constituted the meaning of art works. Works of the highest level of form that are meaningless or alien to meaning are therefore more than simply meaningless because they gain their content (*Gehalt*) through the negation of meaning. (Adorno, 1997: 153–4)

The crucial point, then, is that, for Adorno, Beckett's work is not 'simply meaningless' – this, as he says, would make it 'simply irrel-evant' – rather, through its 'formal principle', the 'meaninglessness' of the work is determinately 'enunciated', via its realization in 'the aesthetic material', thus becoming a kind of *aesthetic meaning*. The task, *for philosophy*, therefore, becomes one of 'concretely reconstructing the meaning of the fact that it [*Endgame*] has no meaning', of tracing the meaning of its negation of meaning. What precisely this entails, for Adorno, is a question addressed in the final section of this essay.

III

According to his biographer James Knowlson, in 1940, at Arcachon on the Atlantic coast, Beckett met and became friends for a time with Marcel Duchamp. Duchamp was staying in the town with his lover Mary Reynolds, already a good friend of Beckett, and the two took to playing regular games of chess in a seaside cafe; games which Duchamp invariably won (Knowlson, 1996: 300–1). One can imagine a short drama (scripted perhaps by Stoppard or Frayn), fictionalizing this brief period of friendship and seeking, through an imaginary reconstruction of the conversations that might have taken place, some commentary upon the meaning of modern art. If such a drama will no doubt remain unwritten it is most obviously because such conversations as did take place probably revolved not around contemporary questions of aesthetics but rather those of chess. Biographical accounts of both certainly suggest that neither would have been over-enthusiastic to talk about their work. Indeed, it is hard to think of two artists more associated with a form of stubborn silence concerning their art. Both are renowned for and in their absence; an absence constituted by their refusal to interpret or explain what they sought to set to work in their works. As Adorno says, 'interpreting Beckett' is something Beckett himself 'declines to concern himself with' (Adorno, 1991: 244). The same could easily have been said of Duchamp.

Marjorie Perloff's description of Beckett's works as 'enigma texts' seems equally suited to those of Duchamp:

> To read enigma texts like these is rather like being sent out on a snipe-hunt, that popular children's game in which the players disperse in the dark, equipped with pillow-cases, flashlights, sticks, and a set of rules, in search of birds they know are not to be caught. (Perloff, 1981: 208)

Robert Lebel, who wrote the first monograph on Duchamp in 1959, similarly concluded that his works constitute an enigma that 'insolently rejects any solution, any key which might be applied' (quoted in Kuenzli and Naumann, 1990: 5).

Yet, of course, any enigma always brings with it a certain temptation: a temptation to solve the riddle. As Adorno himself asserts, if 'interpretation inevitably lags behind Beckett', none the less the 'enigmatic character' of his work seems to call for interpretation' (Adorno, 1991: 244). Beckett, despite (or because) of the famous renunciation of symbolism, seems to invite such decoding. What is the name 'Godot' if not an invitation to make the leap, take the bait, fill in the (obvious) meaning? As Bersani and Dutoit suggest of this play:

> With remarkable perversity, Beckett appears to have done everything to encourage just that kind of interpretation he was inclined to reject. Given the guide they are so trustfully following, it is hard not to sympathize with all the readers who organize their understanding of the play around the notion of God's absence or nonexistence. Beginning with its title, *Godot* resonates with religious meanings. (Bersani and Dutoit, 1993: 27–8)

As Rosalind Krauss has suggested, Duchamp's work also appears to encourage such a temptation to an interpretation through 'which one can "read" these objects'. To do this, Krauss asserts, 'is to violate the strategic import of Duchamp's work; yet the temptation is irresistible, akin to reaching for a clue the artist himself has held out' (Krauss, 1981: 83–4). And what else, after all, has been the effect of the pages of obscure notes, equations, alchemical scribblings, that Duchamp published to accompany the *Large Glass*?

Jean-François Lyotard, in his book on Duchamp (under the subtitle 'diagnostic'), phrases the philosophical and critical dilemma produced here well:

> So what will you do? These are the little setbacks of the critic. Is it always hard and irksome? Not always, but it is so here because Monsieur Marcel has the critics in his sights to defy him and poke fun at him. You won't get me, that's his obsession. (Lyotard, 1990: 9)

In response to Duchamp's 'ruses', Lyotard offers, then, what he calls a 'counter-ruse': 'In what you say about Duchamp, the aim would be not to try to understand and to show what you've understood, but rather the opposite, to try not to understand and to show that you haven't understood' (Lyotard, 1990: 12).

Adorno's 'trying to understand', Lyotard's 'trying not to understand': how are these responses to the temptations of enigma to be differentiated here? It is clear that the difference is not one that can be conceived of in the terms of simple opposition. Adorno argues that what is entailed by trying to understand is not 'the chimerical aim of expressing the play's meaning in a form mediated by philosophy'. In this sense, trying to understand would always already involve a trying not to understand in terms of the conventional conception of understanding. What, then, for Adorno (by contrast to Lyotard's counter-ruse to Duchamp), is to be understood in the attempt to understand the meaning of Beckett's meaninglessness?

This meaning, the truth-content of Beckett's work, would have to be conceived of as an essentially *historical* meaning. More precisely, the meaning of Beckett's meaninglessness, and the possibility *and* difficulty of interpreting this meaning, is inextricably tied up, for Adorno, with the nature of these works' *modernity*:

> The irrationality of bourgeois society in its late phase rebels at letting itself be understood; those were the good old days, when a critique of the political economy of this society could be written that judged it in terms of its own *ratio*. For since then the society has thrown its *ratio* on the scrap heap and replaced it with virtually unmediated control. Hence interpretation inevitably lags behind Beckett . . . In *Endgame*, a historical moment unfolds . . . After the Second World War, everything, including a resurrected culture, has been destroyed without realizing it; humankind continues to vegetate, creeping along after events that even the survivors cannot really survive, on a rubbish heap that has made even reflection on one's own damaged state useless. (Adorno, 1991: 244)

The meaning of Beckett's determinate negation of meaning is, thus, sited in its relation to (or, indeed, truth-content of), the unfolding of an 'historical moment':

> For Beckett, the human being – the name of the species would not fit well in Beckett's linguistic landscape – is only what he has become . . . The individual is revealed to be a historical category, both the outcome of the capitalist process of alienation

and a defiant protest against it, something transient himself. (Adorno, 1991: 249)

As an attempt to understand the meaning of *Endgame*'s meaninglessness, this, of course, relies upon its relation to Adorno's own critical analysis of post-war capitalism and of the historical unfolding of modernity, developed elsewhere. The potential problem here is, therefore, as Zuidervaart notes, that the essay 'makes it hard to distinguish between the meaning to be found in *Endgame* and the meaning Adorno finds' (Zuidervaart, 1993: 156).

There is a sense in which Adorno still wants, as it were, to put Beckett's work to work; a desire which stems from his Hegelian sense of art's truth-content as a kind of apprehension of its own time. It is this, in turn, which guides his readings of the particulars of Beckett's play. Adorno, for example, cites the scene in which Hamm has Clov push his wheelchair to the centre of the room: 'HAMM: Take me for a little turn. (*Clov goes behind the chair and pushes it forward.*) Not too fast! (*Clov pushes chair.*) Right round the world! (*Clov pushes chair.*) Hug the walls, then back to the centre again. (*Clov pushes chair.*) I was right in the centre wasn't I?' (Beckett, 1964: 23). Adorno's reading of this scene understands it as a parody of human autonomy and of the 'loss of a centre ... [which] was already a lie' within a post-war society in which the 'individual is revealed to be a historical category':

> The final history of the subject is made the theme of an intermezzo that can allow itself its symbolism because it reveals its own inadequacy and thereby the inadequacy of its meaning. The hubris of idealism, the enthronement of human meaning as the creator at the centre of his creation, has entrenched itself in that 'bare interior' like a tyrant in his last days. There, with an imagination reduced to the smallest proportions, Hamm recapitulates what men once wanted to be, a vision of which they were deprived by the course of society as by the new cosmology, and which they nevertheless cannot let go of. (Adorno, 1991: 271)

It is certainly not a question of suggesting that such an interpretation is *wrong*; there is, in fact, much to recommend it. Yet one might counterpose to this something Beckett himself says, concerning the artist Bram van Velde, in his *Three Dialogues with Georges Duthuit*, written by Beckett, after the fact, as a reconstruction of their conversations:

B: I suggest that van Velde . . . [is] the first whose hands have not been tied by the certitude that expression is an impossible act.

D: But might it not be suggested, even by one tolerant of this fantastic theory, that the occasion of his painting is his predicament, and that it is expressive of the impossibility to express

B: No more ingenious method could be devised for restoring him, safe and sound, to the bosom of Saint Luke. But let us, for once, be foolish enough not to turn tail. (Beckett, 1965a: 121–2)

Is this, perhaps, the risk still run by Adorno's attempt to understand a meaning of Beckett's negation of meaning – of returning Beckett to 'the bosom of Saint Luke'?

In asserting Beckett's materialism, and thus mimetic respect for the non-identical (by contrast to what he perceives as the idealism of Sartre's rendering of the absurd as 'something universal'), Adorno suggests that, in Beckett, 'the absurd turns into forlorn particulars that mock the conceptual, a layer composed of minimal utensils, refrigerators, lameness, blindness, and the distasteful bodily functions' (Adorno, 1991: 252). (Is this perhaps in part what Derrida also has in mind when he talks of 'this remainder which remains'?) Yet, one might suggest, the danger inherent in Adorno's approach is that such particulars are, in fact, ultimately recuperated by the philosophical conceptuality, which they 'mock', in the assignment of some identifiable and totalizable meaning to the negation of meaning at work in *Endgame* as Adorno reads it. The interpretation of the particulars, such as the wheelchair scene cited above, would then threaten to work in such a way that they become, once again, mere exempla of the meaning (of meaninglessness) that the play has as a whole; that is, its truth-content of expressing the historical unfolding of 'the impossibility to express'.

What might then happen if, as Beckett's suggests, one was, by contrast, 'for once . . . foolish enough not to turn tail'? Is this perhaps where the difference between Adorno's trying to understand and Lyotard's trying not to understand ('and to show that one did not understand') might emerge? Lyotard's foolishness would be in the attempt to fail to understand even a meaning of a certain incomprehensibility which might allow philosophical conceptuality, in however fragile a fashion, to reclaim those 'forlorn particulars' which scatter Beckett's works. No doubt this is 'foolish enough' to the extent that such an attempt to fail to understand could itself only ever fail (as the book on Duchamp which follows Lyotard's words cannot help but reveal). Perhaps, though, the interminable enacting of this inevitable failure is (as in a different way would be the case for Duchamp's own enigmatic works), the real 'challenge' that Beckett's work makes to us.

In this sense Adorno is correct that the task becomes one of tracing the negation of meaning at work in Beckett's texts. The question, however, is whether such a tracing amounts to the achievement of an understanding of the meaning of this negation or an interminable showing that one has not understood. Perhaps one cannot choose to the extent that each would necessarily encounter its own limit of impossibility (in which something would always remain) – the impossibility of understanding and the impossibility of not understanding. Yet, in recognizing this, the challenge that Beckett's work makes to us is not a demand that one stops reading but rather that one not finish, that one not ignore the obligation to keep going without ever quite knowing where one is going to. What emerges from this obligation is not an answer to the enigma of Beckett's work, but rather the persistent retention of its open status as a question. 'Make sense who may. I switch off' (Beckett, 1984: 316).

References

Adorno, Theodor W. (1980) 'Commitment'. In *Aesthetics and Politics*, ed. Ronald Taylor. Verso, London and New York.

Adorno, Theodor W. (1991) 'Trying to Understand Endgame'. In *Notes to Literature II*, trans. Shierry Weber Nicholsen. Columbia University Press, New York.

Adorno, Theodor W. (1997) *Aesthetic Theory*, trans. Robert Hullot-Kentor. University of Minnesota Press, Minneapolis.

Beckett, Samuel (1964) *Endgame*. Faber & Faber, London.

Beckett, Samuel (1965a) *Proust and Three Dialogues with Georges Duthuit*. John Calder, London.

Beckett, Samuel (1965b) *Waiting For Godot*. Faber & Faber, London.

Beckett, Samuel (1984) 'What Where'. In *Collected Shorter Plays*. Faber & Faber, London.

Bernstein, J. M. (1990) 'Philosophy's Refuge: Adorno in Beckett'. In *Philosophers' Poets*, ed. David Wood. Routledge, London.

Bersani, Leo and Dutoit, Ulysse (1993) *Arts of Impoverishment: Beckett, Rothko, Resnais*. Harvard University Press, Cambridge, MA.

Critchley, Simon (1997) *Very Little . . . Almost Nothing*. Routledge, London.

Derrida, Jacques (1992) '"This Strange Institution Called Literature": An Interview with Jacques Derrida'. In *Acts of Literature*, ed. Derek Attridge. Routledge, New York and London.

Jarvis, Simon (1998) *Adorno: A Critical Introduction*. Polity Press, Cambridge.

Knowlson, James (1996) *Samuel Beckett: Damned to Fame*. Bloomsbury, London.

Krauss, Rosalind (1981) *Passages in Modern Sculpture*. MIT Press, Cambridge, MA.

Eds Kuenzli, Rudolf E. and Naumann, Francis M. (1990) *Marcel Duchamp: Artist of the Century*. MIT Press, Cambridge, MA.

Lyotard, Jean-François (1990) *Duchamp's TRANS/formers*. Lapice Press, Venice, CA.

Perloff, Marjorie (1981) *The Poetics of Indeterminacy*. Princeton University Press, Princeton.

Zuidervaart, Lambert (1993) *Adorno's Aesthetic Theory: The Redemption of Illusion*. MIT Press, Cambridge, MA.

9
Philosophical Adjacency: Beckett's Prose Fragments via Jürgen Habermas

Philip Tew

Samuel Beckett and Jürgen Habermas would seem to be unlikely bedfellows. Habermas works within the Western philosophic tradition attempting to reconcile the tensions between the rationalizing and deconstructive elements of modernity, a very specific mode of detailed cultural and critical exegesis. Beckett writes fiction in conflict with the normative modes of narrative and the imaginary. Hence, the trajectories of their different projects suggest that any attempted comparison of the two would result primarily in a series of contrasts, but Habermas's reference in *Autonomy and Solidarity* to the need 'to advance just one step beyond this scene out of Beckett', and Adorno's self-negating philosophy mediated by a clear admiration of the power of Beckett's texts, suggest some mileage in such a comparative analysis (1992a: 99).

Placing Beckett as a textual experience indicates the qualities of the critique of both narrative and being expressed in his fiction. In terms of direct meaning and understanding, Beckett's work is problematic and the grounds of its unsettling effects are perhaps the basis for understanding its implicit themes of the incomprehensible or bizarre. This is most apparent in his later work, particularly his prose fragments. Beckett's humour delights in refuting the text's tendency to appeal to apparently underlying and yet complacent notions of causality and stability, a process of narrative repetition and sterility that becomes an internal dialogue for the author in which he interrogates or undermines his own activity:

Imagination dead imagine.
Imagine a place, that again.
Never ask another question.
Imagine a place, then someone in it, that again. (1995: 272)

To imagine the elements of life, of light and existence becomes a reflection or paradigm of the greater ontological process of an existential void in which narrative is embedded. 'When it goes out no matter, start again, another place, someone in it, glaring, never see, never find, no end, no matter' (1995: 273).

Are Beckett's uncertainties celebrations of either an overall nihilism or a specific lack of faith? Certainly, at whatever point on this range of possible negative coordinates one places him, Beckett's world-view would seem opposed to the ultimately positive account of the ontological priority of normative values outlined by Habermas in *The Philosophical Discourse of Modernity* where those values define human involvement in being and are such that they are seen as potentially providing further enlightenment (1990: 151–2). Habermas is sceptical of the inversion and subversion of human norms; he concludes, 'We cannot exclude from the outset the possibility that neoconservatism and aesthetically inspired anarchism, in the name of a farewell to modernity, are merely trying to revolt against it once again. It could be that they are merely cloaking their complicity with the venerable tradition of counter-Enlightenment in the garb of post-Enlightenment' (1990: 5). Hence in Habermas's terms, Beckett would seem a likely candidate for an *aesthetically inspired anarchism* that is opposed to rationality. In 'The End', Beckett's text positions together elements of nature and the social process of family in a manner that defies normative expectations. 'The earth makes a sound as of sighs and the last drops fall from the emptied cloudless sky. A small boy, stretching out his hands and looking up at the blue sky, asked his mother how such a thing was possible. Fuck off, she said. I suddenly remembered I had not thought of asking Mr. Weir for a piece of bread. He would surely have given it to me' (1995: 81). A broad sense of life's disjuncture, of various modes of confusion and a general lack of any coherent primordial under-standing mark out both the trilogy and the prose fragments, all of which texts vacillate around both the grotesque and numerous trajectories toward the nonsensical.

As soon as a reader relates as any kind of progression the different elements of the prose fragments, the attempt is thwarted by an impression of the text being organized as a sequence of numerous disparities, a collocation of the bizarre and the unaccountable, thereby producing a jumble of events and perceptions. In 'The End' the vague reference points of a *cloister* or a *street* or that of reference to family and a tradition of naming all become absorbed into a *vacuum* of reference, the *rejection* of relations, a *disordering*. The narrator reflects 'There were streets where I remembered none, some I did remember had vanished and others had completely changed their names. The general impression was the same as before. It is true I did not know this city very well. Perhaps it was quite a different one' (1995: 81). As if to contradict any dignity of life, the narrator retreats into a box where the excremental (existential) necessities overtake and disgust him. 'Arched and rigid I edged down my trousers and turned a little on my side, just enough to free the hole. To contrive a little kingdom, in the midst of the universal muck, then shit on it, ah that was me all over. The excrements were me too, I know, I know, but all the same' (1995: 98). How can one account for this curious mix of reference and absence except by an ideology or aesthetics of negativity? What kind of critical process can recover a critical relevance and perspective? It is possible one might conceive in Beckett something of an inversion of that which Habermas perceives in Benjamin's quest of the motif of the dandy 'to distill the eternal from the transitory ... to find a solution to the paradoxical task of obtaining standards of its own from the contingency of a modernity that had become simply transitory' (1992a: 10). Quite how this might be done seems undermined by the organizing principles of provisionality and reductiveness expressed within Beckett's texts.

Nevertheless rather than accept the presence of a void, further progress can be made by drawing from several snippets to create or at least suggest what one might term with a Beckettian sense of dissipated irony two critical mini-fizzles that contain both the fragmentary and the schematic. First, as Beckett comments perhaps punningly in his *Dante ... Bruno ... Vico ... Joyce* piece: 'literary criticism is not book-keeping' (1983: 19), so simply recording or sifting the texts cannot suffice as an account. Certainly for the critic to note content and influence provides an insufficient explanation of Beckett's texts, even for the most fragmentary. In their very elusive allusiveness – for they are about something even if that concerns the vacuity of expression – where are they directed? Simultaneously, they appear to suggest and refute meaning and interpretative space. The flurry of detail denies itself. Can this ebb and flow of elements be regarded in itself as a suggestive closeness, an action and reaction of synthesis as a mode of expression in process? This concept leads me to Lance St John Butler, who in *Samuel Beckett and the Meaning of Being: A Study in Ontological Parable* (1984) raises the potentially interesting and yet constraining concept of an analogue of Beckett's texts and philosophical expression. In the light of a dialectical need to refuse the kind of critical closure implied in the very exegetical structure of an admiration of Beckett's expressed analogue, I would prefer to define this relationship via a notion of adjacency of the two elements, where any attempt at comparison effaces itself by drawing attention to its own provisionality and therefore reflects a fragility of causality seems implied in the circumstances of Beckett's shorter texts.

In this manner of indirect interconnection I wish to consider the implications of the two oblique and perhaps surprisingly approving references to Beckett made by Habermas in *Autonomy and Solidarity*. The philosopher implies that Beckett's positivity lies in the reader understanding his fictional texts' capacities 'in a world transformed by Auschwitz. Our moral-practical reflections and discourses are affected by this productivity, precisely to the extent that it is in the light of such innovations that we can say what we *really* want, and above all: what we *cannot* want' (Habermas, 1992b: 169). What is unexpressed or understated in this judgement is revealing. Habermas has assumed a moral and exteroceptive aspect of the text that appeals to a meta-dimension outside of the text, one divorced from what the texts say and what set of relations they relate in themselves about reality by the nature of their internal structure. Habermas's idea of a communicative community replete with reference would seem at odds with Beckett's prose at least in its immediacy of content and impression. Why then the positive response? I suggest that the astute critic needs to acknowledge in Habermas's two cursory, almost off-hand references an absorption of presuppositions of the trans-formative capacity of negativity and the *avant-garde* in terms of cultural rather than textual reference points. His critical assumptions manage to misread the significance of Beckett by acceding to an overview before considering the detail of his prose. In doing so Habermas conforms to a general notion that the formal position and properties of Beckett's *avant-garde* status supersede the specificity of his texts. Such a reading assumes that the textual and exegetical structures outperform any content in terms of reference in a manner that means content can only secondarily raise its contradictory series

of world-disclosing possibilities after such an overall frame of critical signification has been created. Content transformed into
performative structures allows a loosening of priorities and the revision of the teleology of any time-line of reading strategies. If one
suspends the immediacy of comparison, the theoretical paradigm of
philosophic adjacency allows us to consider different potential dimensions. One is whether Beckett's prose fragments, for instance,
can be perceived as *marginalia*, gaining legitimacy only in their
passage toward more significant forms, set apart from the experien-
tial and material. Another is whether in a world attempting to
de-legitimize universals and centralities, we should conceptualize
the fragments in their own right as intersections with the metaphysical and the material? These critical interrogations extend us
well beyond any localized arguments over genre boundaries and
how such boundaries might be variously defined, of the differentiation between the fragment, the short story and the novella. In this
light of theoretical problematizing perhaps we might extend our
understanding of Beckett's aesthetic by utilizing the apparent con-
tradictions inherent in reading Beckett's work via the philosophical
project of Habermas, using practical and theoretical tensions elided by
Habermas himself.

Taking from Beckett's work on Proust his under-theorized recognition of communitarian and intersubjective presences, where
'life is a succession of habits, since the individual is a succession of
individuals' (1965: 19) and where 'The mortal microcosm cannot
forgive the relative immortality of the macrocosm' (1965: 21), and
placing them within a notion of an 'intrinsic flux', the tenor and
substance of Beckett's prose seems obsessed with a series of what he
called at one point 'dispeopled kingdom[s]' (1995: 31), in which a
stinking wanderer can muse humorously: 'Stables have always been
my salvation' (1995: 87), in a logic of his own or the author's making.
From where does this negation of life-world norms and notions of
the comprehensible derive? Such Beckettian subversions mirror
Charles Sanders Peirce, who in *Reasoning and the Logic of Things*
notes that ratiocination appeals to our own hypotheses, to prob-
abilities and to our instinct, all of which he categorizes as egotistical,
all progressing to a sedimentary sentiment that he refutes in favour
of instinct (111–12). For Peirce, 'The only effect which real things
have is to cause belief, for all the sensations which they excite
emerge into consciousness in the form of beliefs. The question therefore, is, how is true belief (or belief in the real) distinguished from

false belief (or belief in fiction)' (53–4). My analysis of any potential relationship between Beckett and Habermas requires understanding, a different kind of instinctive Peircian rationality as expressed tentatively within the work of both men in their different fields, that underlies their confrontation of this dialectical relationship of puzzling out the dimensions within communicative consciousness of the real. If Habermas's admiration of Beckett has any validity and coherence in terms of his own project, one must necessarily thematize both self and society as contextualized and decontextualized by these two very different writers in order to consider whether there is any sustainable adjacency, affiliation or dialectical tension as a kind of tangential commonality. Both writers demonstrate central, coterminous territory in enacting and perceiving critical interrogations of the topography of the subject; their relative placements of consciousness allow a dissection of the implied radicality of Beckett's texts. Habermas foregrounds the contraction of the subject as a major and ongoing element of the crisis which constitutes a modernity which positions and expresses oppressive socio-political relations.

That Habermas applauds Beckett should not be seen as a matter of course since he rejects what might at least superficially be regarded as similarly-positioned writers. In *The Philosophical Discourse of Modernity* Habermas outlines the constrictive influence of his category of so-called *black* writers that includes primarily de Sade and Nietzsche (Habermas, 1990: 106), where criticism problematizes the relationship between art and life (Habermas, 1990: 340) and reason becomes separated from validity claims and: 'The critical capacity to take up a "Yes" or "No" stance and to distinguish between valid and invalid propositions is *undermined* as power and validity claims enter into a turbid fusion' (Habermas, 1990: 112). All such undermining trajectories are reflected in Beckett's writing, where validity is undercut, and art unsustainable since apparently life appears unendurable. In *Autonomy and Solidarity* Habermas accuses Adorno as necessarily co-opting an intersubjectivity that he seeks to deny in his philosophical expositions (1992a: 100). Could this charge be levelled at Beckett's world of solipsism and negativities since its coordinates however topographically bizarre have a familiarity; from the feeling of people lurking behind curtains away from the empty streets in 'The Calmative' (1995: 65) to the barrel of Guinness in 'Texts for Nothing' (1995: 111)? Surely for Habermas, Beckett can only be separable from the category of *black* writerliness if Beckett's prose represents a critique upon such negativity and weaves a positive interconnection with a discourse of a potentially expanded rationality of the life-world. To postulate the simply literary or self-referential would be to fall within Habermas's objection to any 'knowledge specialized in only one validity claim, which, without sticking to its specific context, bounces across the whole spectrum of validity, unsettling the equilibrium of the lifeworld's communicative infrastructure' (Habermas, 1990: 340). Perhaps that might be better applied to the species of critical commentary that over-determines Beckett's so-called silences and negativities.

Much of Habermas's work is centred ultimately if subcutaneously on intersubjectivity. Where does this leave Beckett's structural resistance to the exact interweaving of aesthetic and personal meaning which functions as the centre-point of his polarities of self-referentiality where reflection proceeds into absence by losing or doubting any contextuality? 'Texts for Nothing' begins:

> Suddenly, no, at last, long last, I couldn't any more, I couldn't go on. Someone said, You can't stay here. I couldn't stay there and I couldn't go on. I'll describe the place, that's unimportant. The top, very flat, of a mountain, no, a hill, but so wild, so wild, enough. (1995: 100)

Yet, he does continue in this dialectical tension with the other. Even if the other is self-absorption it must represent the residue of alterity as does the shifting categorization of the environment, as does the ambiguous and hanging *enough*. Perhaps, Beckett sets up an impenetrable matrix of formal and perceptual oppositions that cannot be seen as simply bipolar opposites, rather as an off-centre gyration that nevertheless reflects a germane and concrete world. This movement in itself can be seen as a resistance, a refusal to settle into the socio-political constraint of conformity.

In Habermas's concept of meaningful expression, at some level Beckett cannot refuse the intersubjective dimension, however solip-sistic his fears, without reconfirming these limits set by modernity. Always as in the transposition detailed by a narrator in 'The Calma-tive': 'lying at the feet of mortals, fathom deep in the grey of dawn, if it was dawn. And reality, too tired to look for the right word, was soon restored, the throng fell away, the light came back and I had no need to raise my head from the ground to know I was back in the same blinding void' (1995: 76). The collective or angelic throng sub-sides; reality can only give way to that which cannot be faced or expressed, the struggle of fragments of life against the act of representation. Beckett intersects what is for Peirce an impossibility of nullity. Beckett fictionalizes what Peirce calls 'A system of multitude *zero* [which] is no system at all' and of which he concludes that 'the multitude of all possible different finite multitudes' (157) produces 'the multitude of irrational quantities' (157). Beckett's fictional world of variability, chaos and dispersion seems to parallel the complexity of scientific possibilities that for Peirce mean man has 'to search blindfold for a law which would suit the phenomena, our chance of finding it would be as one to infinity. The further physical studies depart from the phenomena which have directly influenced the growth of the mind, the less we can expect to find the laws which govern them "simple", that is, composed of a few conceptions natural to our minds' (160). Yet, Peirce's theorizing of the irrational suggests a need to expand to Beckett's apparently irrational world via the significance of Habermas's comment in *Moral Consciousness and Communicative Action* that: 'For Peirce problems always arise in a specific situation' (1992b: 10), since the critical search (whatever the architectonic qualities of the theories) returns to the phenomenology of nature (125). And so too for Beckett, since however nonsensical the elements of his descriptions, underlying the incongruities is the text's capacity to draw attention to what Peirce describes as a human and animal need for a phenomenological coherence where in Peirce's words 'forces depend upon relations of time, space, and mass' (125). Beckett plays with these concepts to disturb human expectations. 'I only saw one cyclist! He was going the same way as I was. All were going the same way as I was, vehicles too, I have only just realized it. He was pedalling slowly in the middle of the street, reading a newspaper which he held with both hands spread before his eyes. Every now and then he rang his bell without interrupting his reading' (1995: 71). The image resists norms and yet draws from normative experiences in a comic and subtle fashion. The reader delights in the vulnerability and rebelliousness of Beckett's moment and yet the residual feasibility of the vaudevillian underwrites the physical reference of his image. The image circles its own subversion by performatively suggesting the clownishness and creativity of life, where the reader experiences the very epiphany Habermas sees denied in the counter-enlightenment of the black writers, whereas in Beckett one finds 'the lightning flash of *insight* into some confusion threatening identity that causes shock, the way *understanding* the point of a joke causes liberating laughter' (1990: 127).

In my own readerly world of the critically real, my ultimately retroductive understanding of Beckett stresses that the possibility of textual specificity is precisely what features on the page before our eyes in any act of interpretative possibility. Such textual moments may be corrigible, but they remain in some senses ineradicable. In 'The Calmative' the narrator apparently returns to life in some fashion. After dozing off he encounters a man seated beside himself:

> What's that you said? He said. Unfortunately I had said nothing. But I wriggled out of it by asking him if he could help me find my way which I had lost. No, he said, for I am not from these parts and if I am sitting on this slab it is because the hotels were full or would not let me in, I have no opinion. But tell me the story of your life, then we'll see. My life! I cried. Why yes, he said, you know, that kind of – whay shall I say? He brooded for a time, no doubt trying to think of what life could well be said to be a kind. In the end he went on, testily, Come now, every-one knows that. He jogged me in the ribs. No details, he said, the main drift, the main drift. But as I remained silent he said, Shall I tell you mine, then you'll see what I mean. The account he gave was brief and dense, facts, without comment. That's what I call a life, he said, do you follow me now? It wasn't bad, his story, positively fairy-like in places. (1995: 72)

Almost because set *in extremis*, Beckett's prose fragments are most frequently read as attempting to create or to represent a liminal space, a realm of the abandoned and unabandoned, an supposed incoherence of a void in terms of structure (or via its absence), a refutation of referentiality. In 'The Calmative' Beckett begins with that which is purportedly a state beyond the end of subjectivity as we know it, a breach in its ontological impassability into an afterlife:

> I didn't know when I died. It always seemed to me I died old, about ninety years old, and what years, and that my body bore it out, from head to foot. But this evening, alone in my icy bed, I have the feeling I'll'be older than the day, the night, when the sky with all its lights fell upon me, the same I had so often gazed on since my first stumblings on the distant earth. For I'm too frightened this evening to listen to myself rot, waiting for the great red lapses of the heart, the tearings of the caecal walls,

and for the slow killings to finish in my skull, the assaults on the unshakable pillars, the fornication with corpses. So I'll tell myself a story, I'll try and tell myself another story, to try and calm myself, and it's there I fell I'll be old, old, older than the day I fell, calling for help, and it came. Or is it possible that in this story I have come back to life, after my death? No, it's not like me to come back to life after death. (1995:61)

We must set ourselves some parameters of a narrative, however provisional. Firstly, note the assertion of the factuality of death and the interdeterminacy of placing that event in his opening sentence. A tension is created, a schism that suggests uncertainty rather than grammatical assurance. *Seemed* stresses appearance and viewpoint. The fear and the evasion of death as conclusion of the failing of a state of living seem to evoke more of an existential terror of being extinguished than the metaphysical hinterland of a world adjacent to that of Emily Dickinson. Of the opening of 'The Calmative' can we take this as a literal death, or a space that parodies by the immanence of finitude in its amplification of the familiar that is decontextualized, erasing and yet incorporating the very apparent certainties of the quotidian and familiar? Such paradox is familiar to the literary, with narrative's incorporation of an ontological mode resistant to its form. Starting from a recognition of literature as a social phenomenon (1995: 3), Helmet Gaus reflected in *The Function of Fiction: The Function of Written Fiction in the Social Process – An investigation into the relation between the reader's real world and the fictional world of his reading* (1979), that both fiction *and* future, planned acts are imaginary: 'The real and the imaginative consciousness can never exist simultaneously, or side by side. They can present themselves only successively. It is, in essence, the same consciousness which only assumes another structure' (Gaus, 1979: 97). Fiction is no more detached than anticipation which re-orders the possible. In 'The Calmative' the sharer of the bench discusses erections, a Beckettian motif. 'It thickens, lengthens, stiffens and rises, he said, does it not? I assented, though they were not the terms I would have used. That is what we call an erection, he said. He pondered, then exclaimed, Phenomenal! No? Strange right enough, I said. And there you have it all, he said' (1995: 73). His phenomenological amazement underpins the exchange, as the phenomenological underwrites the whole of Beckett's questioning. As with forward thinking we are familiar with extending the real both via and as a disruption of immediacy. *Molloy* begins with obsessive self-location, self-reflection and the repetition of I (1979: 9), reflecting a world where: 'you would do better, at least no worse, to obliterate texts than to blacken margins, to fill in the holes of words till all is blank and flat and the whole ghastly business looks like what it is, senseless, speechless, issueless misery... To restore silence is the role of objects' (1979: 14), but this diminution of either perspective or the subject is never enacted. Beckett voices character and viewpoint however apparently nihilistic or bizarre. We recognize some of the coordinates or the relations of self-reflection impacting with an ill-understood alterity.

Habermas in *Postmetaphysical Thinking* analyses the Peircian attempt to account for the objectivity of experience (which is ultimately communicative in nature) that is a central theme for Beckett (Habermas, 1995: 98–103, 107). Two elements intercede into any semiotic model of which fiction is one element: objective form itself and intersubjectivity. In the realm of mutual understanding, reality has an impermeability that the imaginary never transcends. Beckett is faced with the problem of a kind of adjacent incorporation in the representation or imagination of post-death existence or non-existence requiring assumption of another structure within the stuff of the real. Significantly, in the opening of 'The Calmative', death is the focus in its avoidance, its fearfulness and the need for distraction for the narrating subject. The mode is constituted as one might imagine in life itself with its fears of its absence. The narrative moves to reflect on a hinterland with trees, childhood memories, trams, hats on strings and the conclusion: 'I wasn't returning empty-handed, not quite, I was taking back with me the virtual certainty that I was still of this world, of that world too, in a way' (1995: 69–70), a conviction at odds with the opacity of this environment. In this very reductiveness of the post-physical imaginary, the reader and Beckett face what Gaus conveyed as the irreducible poverty of imagined consciousness in all its forms with an ineradicable (unerasable) reductive selectivity when faced with real everyday consciousness (Gaus, 1979: 95). The latter tension as implicit dialectical mode of narrative structures underpins all of Beckett's searches for or within the irreal. Although Gaus reflected that the *novel-concept* allowed a mode of almost lapidary separation from the everyday reality of facts, thus allowing 'affective tensions' (81), he recognized that an emotional underpinning (77) reinforces the objective existence and interconnection of language with reality

(46, 69, 71). In their interrogative intention, Beckett's fragments can be seen to offer themes and contexts as a mode or paradigmatic feature that many critics regard as permeating much of his work. Stanley Gontarski theorizes of the fragment itself that it lies between completion and incompletion, implying structurally a flux between the particular and a transcendent possibility. A primary coordinate is that this apparent literary indeterminacy is expressed vividly in the shorter prose fiction via content and form, a narrative substance that appears dialectically as itself and its own dissolution. Also, this interrogation is inter-fused by a theoretical dimension, Lance St John Butler's philosophical analogue or my own critically real adjacency.

Habermas's critique of presence and communicative effort serves to interrogate the narrative structure and subtexts of Beckett's work, subverting the critical position that any interior, inward, self-projecting voice might fracture the subjective contractions of 'bourgeois culture' rather than constitute an element of those relations. Such an analysis confirms the Beckettian voice as being defined by defeat and denial. Beckett's interrogations are elucidated as epistemologically and topographically constrained in the sense that any refusal of life-world and transcendent possibilities means accession to or confirmation of the very construction of subjective self at the heart of modernity's negation of alternative expansion, and growth beyond the confinement of self through value spheres already themselves determined by external ideological constraint. Hence my reading must question whether Beckett can merely document internality without the parameters of his vision possessing implicitly such referentiality, even when dealing with death or non-being; as foundations, contraction and retreat leave their imprint and signify a constellation of determining and typifying coordinates even without their direct or explicit avowal or narrativization. In *Postmetaphysical Thinking* Habermas assumes a life-world as implictly networked and of narrative overflowing to relate to these contexts of the real stretching beyond the human (1995: 107–8) that would in itself contain the nihilism of Beckett's negative dialectic.

Although Habermas indicates traditional literary texts arrest the transfer of validity claims at their margins, in *Postmetaphysical Thinking* he does indicate the emergence of a different kind of text where this decoupling is not facilitated and invites the reader effectively to destroy the fiction (223–4). This mode in which one must surely place Beckett as one of Habermas's philosophical and scientific authors has implications. At the level of deep structure, in terms of the ontology of presence and text, Beckett's narratives can only reconfirm a centrality that appears ludic, but remains derived from a pre-programmed and already experienced level of consciousness, the whining angst of subject positioning and ultimately a refusal to place the presence of the individual in an interworld by which its defeat and abjection have been constellated. His game position is that of eternally rehearsing defeat before the end-game itself. Beckett's ambiguity is that subjectivity is dominant and absorbs the embodied, perceptually free self. However, the notions of the abject and of defeat depend upon the intersubjective construction of complex definitions and denials, an evaluation of self by the configuration of an implacable singularity that is unsustainable. The terror is external and relates to rejection rather than isolation. In a positive light, is Beckett's curious tension constructive in a performative manner or is it the defeat of the communitarian that seeks to refuse the intersubjective at the heart of the human presence? A web of dialectical denial sustains the contracted consciousness, which refutes a series of alternative possibilities: transcendence, acceptance, self-renewal, altered perception or dialectical reconfiguration of the life-world. If Beckett's central notion remains that of defeat, then its very thematics haunt Habermas's attempts at renewal of the project of understanding and socio-philsophical placement that are undercut by his casual literary admiration. Non-meaning cannot be achieved; the web of interrelations of silence is a compression or contraction of the very forces of the life-world that can offer both renewal and defeat. The intersubjective forces are also those of possibility and oppression. The avoidance is a refusal which cannot place the individual anywhere apart from a contracted and always-already abject subject, where social dimensions of evaluation are so absorbed that the psyche plays them out repeatedly in a hinterland of self-absorption which paradoxically reflects external judgement it seeks to avoid. Quite where does one finally place Beckett in terms of Habermas's literary model of a new mode of fiction that concludes *Postmetaphysical Thinking*? 'There is a correspondence between literary form and philosophical conviction: one who understands the rootedness of theory in the lifeworld in contextualist terms will want to discover the truth in the metaphors of narrative' (225).

References

Beckett, Samuel, and Georges Duthuit (1965) *Proust and Three Dialogues*. London: John Calder.

Beckett, Samuel (1979) *The Trilogy: Molloy, Malone Dies, The Unnamable*. London: Picador.

Beckett, Samuel (1983) *Disjecta: Miscellaneous Writings and a Dramatic Fragment*, ed. Ruby Cohen. London: John Calder.

Beckett, Samuel (1995) *Samuel Beckett: The Complete Short Prose 1929–1989*, ed. Stanley Gontarski. New York: Grove Press.

Butler, Lance St John (1985) *Samuel Beckett and the Meaning of Being: A Study in Ontological Parable*. London: Macmillan.

Gaus, Helmet (1979) *The Function of Fiction: The Function of Written Fiction in the Social Process – An investigation into the relation between the reader's real world and the fictional world of his reading*. Gent: Wetenschappelijke Uitgeverij E. Story-Scienta p.v.b.a.

Gontarski, Stanley (1995) 'Introduction. From Unabandoned Works: Samuel Beckett's Short Prose'. In *Samuel Beckett: The Complete Short Prose 1929–1989*. New York: Grove Press, xi–xxxii.

Habermas, Jürgen (1990) *The Philosophical Discourse of Modernity*. Cambridge: Polity.

Habermas, Jürgen (1992a) *Autonomy and Solidarity*. London: Verso.

Habermas, Jürgen (1992b) *Moral Consciousness and Communicative Action*. Cambridge: Polity.

Habermas, Jürgen (1995) *Postmetaphysical Thinking*. Cambridge: Polity.

Peirce, Charles Sanders (1998) *Reasoning and the Logic of Things*. Lincoln and London: University of Nebraska Press.

10
Beckett and Heidegger: A Critical Survey

Steve Barfield

The history of critical accounts that attempt to stage a confrontation between Beckett and Heidegger is a relatively short one. One reason for this is that for many accounts of Beckett and philosophy the governing principle of research is that of evidence of Beckett's interest in a particular philosopher (or vice versa). In the case of Beckett and Heidegger's philosophy, there seems to be no evidence of an explicit or primary nature. A second reason (representing a very different critical standpoint) is that while there has been a considerable growth in accounts of Beckett that link his work to critical theory, Heidegger's own work is often treated like an antecedent to the work of contemporary poststructuralist philosophers such as Derrida, Foucault or Deleuze. Heidegger becomes a figure who can be gestured towards as a figure from the archaeology of poststructuralism, which also saves critics from having to face problematic political questions about Heidegger's work. The fact that Beckett's politics and those of Heidegger were so very different should not dissuade us from examining the connections between the two. (Readers unfamiliar with the complex literature on Heidegger and the relationship, if any, of his work to national Socialism should consult Richard Polt's *Heidegger: An Introduction*, pp. 152–64 for an incisive account.)

Steven Connor's *Samuel Beckett: Repetition, Theory and Text*, for example, is something of a classic of Beckett criticism in so far as it was one of the earliest texts to examine Beckett through the perspective of critical theory. Derrida, Deleuze and to some extent Lacan provide the framework for elaborating the functions that repetition serves in Beckett's work. Heidegger, however is only mentioned once, where his concept of 'being-thrown' – 'Geworfenheit' – is shown as parallel to the position of Beckett's narrators (Connor, 1988: 44). A reading of Heidegger should force us to recognize how crucial repetition is to the very fabric of the Heideggerian text and enterprise, relating Heidegger to the hermeneutic tradition. (This is discussed more fully in Waterhouse 1981.) Like Beckett's *oeuvre*, Heidegger's functions through a continual return in different ways to the same questions and situations, but never seems to close down any line of questioning: 'An on-the-way in the field of paths for the changing questioning of the manifold question of Being' (Frede translates this as Heidegger's final comment for his intended collected works; [Frede, 1993: 66]).

In fact, the handful of significant works that couple Beckett and Heidegger, however uncomfortably, do so under the aegis of post-war existentialism, thus echoing the still established view that relates Beckett's drama to the post-war French theatre of the absurd. For example, Lance St John Butler's, *Samuel Beckett and the Meaning of Being* elaborates the Beckettian protagonist in part as an existential, authentic human subject struggling to define a 'being prior to language'. (Lance St John Butler, 1984). A more sophisticated version of the same problem (Heidegger as 'existentialist') can be seen in the work of P. J. Murphy, one of the most important critics to be concerned with Beckett's relationship to modern philosophy. In work such as *Reconstructing Beckett* and his influential article 'Beckett and the Philosophers' in the *Cambridge Companion to Beckett* (Murphy, 1990 and 1994). The thrust of both of these works by Murphy is in uncovering a relationship between Beckett and Kant (much of which is persuasive) and in arguing that Beckett's main theme is the way language relates to the world, rather than that of an emptying of meaning from language. But like St John Butler he tends to see Heidegger, Sartre and Beckett sharing a similar 'distinction between existence and being,' disagreeing with Beckett's assertion that 'he never understood the distinction between being and existence' (Murphy, 1994: 236).

The problem with the above approaches is that in collapsing the distinction between Sartrean existentialism and Heidegger's own work they obscure the considerable differences between Sartre's and Heidegger's respective philosophical positions. Heidegger's 'Letter on Humanism' argues his work differs from Sartre's in being non-humanist, non-voluntarist and that he does not accept either Sartre's definitions of existentialism or of ethics. Baldly speaking he accuses Sartre of ignoring the investigation of Being that Heidegger himself began in *Being and Time* in preference for a traditional, thus meta-physical notion of the importance of 'Dasein'. Dasein is Heidegger's term for our being in the world. (The full complexities of this encounter between Heidegger and Sartre are beyond the scope of this chapter, but the interested reader can consult Polt, pp. 164–71, and especially Rockmore, 1995, chs 4, 5 and 6.) Yet as Rockmore has made clear it is precisely these differences that underlie the post-structuralist accounts of Heidegger that have dominated the reading of Heidegger since the 1990s. In this way, an examination of Beckett's philosophical relationship to Heidegger would seem to be the missing link between poststructuralist accounts of Beckett and accounts of Beckett and philosophy that are concerned with the relationship of language, existence and the 'human' subject.

How then one does on go about exploring the relationships between Beckett's work and that of Heidegger? One way is evinced by Simon Critchley's significant work *Very Little . . . Almost Nothing.* This book argues that Beckett's work is 'perhaps uniquely, resistant to philosophical interpretation' (because it does not recuperate or work meaninglessness into meaningfulness). An attempt to respond to this singular quality of Beckett's texts leads in turn to a critical book in which Beckett's and Heidegger's texts never properly meet, but where instead their confrontation is deferred across the space of the volume through awkward intermediaries like Adorno (Critchley, 1997: 141). In this way Beckett meets Heidegger only through the implications of Critchley's exploration and critique of Adorno's criticism of Beckett. Another possible way of exploring the relationship would be to read backwards, from our existing 'poststructuralist' Beckett to Heidegger. If this has not to my knowledge been attempted in any sustained way, then Richard Begam has at least paved the way by placing Heidegger in the frame as one of the founders of postmodernity (Begam, 1997).

In this chapter I argue that the texts of Beckett and Heidegger have an uncanny and unsettling relationship to one another, which shows similar preoccupations but does not necessarily mean any influence of one to the other. The main topics which will be used to bring Heidegger and Beckett into proximity will be the way in which the subject existing in the world as relates to the world as/ of things, as/of community, to death, and finally to time and memory. These are not the only points of comparison possible, nor is it the case that there is one stable and consensual Heidegger or Beckett which this very limited choice of texts under discussion can exemplify. (Particularly in the case of Heidegger there are major questions as to whether his later work is fundamentally different or not, from *Being and Time*. On this question, amongst others, see the useful essays by Dorothea Frede and Frederick Olafson in Guignon (ed.), *The Cambridge Companion to Heidegger*.)

For the Heidegger of *Being and Time*, 'worldliness' (in the sense that there is nothing beyond our world) is the inescapable fact of a subject's existence. The condition of our subjectivity in the world is 'being-thrown'. The alternative to a phenomenological account of Being-in-the-world (of the type that Heidegger gives) would be the type of idealist myth of a transcendent meaning beyond the world we live in that Nietzsche had so forcibly condemned. It is for this reason, that so much of the early part of Division 1 of *Being and Time* concentrates upon the apprehension of things in the world not as items of perception, but as things which affect us through their own specificity as part of a meaningful whole which is the environment in which we exist. It is in sharp contrast to the Cartesian subject–object distinction and accompanying sceptical doubts over existence of the external world. The world in which we live is something we experience before we can know it. Heidegger states that 'world' is 'the totality of those entities which can be present-at-hand' (Heidegger, 1962: 93), and as he explains in the example of the hammer, that the hammer is, for the person using it, not just present-at-hand but rather ready-at-hand (Heidegger, 1962: 98). It is an effective, untheoretical demonstration of the instinctual way we relate to objects.

This intractable singularity of things in the world is also a distinctive part of Beckett's texts and their worldliness, in Heideggerian terms. In some ways the sheer physical 'life' or being of things is something we often forget about in Beckett's text, because as Heidegger might argue we tend to intellectualize them as objects and not experience them as part of our 'world'. Beckett's characters are embedded in a world of things present-to-hand which can quickly become things ready-at-hand. For example, take the celebrated 'sucking stones' in *Molloy*. In one sense they are no more and no less specific than tools to pass the time. The game of substitution and mathematics would be the same with other objects, but would it have the same quality to it? We could further say that Beckett's interest in the physicality of slapstick using commonplace objects (which works as a type of comedy precisely because of the 'thingness' of the things) extends into the theatre as a reasonable consequence of this. It perhaps reaches a summation in the use of the famous banana in *Krapp's Last Tape.*

But there are some important differences. First, if the items in the world of 'The Trilogy' have their own specificity, it is one which is often indeterminate, as if it were subject to the curious mutability and alterity of dreams. 'He moved with a kind of loitering indolence which rightly or wrongly seemed to me expressive. But all that proved nothing, refuted nothing ... A little dog followed him, a pomeranian I think, but I don't think so. I wasn't sure at the time and I'm still not sure, though I've hardly thought about it' (*Molloy*, 13). In a similar fashion items of the body can seem to waver between being things and parts of the self: 'But man is today, at the age of twenty-five, at the mercy of an erection, physically too, from time to time' (from 'First love,' *Collected Shorter Prose*, 6). Second, in much of Beckett's slapstick things seem not to be just resisting our powers of objectification, but threatening to go beyond the boundaries of the present-at-hand and take on an excessive life. Is Krapp playing with the banana or is it playing with him? This is exactly the element that makes a good theatrical presentation of that play both funny and slightly worrying. The narrator of *First Love* says, 'it was things made me weep' (*Collected Shorter Prose*, 11).

Third, and perhaps most distinctively non-Heideggerian, is the way in which for every anti-cerebral movement towards the experience of things, there is a counter-movement towards the intellectual. Language leads both ways at once, especially for Beckett's narrators. Heidegger's example of the hammer is necessarily produced in language, but the link to the referent in the real world is paramount for his argument to work. Beckett's examples of things are led by language into dense allusions to intellectual realms or to endless series of permutations and variations. Hatchets, hammers, sticks, umbrellas, pencils, pens seem to substitute for one another throughout 'The Trilogy', which undermines their status as things in themselves. Malone more or less recognizes this in *Malone Dies*, 'or with it or with his hammer or with his stick or with his fist or in thought in dream I mean ... or with his pencil or' (*Malone Dies*, 289).

Before I begin to consider the importance of this pattern of similarities and differences there are two further areas that need to be explored. The first of these is the question of Dasein and the community in Heidegger and the second the relationship of Dasein to death. Dasein might be translated as 'Being there', and Heidegger attempts to explain what it means by suggesting it is the particular

type of Being which pertains to human beings and which necessarily contains within it an understanding of Being. It is our type of
being as humans, but is not identical with traditional notions of
humanity or mind or even strictly speaking subjectivity. It is, however, apprehended by us as individuality. Dasein has a particular
relationship to Being in so far as Dasein's own Being is an issue for
it. 'Dasein, in its Being, has a relationship towards that Being – a
relationship which itself is one of Being' (Heidegger, 1962: 32). Do
Beckett's characters and narrators look at their existence as if it
'were an issue for it'? In one sense the answer to this is yes. The
voices of 'The Trilogy' consistently seem concerned as to why they
are there or even alive at all. Even the system of displacements and
substitutions which underlie the narration seem preoccupied by the
notion of existence as an issue. 'People with things, people without
things, things without people, what does it matter . . .' (*The Unnamable*,
294). 'Anxiety' as Heidegger argued is an elemental form of Dasein
recognizing that existence is an issue for it. This is not of course to
say that there is not, as Leslie Hill pointed out, a characteristic
counter-force of 'indifference' in Beckett's texts (Hill, 1990). It is
instead to argue that indifference and anxiety seem to be part of a
continually oscillating and repetitive movement.

For Heidegger, the subject can recognize himself in the world
through an embedding of Dasein within a specific community; in
this sense we recognize others because they too are Dasein. However, this embedding of Dasein is something of a double-edged sword
for the individual. In one sense Dasein can never not be located in
a specific community and historical moment – it cannot exist in a
radically ahistorical formulation. But at the same time this is inevitably fraught with domination by what Heidegger terms 'they': the
very community in which the Dasein of an individual subject has
to be located (Heidegger, 1962: 114–36). At first sight, the dynamics
of Beckett's texts seem to suggest quite different dynamics with regard to the relationship between the subject and the community.
Being by oneself, isolated and outside of the community would seem
to be the norm for his characters and is a commonplace of Beckett
criticism. However, it could also be argued that while the texts do
enact some form of resistance to the acknowledged 'they', the texts
also tell of a form of internal community. If all of the characters
the voice of the Unnamable seeks to be done with, are the 'world'
of the voice, then it is as if the they have been internalized, presenting us with a world within an individual subject.

I'm all these words, all these strangers, this dust of words, with no ground for their settling, no sky for their dispersing, coming together to say, fleeing one another to say, that I am they, all of them, those that merge, those that part, those that never meet, and nothing else, yes, something else, that I'm something quite different, a quite different thing, a wordless thing in an empty place . . . (*The Unnamable*, 357)

Although one could assert that this breathless passage is like the resistance between an anguished subject's Dasein and the pressure of the 'they', I think there is something both structurally similar and different in quality at stake here. The 'they' tend to force the individual 'Dasein' into everydayness and inauthenticity in Heidegger's account, whereas here the tone is very different. Furthermore, if the language of the 'they' is liable to be clichés, then Beckett's texts, as Christopher Ricks has pointed out, work most effectively through enlivening clichés and language that seems to have lost the force of originality (Ricks, 1993). In a similar fashion Beckett's texts are clearly not a-historical but seem to pitch themselves far away from their original community, not least of course by their bilingual status. (For an important discussion regarding Beckett and bilingualism see Hill, 1990.) If the later Heidegger writes repeatedly of the need to be home and that 'language is the house of Being' (Heidegger, 1978: 217), it is tempting to see Beckett's work as asserting the unavoidability of exile 'with now and then a postcard from the homeland' ('First Love' in *Collected Shorter Prose*, 6).

Probably the most well-known sections of *Being and Time* are those that deal with the way individual Daseins engage through moods such as 'anguish' to finally end with the meaning of their own possible death (not their simple physical end but the fact that this makes life meaningless) and their consequent finitude (Heidegger, 1962: 291–311). Death is explained as that possibility which is 'one's ownmost, which is non-relational, and which is not to be out-stripped' (Heidegger, 1962: 294). 'Authenticity' is to make a choice of whom to be, based on the recognition that this moment might be one's last. Through this process the individual Daseins grasp finitude and with it recover as Dasein their authenticity and a proximity to Being. As well as being well known these are also very controversial passages. This seems to some philosophers to be where Heidegger is closest to a representation of the individual's Dasein as the very type of anthropomorphic subject he later considered to be Sartre's error, when Heidegger discusses this in 'The Letter on Humanism'. Furthermore, only through authenticity can we grasp the temporality of our Being and this means being aware that we are choosing deliberately. It hardly needs pointing out that Beckett's texts feature characters that are dominated by thoughts of their own death. However it would be a very resolute Heideggerian indeed who would assert that a being-towards-death offers Beckett's characters and narrators in 'The Trilogy' and elsewhere any of that authenticity of feeling that Heidegger intended. If the narrator of *The Unnamable* at times wishes for death, it is for an end that would be 'non-relational' and 'not to be outstripped' but which would also offer an end to any possibilities of choice whatsoever. In a sense this is a moot point because death in Beckett's 'The Trilogy' is never there except as a continuing stripping down to an even more minimal next stage. Ghosts merely become more ghostly.

Whereas death as finitude offers the beginning of the affirmation of Dasein as proximity to Being for Heidegger, death is both more uncertain for Beckett and seemingly incapable of offering more than the phantom promise of a cessation of existence. A promise that may be little more than to be 'a wordless thing in an empty place' and one which seems never to be fulfilled nor absolutely grasped in Heidegger's terms. Perhaps the most interesting way in which Beckett's texts undermine the meaning of death as finitude for Dasein is through that atypical Beckettian image of the birth–death. Paul Davies applies a Jungian perspective to the characters and finds that 'birth is something that happens *to* them; that, therefore, individuation as a person was somehow an event which the pre-existent being might have avoided or postponed' (Davies, 1994: 48). By linking birth and death together being-towards-birth becomes if not quite as powerful, then far more disturbing than being-towards-death. It produces an atemporal disjunction that ensures Beckett's characters are between birth and death in that liminal space that so many of the later dramas enact. Death becomes not the end of life but a possible new beginning where birth seems like it could be the end rather than any new start. It could also be said to reintroduce a humanist, voluntarist aspect precisely where Heidegger would assume that the rigorous decidability of 'death' prevented the subject as a determinate structure from backsliding into the everyday world of a false subjectivity that would be further away from Being.

Before I conclude with a discussion of temporality in Beckett and Heidegger, it is worthwhile recapitulating what type of pattern of relationship has emerged. It is a relationship with surprising parallels but also noticeable differences. Both Beckett and Heidegger present the 'thingness' of things in contrast to Cartesian models of subjectivity. But Beckett presents patterns where things threaten to exceed the boundaries necessary to structure Dasein from a Heideggerian perspective or to maintain the anti-Cartesianism of the Heideggerian project in a pure form. 'I'm neither one side nor the other, I'm in the middle, I'm the partition, I've two surfaces and no thicknesses, perhaps that's what I feel, myself vibrating, I'm the tympanum, on the one hand the mind, on the other the world' (*The Unnamable*, 352). Beckett in 'The Trilogy' and elsewhere appears to also assert worldliness (as opposed to any form of idealism) as a brute fact of the subject's existence, while also undermining the division between Dasein and the community. The 'they' that would inform Dasein's possibility to become authentic, according to Heidegger, are more internalized than external, and for this very reason more indeterminable. In a related fashion the Heidegerrian logical opposition of 'anguish' and the 'everyday' is subjected to a destructuring which renders it more difficult to determine which is really which in the Beckettian text. Finally, if death and the possible discovery of finitude provide a structure by which Dasein can apprehend its true authentic Dasein nature and thus grasp Being, then Beckett's texts would appear to question the force and direction of Heidegger's central path.

The relation between the subject and time is also of crucial importance to both Beckett and Heidegger. For Heidegger the analysis of time provides a means to understand the ontology of *Dasein* where 'temporality's essence is a process of temporalising in the unity of ecstases' (Heidegger, 1962: 65). This in turn leads to his recognition, that while we may live in time as past, present and future, this only serves to establish the relationship between Dasein and Being, rather than time existing independently of the Being of Dasein. It is for this reason that our everyday categories of time seem to be both violated and confirmed in Hedidegger's account, where time is always in one sense marked as that of the future. The past tense is, as David Farrell Krell states, something Heidegger abjures, 'what human existence never is, not when alive, not even when dead' (Krell, 1990: 240). Heidegger writes in 'The Letter on Humanism' that 'The history of Being is never past but stands ever before' (Heidegger, 1978: 219). For Beckett, too, time, and in a distinctive way memory, are the fabric of the texts and accompanying narrative structures of the texts themselves. Our ordinary and everyday understanding of time as past, present and future becomes in them just as unstable as it is in Heidegger's work. But I hope to argue that there is also a crucial difference. For Beckett, while the past never returns as what it was, neither is the future ever quite the same as it might be, even when we are projected forward like Dasein. The future often leads back to the past for characters who so often describe themselves as not having been 'properly born,' or who, like Molloy, are in search of their future via their origins in the shape of their relationship to their mother. 'What am I to do what shall I do, what should I do, in my situation how proceed? By aporia pure and simple?' (*The Unnamable*, 267). Tenses seem almost interchangable here, and the present or past tenses are neither better nor worse than the future. Although we might think of the aporia as primarily relating to the procedure of establishing an intellectual or spatial direction, it could just as easily also mean in this context that of establishing a sense of time through linguistic tense structures. Memory functions in Beckett's texts as an ambivalent figure of lived time, neither reliable, nor avoidable and which if it does not continuously affirm the boundaries of a self or subject, it does not straightforwardly negate the boundaries of the subject either. It is not just the relationship between birth and death and the consequent complication of the trajectory of Dasein's being-towards-death that is affected here. Memory itself is highly unstable – which events are past, which are present and which are future for Beckett's narrator? 'Thats all I know, its not mine, it's the only one I ever had, that's a lie, I must have had the other, the one that lasts, but it didn't last, I don't understand, that is to say it did, it still lasts . . .' (*The Unnamable*, 381).

Beckett suggests his texts expose an 'ontological indecency' (Juliet, 1995: 146). In a similar fashion the Unnamable remarks that it is 'sufficiently stupified with all their balls about being and existing' (*The Unnamable*, 320). But what sort of approach to ontology, the philosophy of the nature of being, warrants this coupling of the ontological and the indecent? I think we can take these two remarks by Beckett in an almost literal way. What is indecent or obscene is the display of being and existence is that it is just always too much, in excess of the way being and existence are recuperated by traditional ontology. In the spirit of Beckett's language we might say what we have is an ontology pulling down the trousers/skirts of being. Heidegger's account of the distinction between Being and Dasein opens up to us the history of how Being has been thought, as opposed to a metaphysical nature for being which is unchanging and synonymous with God. This begins the process of obverting the connections between ontological investigation and its objects which the Beckettian texts push to its limit. The connection of Heidegger and Beckett is not a simple carnivalization or undermining of Heidegger's work through Beckett's texts, rather the Beckettian texts act in an uncanny fashion with Heidegger's work and remind us that any thinking about being and existence is inevitably exceeded by these very objects of attention. Heidegger in certain moments is not beyond glimpsing a view very similar to the day-to-day one in which Beckett's characters and narrators live. The difference is that Heidegger would probably presume that the condition of unnamability should lead us closer towards Being and offer us solace, whereas for Beckett the second of these propositions appears particularly unlikely.

> But if man is to find his way once again into the nearness of Being he must first learn to exist in the nameless. In the same way he must recognise the seductions of the public realm as well as the impotence of the private. (Heidegger, 1978: 223)

The difference between Heidegger and Beckett might finally lie in the hesitation of this little word 'if'.

References

Beckett, Samuel (1979) *The Beckett Trilogy: Molloy, Malone Dies, The Unnamable*. London: Picador.

Beckett, Samuel (1984) *The Collected Shorter Prose 1945–1980*. London: John Calder.

Begam, Richard (1997) *Samuel Beckett and the End of Modernity*. Cambridge: Cambridge University Press.

Butler, Lance St John (1984) *Samuel Beckett and the Meaning of Being: A Study in Ontological Parable*. London: Macmillan.

Connor, Steven (1988) *Samuel Beckett: Repetition, Theory and Text*. Oxford: Blackwell.

Critchley, Simon (1997) *Very little . . . almost nothing: Death, Philosophy, Literature*. London: Routledge.

Davies, Paul (1994) 'Three Novels and Four novelles'. In John Pilling (ed.), *The Cambridge Companion to Beckett*. Cambridge: Cambridge University Press.

Frede, Dorothea (1993) 'The Unity of Heidegger's Thought'. In Charles Guignon (ed.), *The Cambridge Companion to Heidegger*. Cambridge: Cambridge University Press.

Krell, David Farrell (1990) *Of Memory, Reminiscence and Writing: On the Verge*. Bloomington: Indiana University Press.

Heidegger, Martin (1962) *Being and Time*, trans. J. Macquarrie and E. Robinson. Oxford: Blackwell.

Heidegger, Martin (1978) 'Letter on Humanism'. In *Basic Writings*, ed. David Farrell Krell. London: Routledge and Kegan Paul.

Hill, Leslie (1990) *Beckett's Fiction: In Different Words*. Cambridge: Cambridge University Press.

Juliet, Charles (1995) *Conversations with Samuel Beckett and Bram Van Velde*, trans. J. Tucker. Leiden: Academic Press.

Murphy, P. J. (1990) *Reconstructing Beckett: Language for Being in Samuel Beckett's Fiction*. Toronto: University of Toronto Press.

Murphy, P. J. (1994) 'Beckett and the Philosophers'. In John Pilling (ed.), *The Cambridge Companion to Beckett*. Cambridge: Cambridge University Press.

Olafson, Frederick (1993) 'The Unity of Heidegger's Thought'. In Charles Guignon (ed.), *The Cambridge Companion to Heidegger*. Cambridge: Cambridge University Press.

Polt, Richard (1999) *Heidegger: An Introduction*. London: UCL Press.

Ricks, Christopher (1993) *Beckett's Dying Words*. Oxford: Oxford University Press.

Rockmore, Tom (1995) *Heidegger and French Philosophy: Humanism, Antihumanism and Being*. London: Routledge.

Waterhouse, R. (1981) *A Heidegger Critique: A Critical Examination of the Existential Phenomenology of Martin Heidegger*. New Jersey: Humanities Press.

11
Beckett and Nietzsche: The Eternal Headache

Richard Lane

This chapter will comment upon two texts – Beckett's play *Krapp's Last Tape* and Nietzsche's *Ecce Homo*, (in particular, with the latter, the section titled 'Why I Write Such Good Books') – while exploring the larger issue of the relationship between Beckett and Nietzsche. Does this mean Nietzsche *in* the work of Beckett? Or Beckett *in* the work of Nietzsche (ignoring a certain chronology)? Or could this mean Beckett *as* Nietzsche or Nietzsche *as* Beckett? The former can be read or thought of in two ways: the banality of saying that Beckett was influenced by Nietzsche, or the more unusual statement that Nietzsche was influenced by Beckett; either of these options are essentially predictable, leading me to assert the far more interesting notion that there is a Beckettian and Nietzschean textual moment found *denied* in both, yet *shared* by both.

The notion of an intertextual relationship which functions both ways, so to speak, between Beckett and Nietzsche, can be found in a more extended and rigorous discussion of Beckett and post-structuralism in Begam's study *Samuel Beckett and the End of Modernity*. Begam reverses the standard poststructuralist approach to Beckett by arguing that not only can Beckett be read through poststructuralism, but poststructuralism can be read through Beckett (1996: 10–11). The importance of Nietzsche for Begam's project is made clear with his discussion of *différance*, unnamability and postmodernity:

> Nietzsche's work effectively set the agenda for what was to become the 'end of modernity' discourse. Not only did he attack the empiricism implicit in Descartes, but he extended his critique to humanism, rationalism, and scientism – in short, those habits of mind most often associated with the Enlightenment. As is well-

known, Heidegger takes up and further develops the critique of truth that Nietzsche initiated. (1996: 19)

A recent extensive study of the interconnections and relationship between Beckett and Nietzsche in light of Derridean poststructuralism is Richard Cope's 'The Expression of Failure or the Failure of Expression' (1998). Cope approaches the subject via Beckett's conversations with Bram van Velde, exploring in the process the more widely known relationship between Beckett and Schopenhauer. However, Cope's approach via philosophy, theory and aesthetics enables him to explore 'the impossibility of expression made complex by the obligation to express' (1998: 10), thereby examining not simply the influence of 'x' upon 'y' (or 'y' upon 'x') but rather the tensions between/within a complexly interacting web of philosophical and aesthetic problematics:

> The difference lies in the fact that for Nietzsche, expression is inadequate, existing only within relations, but for Beckett, it is impossible, due to a complete breakdown of these relations. Nietzsche still allows for expressive attempts, but remains adamant of the open-handedness of interpretation, whereas Beckett willfully destroys the notion of expression, but can only do so by leaving his methods open to interpretation ... Beckett's claim that 'there are many ways in which the thing I am trying to say in vain, may be tried in vain to be said' is at once affirmed and negated, by the fact that he does say it in vain, but in doing so relies on such unexplainable, because fictitious, terms as the obligation. For Nietzsche the realization that 'adequate expression matters little', is placed beside the knowledge that we are still driven towards an attempt at such, an action that continues to feed our delusions, from which we must free ourselves. (Cope, 1998: 14)

Cope goes beyond the traditional Beckett–Schopenhauer relationship/ critical account, by examining in some detail the Nietzsche–Beckett and Nietzsche–Derrida relationships, focusing not just on shared strategies, but more importantly for his argument, respective differences; the result is a pairing 'Beckett–Derrida': 'Derrida allows for a multiplicity in his readings and writings, that at once protects the text, but also opens it up for infinite interpretations. Beckett's discursive writings, while being stable and systematic, are also aware of their status as a fictive residue of philosophy, self-conscious of their flaws and trappings, and [thus] can be read as being self-deconstructive' (20). In this chapter, I am going to take another slightly unusual approach, one that examines the writing lives of Beckett and Nietzsche, and the interconnected positioning of the two writers *as* characters in one another's texts.

In *Ecce Homo*, Nietzsche theorizes an extreme case of writing: a book that 'speaks of nothing but events which lie outside of the possibility of general or even of rare experience' (1993: 70). He calls this 'the *first* language for a new range of experiences', yet at this point we would have to assume that it is either the language of an ontological void, or, a speaking from the void. It is a language where 'nothing is heard' as Nietzsche theorizes it, especially in relation to his own work: 'In this case simply nothing will be heard with the acoustical illusion that where nothing is heard, there *is* nothing . . .'. But that is not to say that Nietzsche's writing is not 'weighty' – in fact it is so 'weighty' it has been throwing all other literature off balance (Nietzsche, 1993: 70). Thinking about this situation in relation to *Krapp's Last Tape*, we have the acoustical illusion that we have been *about* to hear something, therefore, even with all its cutting (or editing) irony and humour, we *have* heard something in the resounding silence of *where it would have been said*:

> What I suddenly saw then was this, that the belief I had been going on all my life, namely – [KRAPP *switches off impatiently, winds tape forward, switches on again*] – great granite rocks the foam flying up . . . clear to me at last that the dark I have always struggled to keep under is in reality my most – [KRAPP *curses, switches off, winds tape forward, switches on again*] – unshatterable association until my dissolution of storm and night with the light of the understanding and the fire – [KRAPP *curses louder, switches off, winds tape forward, switches on again*] – my face in her breasts . . . (1990: 220)

The joke here is, of course, the fact that as readers we do not get to hear the epiphanies, we do not get to share the vision; a kind of anti-*Portrait of the Artist* approach. But I think this editing or cutting also needs to be taken seriously, in relation to what it signifies as Krapp gets older, and reviews not only his past life, but his past work: his writing life. As Andrew Kennedy puts it: 'Krapp is no passive listener, but his own "programmer", re-arranging his minimal autobiography' (1991: 69).

My overall argument is that Nietzsche cannot escape the reading of his work as void (charges of nihilism or just simply ignoring it), however weighty his literature, however off-balance he throws other writings, whereas Beckett cannot escape the plenitude that he appears to be asserting no longer exists in a non-redemptive world (for example, the proliferation of meaning in a meaningless universe). Both share in a sense 'acoustical illusions' in how they articulate these positions. Nietzsche has to write a text called 'why I write such excellent books' to fill this impossible void, whereas Beckett constantly writes minimalist books in an impossible gesture of wiping out the plenitude with the void.

Rhetorically speaking, Beckett and Nietzsche share a non-teleological *enantiodromia*, or the tendency of things to turn into their opposite (the notion is derived from the Pre-Socratics). Clearly this functions at the level of *character* in Beckett, with pomposity, for example in Krapp, turning into cynicism and a worldly weariness, or, elsewhere in Beckett's work, transformations that include entire character shifts into other characters (or, the reduction to the same, for example, *The Trilogy*). This *enantiodromia* should not be thought of as an eventual balancing of opposites to form some kind of holistic equilibrium (see Clarke, 1992: 150), neither should it be thought of as a 'proof' that the individual in Beckett and Nietzsche is eventually subsumed by a system, such as Hegel's World-Spirit. The *enantiodromia* is non-teleological, operating as a force which is both welcomed and feared by both authors, because it is a blind force in a secular world. The first paragraph of the foreword to *Ecce Homo* ends with a passage in italics: '*Listen to me! for I am thus and thus. Do not, above all, confound me with what I am not!*' (33). Nietzsche situates himself as a character in his own work, a work which leads inevitably to a reversal of characterization, a switch into the 'what he is not' – his entire philosophy prepares the way not only for this profound revaluation, but also the turning of concepts into narratives, which enables the switch to take place. Without, of course, the switch having ever taken place at all. With a non-teleological *enantiodromia*, the switch *might as well not have taken place*, indeed, *doesn't take place if the sense of a switch or reversal is located so to speak in the direction with which it is travelling*. Think of Hegel's *Phenomenology of Spirit*: without World-Spirit being there from the start and at the end, the whole narrative just doesn't make sense. Or, it makes too much sense and prepares the way for contemporary philosophy. In *Krapp's Last Tape*, we have a sort of unhappy consciousness reviewed, cynically, at a higher level, but then this doubling is *in turn* reviewed at 'a higher level', and we see that the reversal – from idealism to cynicism – needs to start all over again, or never really took place. There is a danger here of putting Hegel rather confusingly in the body of Beckett's work – although that is part of the plenitude: out of the unspoken word in Beckett, for reasons unknown, pours a multitude of philosophical and theoretical voices: so many that the critical responses to Beckett, the mapping of this multitude, resemble some kind of babbling or *babeling*.

Richard Begam approaches the issue of the other in Beckett's text partly through the imagistic rather than vocal notion of 'mirror-play' where 'two mimes stand face to face and like a man and his reflection, begin to move in perfect synchrony, just as Watt and Sam do at the asylum' (1996: 98). For Begam, apart from it being funny, with its vaudeville act qualities, this raises a number of ontological questions: 'given the two mimes, how do we determine which represents the man and which the reflection?' More generally, what are the criteria, within any perceptual schema, for establishing where reality ends and imitation begins? Finally, to what extent does the mirror-play function as a piece of metacriticism, one that mimes its own mimesis, or stages its own staging?' (1996: 98–9). Begam goes on to talk about Beckett's notion of a 'narrator/narrated' character and the way in which this dualism deconstructs itself in a kind of foreshadowing of Derrida's ideas of supplementarity and *différance*. This is then related to Baudrillard's notion of the hyperreal, where the copy doesn't stand in for the original but replaces or surpasses it, a notion developed from writers such as Marshall McLuhan and Guy Debord. Rather than developing these ideas along the poststructuralist lines laid down by Begam – which he does brilliantly anyway – I want to borrow this more theorized notion of the two mimes and call them Beckett and Nietzsche, or B and N.

We could decide that B and N function according to the rule of Bruno's 'identified contrary', where: 'The maxima and minima of particular contraries are one and indifferent. Minimal heat equals minimal cold. Consequently transmutations are circular. The principle (minimum) of one contrary takes its movement from the principle (maximum) of one another ... Maximal speed is a state of rest. The maximum of corruption and the minimum of generation are identical: in principle, corruption is generation' (Begam, 1996: 101). I think it is limiting to only apply such rules to the texts that seem to be most expressive of them, such as *Murphy* and *Molloy*. Rather,

I see the two mimes B and N in both sets of life-works; B is N, and N is B, but only because of certain rule-bound structures which ultimately obey no rules, such as *différance* and the identified contrary.

But after this detour through an imagistic notion of the mimes, leading to a logical or functional notion, whereby each performance generates rules in the later Wittgensteinian sense of the *Philosophical Investigations*, I want to return to the mime performance in a vocal sense, where *writing* becomes not some kind of anti-mimetic performance art but rather an acoustical illusion in the sense of taking text and turning it into audio-tape, or, text as audio-tape, and I mean here spools of magnetic tape, which is to think of text as segments of data that can be reshuffled at a macro and micro level – spools being a slightly old-fashioned word, but then fashion doesn't matter here because this is a philosophical definition of text *as* tape. We get such vocalized positions in the slapstick known as *Krapp's Last Tape*: 'Just been listening to that stupid bastard I took myself for thirty years ago, hard to believe I was ever as bad as that' (1990: 222). Krapp's editing becomes in effect an attempt to deflate the pomposity of a spiritual and aesthetic teleology, replacing teleology with multifarious interjections or *styles* of speaking. We are not sure what he is referring to when he produces his anti-teleological recording, when or where his references take place, or what discourse is being used. This tape is eventually wrenched from the machine in a significant gesture and thrown away; an abandoned text to say the least. But what exactly is Krapp throwing away? His final attempt to say who he is, who he has been? Because, as Nietzsche argues, this is the essential task for the writer, to 'bear witness' about one's self (1983: 33). *Krapp's Last Tape* is perhaps nothing but 'bearing witness' – that is to say, an oral testimony which is an 'acoustical illusion', but also a living proof or evidence of an eternal return of the same. N in the text of B; N and B working as mimes in each other's texts.

How does Nietzsche deal with the effects of his multifarious styles? How does he 'bear witness'? By suggesting that there is a disparity between the greatness of himself and the smallness of his contemporaries, but not necessarily readers. And the latter point is important, because Nietzsche is still waiting for the day that a reader can hear his abyssal voice and recognize plenitude, just as Beckett waits for the day when a reader will come along and recognize nothingness in the texts, such as *Godot* or *Film*, which seem so full to the brim of meaning. Nietzsche wants the certainty of his texts to be preserved, while his texts have inadvertently been edited and cut and spliced beyond all recognition: Nietzsche gives us the art of the fragment and expects each fragment to be received like the whole that is no longer tenable; but rather than interpret the situation as I am, Nietzsche decides that his contemporaries suffer from physiological deficiencies, such as deafness and blindness: 'I have been neither heard nor even so much as seen' (1983: 33). In *Krapp's Last Tape* we have a man and a machine who between them are bathed in light: all else is in darkness. While Krapp breaks the boundaries between audience and stage with his banana skins and the interaction of silence and audience laughter, it is the audience who cannot be seen in *Krapp*, whereas Nietzsche claims to see his audience all too clearly. But if I am arguing that B is in N and N is in B, what about the claims that exist in the two concerning aesthetic and spiritual perfection and/or failure? Nietzsche calls his books 'gifts', implicating the reader in an economy that precedes Western literature and philosophy with the system known as 'potlatch': the system of putting the recipient of a gift in debt and at the same time producing an efficacious result that exceeds that debt (such as the achievement of names or title or rank); this is what Nietzsche says about his potlatch which he calls 'Zarathustra': 'I have with this book given mankind the greatest gift that has been given it. With a voice that speaks across millennia, it is not only the most exalted book that exists ... it is also the most *profoundest*, born out of the innermost abundance of truth, an inexhaustible well into which no bucket descends without coming up filled with gold and goodness' (1983: 35). Zarathustra, that solitary figure, has given us a great gift; if only we could receive that gift, we could enter the contract of the potlatch, a contract which could exist as *Ecce Homo* suggests as it bears witness to the potlatching gesture. But what about that other not-so-great solitary figure: Krapp, bathed in the light while we sit, like Nietzsche's audience, in darkness? Has he no gifts to give us? Krapp does not seem to be giving us anything, just taking away. He does not allow us the transcendental moment of a spiritual and/or aesthetic epiphany, destroying it instead in a moment of pathos and laughter. The epiphanic Krapp is described in the sentence: 'Just been listening to that stupid bastard I took myself for thirty years ago, hard to believe I was ever as bad as that' (1990: 222). The greatest, most powerful form of potlatch, however, is the destruction of the most valuable possessions, spiritually and aesthetically speaking. Klossowski, in *Nietzsche and the Vicious Circle*, examines a dream that Nietzsche experienced, 'doubled' in its recounting (two visits to a scene of removal). The first 'version' of the dream (1858) is as follows:

> At this time I dreamed that I heard the sounds of an organ coming from the church, as if at a burial. As I was looking to see what was going on, a grave suddenly opened, and my father, clothed in his death-shroud, arose from the tomb. He hurries toward the church and almost immediately comes back with a child in his arms. The mound of the grave reopens; he climbs back in, and the gravestone once again sinks back over the opening. The swelling noise of the organ immediately stops, and I wake up.
>
> The day after this night, little Joseph is suddenly taken ill with cramps and convulsions, and dies within a few hours. Our anguish was immense. My dream was fulfilled completely. (1997: 173)

Nietzsche's father is removed from life at age thirty-six; he returns from the dead only to remove the son; Nietzsche is left as a mere shadow of the father/son, divorced from any tortured results of their relationship. Klossowski interprets the doubled dream sequence, in relation to a statement in *Ecce Homo*, as a reversal of the Oedipus Complex. I interpret this dream sequence as an inverted biblical narrative: the *resurrected* father takes the son or destroys his life; the people are left with a shadow and a debt. *Krapp's Last Tape* therefore has N in B, with its extreme potlatching, its removal of the epiphanic moment, its taking away of youthful text and the destruction of text-as-tape; perhaps N is exceeded in the moment of Krapp's textual self-destruction which is also a profound affirmation. When the great Haida chiefs of British Columbia's coast destroyed their most valuable possessions, they became even greater chiefs: invincible, *unpotlatchable* perhaps, but still implicating their people in a circuit which demanded a greater potlatch in future years. Nietzsche makes the mistake of attempting to exceed the greatest ever potlatch by giving us too much, by being afraid to edit or even abandon the mnemonic devices that will lead to the continuation of his works; he cannot destroy one fragment, erase one word, negate one piece of poetry, and in the process he becomes the fragment, the word of modernity, and the negation of the poetic. B in N, whether he likes it or not, and N in B, whether he sees it or not.

So we return to my opening generalizations, where Nietzsche has to write a text called 'why I write such excellent books' to fill an impossible void, whereas Beckett constantly writes minimalist books in an impossible gesture of wiping out the plenitude with the void. I want to argue that both Nietzsche and Beckett are involved in a contract with their texts, *a contract with the act of narrative*, an act of faith we could say *in* narrative, which involves having to personally bear witness to the texts as they start reeling out of control. Beckett's extreme minimalism is apparent in many places, but perhaps nowhere more famously than *Breath* (1990: 371):

CURTAIN

1. Faint light on stage littered with miscellaneous rubbish. Hold about five seconds.
2. Faint brief cry and immediately inspiration and slow increase of light together reaching maximum together in about ten seconds. Silence and hold about five seconds.
3. Expiration and slow decrease of light together reaching minimum together (light as in 1) in about ten seconds and immediately cry as before. Silence and hold about five seconds.

CURTAIN

And *Breath* literally did reel out of control, as James Knowlson narrates. Originally offered to Kenneth Tynan as a piece for his erotic revue *Oh! Calcutta!*, Beckett's ironic sketch was immediately reconfigured: 'someone else connected with the production, tampered with Beckett's text, adding the phrase "including naked people" to the clutter of miscellaneous rubbish. When the illustrated book was published . . . the photograph facing his script clearly displayed the naked parts of bodies' (1997: 566). Worse still, Beckett's name was the only one attached to a particular text. Beckett then had to extricate himself from his contract, which he did manage, but after the New York run, as Knowlson makes clear. 'Have I been understood?' asks Nietzsche three times, at the end of *Ecce Homo*. Have we understood *Breath*/Beckett here? What are we to make of *Breath* devoid of its ironic positioning in an erotic review, and its troubled, unauthorized rewriting with the addition of 'naked people' to the rubbish heap? Out of the absence comes presence, out the cutting comes addition, not just in terms of the re-writing, but also the contractually problematic re-presencing of the author. Beckett's attempt to efface himself is dramatically reversed. At the end of *Ecce Homo*

Nietzsche presents himself as the first man, the first to discover the truth, which he then neatly summarizes for the reader as his massive critique of Christianity. Yet in this summary, the last gasps of Christianity do not appear to be superceded by the body of Nietzsche; rather, the celebration of his existence and his name is replaced by the transference into/onto Zarathustra. Nietzsche tries to place himself centre-stage, but is crowded out by the body of the prophet. Nietzsche's autobiography ends, in this sense, in anonymity.

For both N and B to *Personally bear witness* to their narratives also means writing on the body, or presenting the body as the written document of proof; but this in turn starts to pressurize or impact upon the singular body. Nietzsche starts suffering from a number of intense illnesses and migraines, he's left with some kind of eternal headache, degenerating, so the crude narrative goes, into madness. Beckett coped with innumerable illnesses and problems, perhaps the most infamous being his cataracts and all that they implied. This is not an attempt to make some kind of biographical or causal point about these illnesses, rather, to suggest that the body is not the stable, legal document that someone like Nietzsche took it to be (even if, as Deleuze notes, the Nietzschean body is constructed via a relationship of forces), whereas bodies breaking down, being dragged uselessly around, or dragging the subject uselessly around, proliferate in Beckett like a series of broken promises. Still, the body bears witness: after its failure in Nietzsche, thinkers such as Heidegger reconstruct the body of his contractual texts (however problematic that act might now seem to be), whereas the failing bodies in Beckett are reinscribed upon a multitude of stages and reinterpreted in a great number of classrooms and research libraries around the world. A contractual relation with the text is an ethical relation and this was perhaps the biggest headache that either writer suffered from, as history itself bears witness to their insights.

References

Beckett, Samuel (1990) *The Complete Dramatic Works*. London: Faber & Faber.
Begam, Richard (1996) *Samuel Beckett and the End of Modernity*. Stanford: Stanford University Press.
Clarke, J. J. (1992) *In Search of Jung*. London: Routledge.
Cope, Richard (1998) 'The Expression of Failure or the Failure of Expression'. Unpublished MA thesis, Goldsmiths College, London.
Deleuze, Gilles (1983) *Nietzsche and Philosophy*, trans. Hugh Tomlinson. London: Athlone.

Kennedy, Andrew K. (1991) *Samuel Beckett*. Cambridge: Cambridge University Press.

Klossowski, Pierre (1997) *Nietzsche and the Vicious Circle*, trans. Daniel W. Smith. Chicago: University of Chicago Press; and London: Athlone.

Knowlson, James (1996) *Damned to Fame: The Life of Samuel Beckett*. London: Bloomsbury.

Nietzsche, Friedrich (1983) *Ecce Homo*, trans. R. J. Hollingdale. Middlesex: Penguin.

Index

DATE DUE

GAYLORD			PRINTED IN U.S.A.